EXPLORING

Superior Country

THE NATURE GUIDE TO LAKE SUPERIOR

Craig Charles

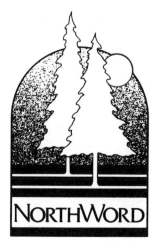

NorthWord

Dedication

*In memory of my boyhood friend, Bo, and
our many Superior Adventures.*

Library of Congress Cataloging-in-Publication Data

Charles, Craig.
  Exploring Superior country : the nature guide to Lake Superior /
Craig Charles.
      p.   cm.
  Includes bibliographical references and index.
  ISBN 1-55971-137-X
  1. Superior, Lake, Region--Guidebooks. 2. Natural areas-
-Superior, Lake, Region--Guidebooks. 3. Parks--Superior, Lake,
Region--Guidebooks. 4. Outdoor recreation--Superior, Lake, Region-
-Guidebooks. I. Title.
F552.C47   1992
917.74'90443--dc20   92-7429
                                                                  CIP

Published by
NorthWord Press, Inc.
Box 1360
Minocqua, WI 54548

Designed by
Lakeland Graphic Design
Minocqua, WI 54548

For a free catalog describing NorthWord's line of
nature books and gifts, call 1-800-336-5666.

ISBN 1-55971-137-X

Printed in the United States of America

TABLE OF CONTENTS

SYMBOL KEY

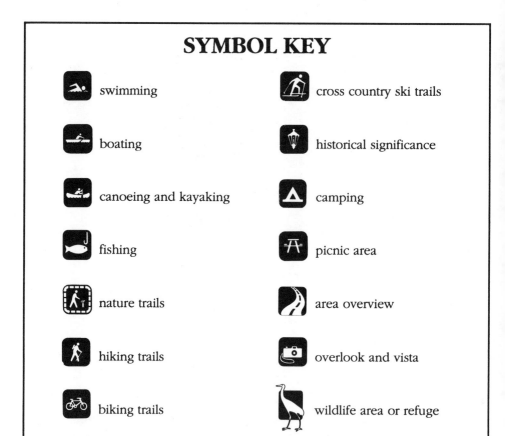

swimming

boating

canoeing and kayaking

fishing

nature trails

hiking trails

biking trails

cross country ski trails

historical significance

camping

picnic area

area overview

overlook and vista

wildlife area or refuge

Preface
SUPERIOR ADVENTURES

Poised like a sentinel guarding the queen of the Great Lakes, the Witch Tree stands twisted but proud along the Minnesota North Shore of Lake Superior. Gnarled by winds and aged by weather, the old cedar has stood for some 400 years. Members of the Ojibwa tribe once left offerings beneath its branches, in the hope that this "Little Spirit Cedar Tree" would provide safe passage on the inland sea they called *Gitchi Gummi.*

I, too, owe Lake Superior an offering. I was on the shores of *Gitchi Gummi* when I hoisted my first backpack and balanced my first canoe on quivering shoulders—events that changed my life.

Fittingly, the Witch Tree today serves as the spiritual symbol of the Inland Sea Society, an organization dedicated to the stewardship of Lake Superior. It's the desire of this diverse group of paddlers, sailors, fishermen, and Lake Superior lovers to return something to the lady who has given so much to them.

As you join me on these Superior adventures, you'll be encouraged to paddle, hike, swim, ski, and just meander, in order to experience this wild northern land in its natural glory. You'll also be encouraged to leave something for the Witch Tree, be it only a memory of your kindness during your visit or a vanishing footprint in the sands of Superior Country.

Introduction
THE LADY, THE LAKE

Straddling two countries, with a crown of iron and a foot of copper, Lake Superior merits her title as queen of the inland seas. She is both loved and feared, admired and respected. Sometimes she's serene and peaceful, at other times turbulent and tempestuous. Her wooded shores, the pristine streams that feed her, and the rugged cliffs that pay homage to her are all dwarfed by Queen Superior herself, greatest of the Great Lakes.

On a planet surface that is seven-tenths water, only a meager three percent is water free of salt. Lake Superior lays claim to one-eighth of the world's life-sustaining supply of fresh water. It's also the northernmost of the Great Lakes and the largest body of fresh water in the world, covering 31,800 square miles and measuring 360 miles across by 160 miles wide. From its surface at 602 feet above sea level, Lake Superior plunges an awesome 1,402 feet at its deepest point. Though it's fed by 336 tributary streams, Superior is drained by a single outlet—the St. Mary's River.

But it's not just the volume of fresh water that makes Lake Superior so vital and appealing. It's also the quality of that water. Lake Superior holds some of the purest and clearest water in the world, a fact that can be attributed to the water's origin. While the bottoms of the other Great Lakes are composed of silt, clay, and sand, the floor of Lake Superior was carved thousands of years ago by glaciers moving across the Canadian Shield, which consists primarily of granite and granite-like rock. Since there is very little mineral or nutrient transfer between water and granite, Superior lacks the nutrients to support abundant aquatic life. This, together with its size, depth, and temperature, means the lake has fewer kinds of aquatic species and smaller populations of those species than its sister lakes.

Nonetheless, it has an adequate fish population, and fishing has always been the chief attraction to Superior shores for both native Americans and white European settlers. One of the earliest white explorers, Pierre Esprit Radisson, said of Chequamegon Bay, "In that bay there is a channel where we take stores of fishes, sturgeons of vast bigness and Pychs (northern pike) seven feet long." Today, unfortunately, sturgeon are a rare find in Lake Superior. Because the bony, armor-plated sides of their bodies tore holes in the narrow nets used to catch them, they were traditionally considered a nuisance catch, and these ancient inhabitants were left to rot or were burned like cordwood on Superior beaches.

Superior remains famous for its delicately flavored lake trout and its equally tasty whitefish. Commercial fishermen began exploiting this seemingly inexhaustible resource in the early nineteenth century. Whitefish were the first "cash crop," but by the 1890s their numbers were diminishing, and lake trout became the highly sought commodity. By the turn of the century, the lake herring harvest surpassed both. Fish hatcheries were in full swing, attempting to replenish the quickly diminishing population. Fortunately the restocking efforts were successful, and for the next 40 years the commercial fishing industry flourished.

In the 1950s an intruder from the Atlantic Ocean entered the Lake Superior ecosystem, upsetting its delicate balance. The Great Lakes are connected to the Atlantic Ocean via the Erie Canal and the St. Lawrence Seaway. When the Seaway was being built in the 1950s, it was believed that saltwater species could not survive in a freshwater environment, so there was little concern about so-called "invader species" upsetting the natural balance of the Great Lakes. The conventional belief was in error. One of these unwelcome visitors, the sea lamprey, managed not only to adapt but to thrive and multiply in the fresh water of the Great Lakes. The eel-like, parasitic creature attaches itself to fish and feeds off their body fluids. Facing no natural predators in the Great Lakes, the lamprey eel proceeded to devastate fish populations in Lake Michigan and Lake Huron, while fishermen fretted over its impending advance into Lake Superior.

Sure enough, the lake trout catch in Lake Superior dropped from 3.1 million pounds in 1950 to just 360,000 pounds by 1960. Drastic measures were needed. Today researchers use a chemical that kills sea lamprey larva without harming other fish. The chemical treatment has drastically reduced the damage caused by this voracious predator.

The story of Lake Superior is also the story of its people. Archaeologists surmise that the Mongol peoples of Siberia migrated from Asia across the Bering Straits, through Alaska, and into North America over an ancient land bridge. These semi-nomadic peoples are thought to be predecessors of modern-day American Indians. Native peoples believed that Superior held mysterious, supernatural powers. The Ojibwa (Chippewa) Indians called the lake *Gitchi Gummi*, or the Big (Shining) Sea Water. They believed Superior was home to Missipeshu, a beach-stalker that devoured children and unleashed the fury of *Gitchi Gummi*. To satisfy Missipeshu, these peoples sprinkled an offering of tobbacco on the water before beginning a journey on the powerful lake.

Superior is a majestic regent. If you grant her the respect she commands, your own Superior adventures will be filled with discovery, beauty, and excitement. If you question her reign, however, beware the wrath of Missipeshu.

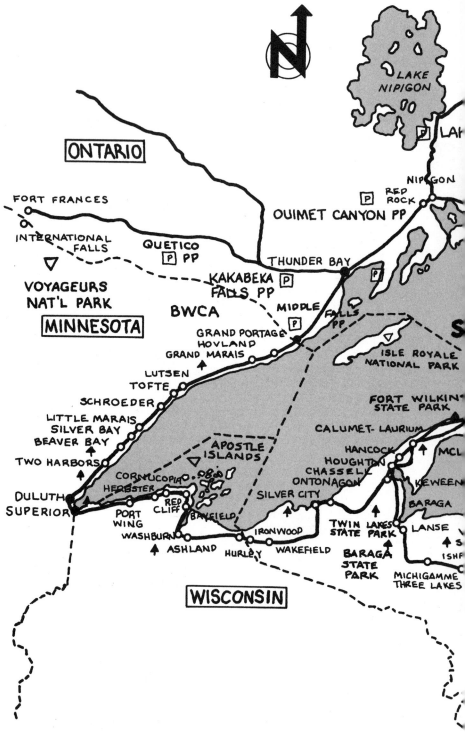

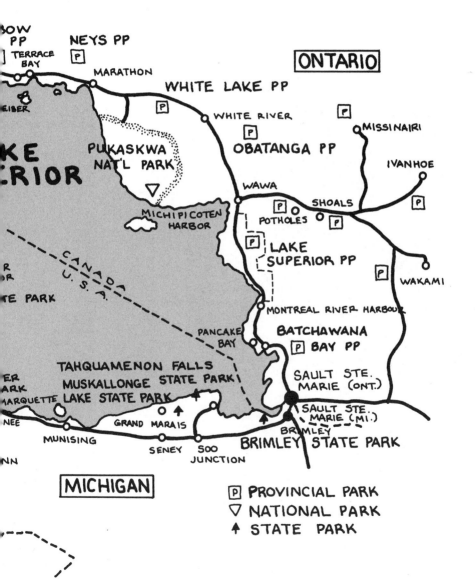

GON PP

BOW
PP   NEYS PP
TERRACE   P   ONTARIO
BAY
      MARATHON
EIBER   WHITE LAKE PP

                    P   WHITE RIVER   P
KE   P   MISSINAIRI
RIOR   PUKASKWA   OBATANGA PP
            NAT'L PARK   IVANHOE

                   ▽   WAWA
                                              SHOALS
            MICHIPICOTEN   P ○   P
            HARBOR   POTHOLES ○ P

      CANADA   P   P
      U.S.A.   LAKE   WAKAMI
R   SUPERIOR PP
OR
TE PARK   MONTREAL RIVER HARBOUR

                         PANCAKE   BATCHAWANA
                         BAY   P BAY PP

      TAHQUAMENON FALLS   SAULT STE.
ER   MUSKALLONGE STATE PARK   MARIE (ONT.)
ARK
MARQUETTE LAKE STATE PARK   SAULT STE.
NEE   ▲   MARIE (MI.)
                   ○ ▲   BRIMLEY
NN   MUNISING   GRAND MARAIS   BRIMLEY STATE PARK
            SENEY   SOO
                    JUNCTION

      MICHIGAN   P PROVINCIAL PARK
                           ▽ NATIONAL PARK
                           ▲ STATE PARK

MINNESOTA'S NORTH SHORE
Rushing Rivers and Sky Blue Waters

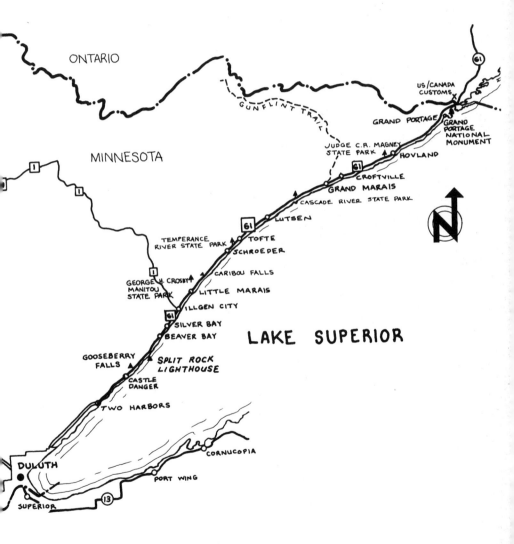

Through the Windshield

Historians tell us that Minnesota is a Dakota Indian word meaning "Land of Sky Blue Waters." As you're traveling Minnesota's Superior North Shore, you'll find that the state lives up to its name. This is a land of rushing rivers and rugged cliffs. It's also a place of placid lakes and peaceful campsites. As you travel the historic route up Highway 61, you'll follow the path of 17th-century French voyageurs. These powerful men paddled mighty Lake Superior in freighter canoes, shuttling cargoes of beaver pelts to remote trading posts across the inland sea.

Duluth, Minnesota (pop. 83,650), located just a bridge away from Superior, Wisconsin, is your starting point on this journey. Perched on the edge of Minnesota's wild North Shore, Duluth is an industrial port city, rich in history and architectural grandeur. The city takes its name from French explorer Sieur Du Lhut, who recorded his journey up Wisconsin's Brule River to Lake Superior in 1680.

The Duluth/Superior harbor stands at the mouth of the St. Louis River, where the sands of time have created two barrier beaches known as Minnesota Point and Wisconsin Point. These wooded sand dunes afford the port protection from the wrath of Lake Superior's storms. Although Minnesota Point is the site of several homes and a seaplane base and airport, the forested dunes still attract migrating shorebirds and resident sea gulls. Park Point, a protected natural area on the dunes, is a popular spot for birders to congregate, especially in the late spring and in August, when shorebirds are migrating. In winter, the ice ridges heave and crack, creating an arctic spectacular for those willing to brave the icy chill.

Black bear alerts have been posted during years when berry crops have been light, since bruins have been known to leave their wilderness retreats for the lure of city garbage. Moose have also made an occasional trip to Duluth, startling visitors and residents alike.

For many, the most appealing time to visit Duluth is during the annual hawk migration. From mid-August through December, thousands of birds of prey swoop down on Duluth from points further north. Hawk Ridge, a 115-acre preserve situated eight hundred feet above Lake Superior, is the center of activity. Protected since 1972 and managed by the Duluth Audubon Society, Hawk Ridge is a natural funnel for migrating birds following the shores of Lake Superior. Peak migration typically occurs around mid-September. Thousand of birds have been counted in a single day by trained professionals, and many activities are scheduled to celebrate the migration. To reach Hawk Ridge, follow Skyline Drive and watch for a wooden sign directing you down the one-mile dirt road to the preserve.

Sidetracking from the North Shore, you'll find U.S. Highway 53, which stretches 163 miles to Voyageurs National Park. The park is christened in honor of the canoe-paddling French-Canadians who once transported beaver pelts and trade goods between Montreal and the wild border lakes of the northland. Today, boats still provide the only transportation through this roadless park, and guided tour vessels cater to those without their own watercraft.

Back on the Minnesota North Shore, your journey continues at the bridge over the Lester River in Duluth and heads up Highway 61 all the way to the Canadian border. Here you have two choices. The scenic route hugs the shoreline on two-lane County 61, while a four-lane divided freeway provides a speedy 20-mile trip down U.S. 61. Bicyclists and travelers with leisure time will enjoy the scenic county highway, which crosses the French and Sucker rivers. Sharp-eyed bicyclists may happen upon wild strawberries in season along this route. Fishermen may wish to visit the French River Fish Hatchery, operated by the Minnesota Department of Natural Resources. Herring, walleye, Atlantic salmon, and rainbow trout are among the fish raised at the hatchery, and visitors are welcome to tour the facility weekdays from 8 a.m. to 4 p.m. For information, call 218/723-4881.

About five miles north of the French River, a plaque commemorates the founding of Buchanan, a settlement named after President James Buchanan. Platted in 1856, Buchanan was the home of the *North Shore Advocate*, the area's first newspaper.

Continuing to Knife River, you'll find opportunities to purchase fresh and smoked fish from the handful of commercial fishermen who still operate from this community. Knife River takes its name from the Indian term *Makomani*, which means "sharp rocks in the river bed."

At the entrance to the city of Two Harbors, County 61 meets the U.S.61 expressway. Not surprisingly, Two Harbors (pop. 3,650) was named after its two good harbors, Agate Bay and Burlington Bay. This was once a popular Ojibwa fishing grounds, but today Two Harbors is noted for its significance as an iron ore shipping port.

While in Two Harbors, you may enjoy a visit to the Agate Bay Lighthouse Station, built in 1892. The Lake County Historical Society now owns the station and an adjacent pilot house from an iron ore freighter. Both facilities are open to visitors daily from late April to late October.

Campers looking for a place to rest can pitch a tent or wheel an RV into the 76-unit Burlington Bay municipal campground. The campground accepts reservations, and even though it's in the shadow of the highway, it offers a fine spot from which to prepare for a trip to the nearby Boundary Waters Canoe Area Wilderness (BWCAW). For information, call 218/834-2021.

Continuing on Highway 61, you'll reach the 1,662-acre Gooseberry Falls State Park (listed separately). The Gooseberry River cascades through the park in a series of five picturesque waterfalls. The Ojibwa name for this river was *Shavonimikani*, or "place of the gooseberries." Today the state park is a popular resting spot for day visitors who park their cars at the wayside bridge and walk the falls trail. Budget additional time if you wish to leave the crowds behind and view each of the spectacular drops. This is also a popular destination for campers, so advance reservations are suggested if you plan an overnight stay.

Minnesota state parks employ Mixtic Corporation, a private reservation system, to book family camping and lodging requests. You can call 800/765-2267, Monday through Friday, from 8 a.m. to 5 p.m. Payment is by MasterCard or Visa, and reservations can be made from three to 120 days prior to arrival. A state motor vehicle entrance fee is also required at state parks.

You may now want to grab your camera and take a few pictures of Split Rock Lighthouse (listed separately), which is visible from the roadside scenic lookout just west of the state park entrance. It's easy to understand why this is the most photographed site on Lake Superior, since the historic lighthouse is planted on a bed of solid rock. The lighthouse was completed by the U.S Lighthouse Service in 1910, its construction prompted by a series of six shipwrecks near the Split Rock River. The lighthouse remains an engineering marvel, and the cost of admission to the grounds is well worth the price. A guided tour of the lighthouse will help you understand the ingenuity and independence required of the builders, as well as the lighthouse keepers and their families.

Continuing your journey, you'll pass Beaver Bay, the final resting spot of the North Shore's best-known mail carrier. John Beargrease became famous for his ability to make the weekly mail run between Two Harbors and Grand Portage regardless of the weather. Each January the annual 500-mile John Beargrease Sled Dog Marathon between Duluth and Grand Portage pays tribute to his memory.

As you approach Tettegouche State Park (listed separately), consider renewing your faith in wilderness at the Baptism River, formerly known as River au Bapteme. Water from the river was at one time used to baptize new converts to Christianity. Today the area surrounding the river has been preserved as the 4,650-acre Tettegouche State Park. The park boasts three waterfalls on the Baptism River—including Minnesota's highest, which drops a spectacular 80 feet to a pool below. The 1.5 mile hike to the falls is worth the effort. If you still have energy, don't miss the self-guided tour to Shovel Point, which begins at the upper trail parking lot. This is a great place to ponder man's insignificance on the calendar of time, since the point is actually a lava flow that occurred 1.1 billion years ago.

Just north of Tettegouche State Park, Highway 1 branches east through Minnesota's Arrowhead Country to Ely. If you're hoping to beat the summer crowds traveling the North Shore, you may wish to leave Highway 1 and head up Lake County Road 7 to George H. Crosby Manitou State Park (listed separately). You'll have to hoist a backpack if you plan to stay overnight in the park, but if you're a trout fisherman you may find the effort rewarding. Both rainbow and brook trout can be found in the Manitou River, which drops 600 feet through the park before finding an outlet at Lake Superior.

Back on Highway 1, you'll make the 60-mile trek through the Superior National Forest (listed separately) to the Iron Range town of Ely, which is pronounced "E-lee." The self-proclaimed "Canoe Capital of America" rests on the edge of the Boundary Waters Canoe Area

Wilderness (listed separately) and resembles an Old West frontier town. Fishermen, paddlers, hikers, mountain bikers, and even city slickers will find something to their liking in the Ely area. Over 500 lakes dot the landscape, and the town's modern lodging facilities, fine restaurants, and plentiful outfitters make the region accessible to everyone. While you're in Ely, don't miss a visit to the International Wolf Center, where educational programs are offered and research is conducted on what may be America's most misunderstood wild animal, the timber wolf.

Continuing up the Minnesota North Shore, you'll pass through the tiny villages of Tofte and Schroeder. Both of these communities were settled in the late 1800s by Scandinavians impressed with the resemblance between the rugged shoreline and their homeland. A granite cross at the mouth of the Cross River in Schroeder has replaced the wooden cross erected by the famed missionary, Father Frederic Baraga. Known as "the snowshoe priest" because of his tireless winter travels across the Great Lakes, Baraga erected the wooden cross to commemorate landing at the river after enduring a terrible storm on Lake Superior.

Tofte lies near the mouth of the Temperance River and at the beginning of the Sawbill Trail. The Temperance is aptly named because, unlike other rivers on Minnesota's North Shore, it contains no "bar" at its mouth. Temperance River State Park (listed separately) provides a campground and hiking trails just three miles from Tofte. Tofte is also one of the gateway communities for interior access to the BWCAW via the Sawbill Trail. Outfitters in the area are available to serve you whether you wish to spend a day or a week in canoe country.

North of Tofte, travelers will find the largest downhill and cross country skiing resort in the Midwest. Lutsen Resort (800/232-0071 from Minnesota, 800/346-1467 elsewhere), established in 1894, today serves thousands who revel in the abundant snowfall of the North Shore. Summer visitors enjoy mountain biking in the nearby Superior National Forest. The resort offers assistance in planning mountain bike routes, as well as all-terrain bicycles (ATBs) available for rental. Those seeking a unique summer thrill will find an ice-free sled track winding down Minnesota's highest peak, the 2,301-foot Eagle Mountain.

From Lutsen the scenic, 20-mile Caribou Trail leads to Brule Lake, an access point to the BWCAW. Mid-September to early October is a popular time to drive the Caribou Trail, since the colors of autumn come earlier to the inland forest than to the shoreline of Lake Superior. The second wave of fall colors arrives along the Superior shore during the first three weeks of October, extending the beauty of the season.

Nearby Cascade River State Park (listed separately) offers a modern campground coupled with the beauty of the Sawtooth Mountains. The park is appropriately named, since the river cascades over a series of beautiful waterfalls and rapids above the highway.

Gateway to the fifty-mile Gunflint Trail and the BWCAW interior, the lakeshore community of Grand Marais is a favorite stop for many North

Shore visitors. You'll see a canoe atop every other car, and this community of 1,100 year-round residents bustles in the summertime. Grand Marais outfitters can supply campers with everything from canoes to freeze-dried food. The district ranger office for the three million-acre Superior National Forest is located in Grand Marais, and it's a must-stop for folks seeking maps, permits, advice, or information on outdoor recreation in the forest or the BWCAW.

Heading up the Gunflint Trail, you'll find Judge C.R. Magney State Park (listed separately). Named after former Duluth mayor and Minnesota Supreme Court Justice Clarence Magney, the park offers a picnic grounds along the banks of the Brule River and a rustic campground (no showers). A hike to Devil's Kettle Falls will reveal a treacherous boil of foaming whitewater. According to legend, the turbulent water is swallowed by a huge pothole, never to surface again.

The Gunflint Trail ends at Seagull Lake, a popular starting point for many canoe country adventures. You'll need a permit to camp in the BWCAW, and the many outfitters along the Gunflint Trail will be happy to accommodate your specific requirements.

Passing though the Scandinavian-settled community of Hovland, you'll again have access to the BWCAW from the Arrowhead Trail, which ends on McFarland Lake. This is the trailhead for backpackers challenging the rugged Border Route Trail, and a wilderness permit is required for overnight visitation.

North of Hovland, Highway 61 passes through the Ojibwa Indian Reservation, and into historic Grand Portage near the Pigeon River. This was once the center of voyageur fur trading activity, and a reconstructed fort commemorates the era at the Grand Portage National Historic Monument (listed separately). The original settlement was constructed in 1721, and today the National Park Service offers guided tours (admission charged) daily from mid-May through October. For information, call 218/475-2202. Resting at the foot of Mt. Josephine and protected by Grand Portage Bay, the modern community of Grand Portage provides access to Michigan's Isle Royale National Park (listed separately.)

Protected as wilderness since 1931, Isle Royale is a roadless preserve that offers outstanding hiking opportunities, backcountry campsites, and lodging facilities. In the backcountry, you may hear wolves howling, and you might encounter moose at any time. Daily roundtrip passenger service is available from Grand Portage via the 65-foot *Wenonah* and the 63-foot *Voyageur II*, both operated by the Sivertson Isle Royale Service (715/392-2100). Both boats land at Windigo, on the shores of Washington Harbor at the island's southwestern corner. The *Voyageur II* continues on to Rock Harbor, where it overnights. Passengers will find lodging facilities at Isle Royale ranging from hotel rooms to housekeeping cottages. For reservations, contact the Rock Harbor Lodge (906/337-4993 from May to September, 502/773-2191 from October to April). Rock Harbor is the spectacular home port of

Isle Royale's National Park Service, and most backcountry excursions begin and end there.

Windigo rests on the remote shore of Washington Harbor. Campsites are available, but overnight lodging facilities are not. Windigo provides access to the rugged Greenstone Ridge Trail, a popular hiking trail that traverses the heart of Isle Royale. Trout fishermen landing at Windigo will be glad they packed a fly rod, as the Grace and Washington creeks are noted for brook trout and no license is required to fish the island's interior lakes and streams.

Near Grand Portage, appearing to grow from solid rock, a twisted cedar tree reaches for the sky from the shores of Lake Superior. For about 400 years, the "Little Spirit Tree" has stood sentinel over Lake Superior. Travelers have left gifts beneath the cedar, also known as the Witch Tree, hoping that it would provide them with safe passage on the inland sea. To secure permission to visit the Witch Tree, stop at the Grand Portage Lodge, operated by the Objiwa nation. For the Ojibwa, the tree remains a spiritual monument, as perhaps it should for all travelers who seek safe passage through Superior Country.

GOOSEBERRY FALLS STATE PARK
1300 East Highway 61
Two Harbors, MN 55616
800/765-CAMP

For eons, the Gooseberry River has tumbled over the rock of Minnesota's North Shore, carving a path to Superior. As it tumbles over five waterfalls, the river reveals the ancient lava flows that shaped the formation of the earth.

The lower Gooseberry River makes up the largest estuary on the North Shore. The river level varies daily, depending on rainfall, as water converges into the narrow rocky gorges. Visitors can park their cars at the wayside by the Gooseberry Park bridge, and most of the falls are visible from the bridge walk. To best appreciate the power and beauty of the Gooseberry, visit early in the morning when you can have the river to yourself. You'll hear the river speak in a language as old as the earth itself.

Five of the park's fifteen miles of walking trails wind along the river, passing through stands of conifer, aspen, and birch while offering views of Lake Superior. The park also offers access to a completed section of the Superior Hiking Trail that will eventually run from Duluth to the Canadian Border.

GOOSEBERRY FALLS STATE STATE PARK

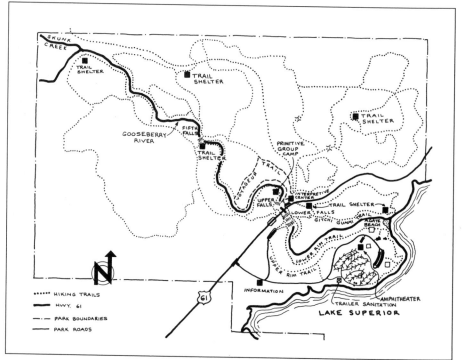

While you're visiting the park, take time to admire the buildings that have earned Gooseberry Falls a place on the National Registry of Historic Places. These buildings were constructed by the Civilian Conservation Corps (CCC) between 1934 and 1940, when 200 men were housed in two camps at Gooseberry. The men drilled and blasted native stone from quarries in Duluth and Beaver Bay. The stone was then trucked back to camp, carefully cut, and formed into the impressive arches, fireplaces, and buildings that visitors admire today. Perhaps most impressive is the massive stone retaining wall located at the Highway 61 wayside. Varying from 15 to 25 feet in height, the 300-foot-long wall contains individual quarried stones that weigh several tons.

The park's modern, 70-unit campground is popular during the summer months, and reservations are recommended. During winter 15 miles of trails are groomed and tracked for cross-country skiing. Snowmobilers can access the North Shore State Trail through the park, enjoying hundreds of miles of groomed trail from Duluth to Grand Marais.

The park's interpretive center is open from mid-May through October, and will help you gain a better appreciation of the region's geology and geography.

SPLIT ROCK LIGHTHOUSE STATE PARK
2010 A Highway 61 E
Two Harbors, MN 55616
218/226-3065

When the fog above Superior is thick and the waves are crashing, it's easy to imagine the fear and uncertainty that turn-of-the-century ship captains must have felt as they crept near the cliffs of the Split Rock River.

The fear was justified. On November 28, 1905, a single storm endangered 29 ships, leaving two of the carriers founded on the rocky coast. After the area was christened "the most dangerous piece of water in the world," Congress in 1907 appropriated $75,000 for construction of a lighthouse and fog signal in the vicinity of Split Rock.

Since there were no roads to the wilderness site in 1908, construction materials had to be hoisted over the cliffs of Split Rock from barges anchored in the lake below. Today the Split Rock Lighthouse and its surrounding buildings remain a marvel of engineering ingenuity. Little remains of the derrick and hoisting engine that brought a lighthouse and its keepers to this unconquered headland, but the lighthouse and the keeper's home have been restored to their original grandeur.

Visitors who take the guided tour up the winding stairs to the beacon will find its history remarkable. Over six tons of precision equipment made the journey from Paris, France, to the site. The beacon was then assembled prism by prism in the lantern room. Its

SPLIT ROCK LIGHTHOUSE STATE PARK

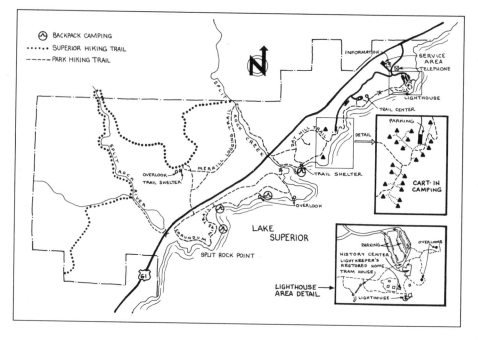

incandescent oil vapor lamp was lit on August 1, 1910, and for the next sixty years the light would flash each night at ten-second intervals across more than twenty miles of Lake Superior's navigable waters.

The lighthouse keeper, his assistant, and family members lived on the grounds, and tours of their homes and the light itself are offered. If you spend an hour on this tour, you'll step into a time when steel met waves and families met the challenge of the Superior wilderness.

After touring the lighthouse grounds, visitors with a flare for adventure will enjoy camping along the Lake Superior bluff at Split Rock Lighthouse's cart-in campground. This unique concept requires that you leave your car at the lighted campground parking lot and wheel a cart to one of 20 secluded campsites. Don't fret about missing the conveniences of modern life. You'll find flush toilets and even hot showers at the campground's comfort station. Plan ahead, however, since these sites book quickly during the summer season.

Hiking is one of the best means of enjoying the park and its surroundings. Split Rock Lighthouse offers 12 miles of well-marked hiking trails, including a two-mile jaunt to the top of Day Hill. Those with more energy will enjoy the eight-mile loop that winds its way past Lake Superior's shoreline, offering a wonderful view of the lake, the lighthouse, and the Split Rock River.

Winter visitors will enjoy the park's seven miles of intermediate cross-country ski trails, including a short lakeshore trail between the Split Rock River and the lighthouse. The park is open seven days a week, but the Minnesota Historical Society's History Center is open only from October 16 to May 14, Friday through Sunday, noon to 4 p.m.

TETTEGOUCHE STATE PARK
474 Highway 61 E
Silver Bay, MN 55614
218/226-3539

A mere 60 miles from Duluth, the inland wilderness lakes and surrounding granite cliffs of Tettegouche State Park demand exploration. Winter may be the best time to plan your visit, since 12 miles of challenging ski trails lead to Mic Mac, Tettegouche, Nipisiquit, and Nicado lakes. If you're a summer traveler you'll find campsites available, but you'll have to leave your car behind and use the carts provided to shuttle your gear to your campsite.

Tettegouche State Park surrounds the Baptism River, long famous for its spring steelhead (rainbow trout) runs. The Baptism River cascades over three waterfalls in the park, including one offering an awesome 80-foot drop, the highest in Minnesota. Fishermen share the river with the kayakers who sometimes challenge the whitewater of the Baptism. Winter finds ice climbers chipping away at the frozen waterfalls, and autumn brings visitors hiking in the brisk air beneath a colorful canopy.

Within the protected boundaries of the park, you'll find Shovel Point. A self-guided nature trail will help you interpret this unique example of an ancient lava flow. Anchored to a thin layer of topsoil, red pines sway in the wind at the top of Shovel Point, sharing the

TETTEGOUCHE STATE PARK

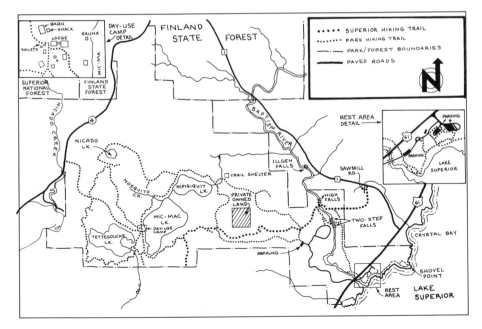

21

space with rare plants including butterwort and lingonberries. Over 90 varieties of lichen are also present, thanks to the influence of Lake Superior and the unique geology of Shovel Point.

After enjoying the point and its magnificent view of the lake, you'll return along the northeast cliff and see spruce trees stunted by the wicked winds and harsh conditions of a Superior winter.

Descending from the parking lot, you'll find a trail leading to a cobble beach on the shores of Lake Superior. This is a great vantage from which to ponder the force of Lake Superior and its effect on all who visit.

GEORGE CROSBY MANITOU STATE PARK
c/o Tettegouche State Park
474 Highway 61 E
Silver Bay, MN 55614
218/226-3539

The Manitou River drops 600 feet through George Crosby Manitou State Park, and you may feel that it's making the journey just for you. Such is the peace and quiet of the park.

Unlike other state parks on Minnesota's North Shore, this one isn't packed with RVs and chinese lanterns lighting the evening sky. There is, however, a price to pay for this isolation, since the park is reserved for backpackers.

Indians called the Manitou River *Manidowish*, meaning "spirit," because heavy mists often cloak the river at the drops, creating an ethereal, ghostly impression. Fisherman will enjoy trying to entice a rainbow or brook trout into snapping a fly on the River Trail that follows the Manitou. The park's 23 miles of trails vary in difficulty, from a flat walk around Lake Bensen to the rigorous mountain vistas of the Humpback Trail.

September and October are the best months to visit, because the annoying bugs are gone and fall colors blanket the hardwoods. The crisp mornings and cool days are tailor-made for a hike in the mountains. You can extend your fall color search by starting your hike at Crosby Manitou and later moving with the colors to the Lake Superior shoreline.

TEMPERANCE RIVER STATE PARK
P.O. Box 33
Schroeder, MN 55613
218/663-7476

Many visitors to Temperance River State Park plan their vacation around the autumn salmon migration, when shore casting along the banks and at the mouth of the river can be very good. A state record chinook salmon has been landed from the Temperance River and, if the river isn't yielding, you can wet your line in many area lakes.

The park offers over one mile of Lake Superior shoreline, and the pebble or sand beaches are fine places from which to enjoy the lake's many moods.

Nearby, the Sawbill Trail provides access to many popular canoe routes in the Boundary Waters Canoe Area Wilderness, but you'll need to pick up a permit if you plan an overnight visit.

There are two campgrounds within the park, one on a hill overlooking Lake Superior and the other right along the lakeshore. This is the only park on the Minnesota North Shore with campsites so close to Lake Superior, and it's a great place for a getaway in mid-July, when the heat of the city is bearing down on your friends back home.

Hiking is a popular way of viewing the river gorge of the Temperance as it winds its way to Lake Superior, tumbling over waterfalls and potholes. An interpretive trail will help you better understand the geology and history of the river bed. Quiet visitors wandering through the park's interior may happen upon whitetail deer, a moose, a black bear, or may even spot the tail end of a timber wolf fleeing from view. Access to the Superior Hiking Trail allows backpackers the opportunity to hike all the way to Grand Marais, but the day hike to Carlton Peak is a more popular trek. At 927 feet, Carlton Peak is the highest point on Minnesota's North Shore, and its summit affords impressive views of the surrounding Sawtooth Mountains and Lake Superior, especially during peak fall colors.

Motorists will enjoy a drive on the nearby Fall Color Tour provided by the Forest Service. Autumn is the best time of the year to spot a bull moose on the roam, especially if you rise early or make a sunset auto tour.

Because it's located about halfway up the North Shore, Temperance River State Park is a popular launching spot for those who intend to explore the surrounding countryside. So, even if the fish aren't biting, you can lace up your hiking boots and enjoy the beaches, mountains, lakes, and rivers of Superior Country.

CASCADE RIVER STATE PARK
HCR 3, Box 450
Lutsen, MN 55612
218/387-1543

Nestled in the Sawtooth Mountain Range, Cascade River State Park offers campers the comforts of home and the rugged surroundings of wilderness.

The Cascade River is a popular fishing spot, especially during the spring steelhead (rainbow trout) season and the fall salmon run. Rainbow and brook trout abound in the upper sections of the river, and anglers are often found casting for lake trout at the river's confluence with Lake Superior.

The park takes its name from the series of steps over which the river cascades while making its way to Lake Superior. Walking over a park footbridge, you'll get a unique view of five different waterfalls. Spring is the best time to visit the cascades themselves, since winter run-off pushes a rushing torrent of frothing whitewater through the gorge. During summer, the misty walls of the gorge are cloaked in ferns and moss, and rainbows are sometimes formed in the mist above the river.

Lookout Mountain, one the park's major attractions, towers over the Cascade River Valley. Backpackers will be pleased to note that the Superior Hiking Trail passes through the park, and hike-in campsites are available both along the shore of Lake Superior and within the park's interior. Hiking trails also traverse the interior, providing opportunities to explore the many streams that feed the Cascade River. Whitetail deer are common in the park, and the appropriately-named Deer Yard Lake hosts Minnesota's largest winter concentration of whitetails.

Winter is a special time here. Miles of groomed cross-country trails await skiers of all abilities. An Adirondack shelter, complete with fire ring, is available for skiers making the venture to Lookout Mountain, and the park's trails are linked with the extensive North Shore Mountains Ski Trail System.

Humans aren't the only visitors to Cascade River State Park. Many migrating birds rest in the park during their spring flights, and it seems that both earthbound and avian travelers find here the renewal they require to continue their journeys.

CASCADE RIVER STATE PARK

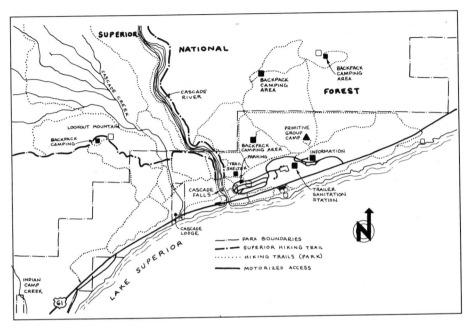

JUDGE C.R. MAGNEY STATE PARK
Box 500, East Star Route
Grand Marais, MN 55604
218/387-2929

The untamed Brule River flows through Judge C.R. Magney State Park, dancing amidst the polished rocks in a whitewater froth before reaching its outlet at Lake Superior.

The late Judge Clarence Magney loved to watch the rivers of Minnesota perform their ancient rituals, and he was instrumental in establishing 11 parks and waysides along Lake Superior's North Shore. Magney State Park commemorates this noted conservationist.

Brule Lake, situated within the Boundary Waters Canoe Area, is the source of the wild and free Brule River. As it makes its way through the Brule River Valley, the river is divided by a jutting rock at Devil's Kettle Falls. Here, the eastern section of the river drops 50 feet into a deep gorge and a pool, while the western portion plunges into a huge pothole and, according to local legend, dissappears forever.

Hiking trails weave through the aspen and birch stands of the Brule River Valley, and quiet walkers may surprise a white-tailed deer or black bear. The park's boreal forest contains a wide variety of plant and animal habitat, ranging from moist canyons along the river to dry, sunny, wind-swept ridges.

The park's rustic campground is usually the last state park campground to fill on busy summer weekends, and those who can live without a hot shower will be rewarded with a peaceful wilderness experience.

Anglers enjoy fishing for rainbow and brook trout in the Brule or its tributary, Gauthier Creek. The river is stocked annually with trout by the Minnesota DNR, and the Brule is noted for its spring steelhead (rainbow) run and its fall pink salmon run.

Minnesota state parks are open year-round, and if you strap on a pair of snowshoes and visit Magney, you're likely to have the Brule River Valley all to yourself.

GRAND PORTAGE NATIONAL MONUMENT
P.O. Box 666
Grand Marais, MN 55604

A journey back to the days of birch bark canoes and beaver pelt currency awaits visitors to Grand Portage National Monument. Established in 1958 just south of the U.S./Canadian border, the site includes a reconstructed stockade replicating the trading post that stood on this spot in the late 1700s.

It was along the banks of the Pigeon River that French-Canadian voyageurs bypassed treacherous rapids by carrying their birch bark canoes overland to Lake Superior. They christened this route the Grand Portage, or "Great Carrying Place."

Businessman Simon McTavish and his Scottish partners recognized that the area was important because it linked Montreal, then the capital of Great Lakes fur trade, with the fur-rich border country of northwestern Canada at the Pigeon River. In 1784, McTavish established the headquarters of the British-owned North West Company and hired hardworking French-Canadian voyageurs to transport the furs from the wilds of the north to the civilized east.

The company's post, located where the Pigeon River meets Lake Superior, proved a convenient meeting place for the voyageurs, because two groups emerged based on geographical distinctions. The north men, called "winterers," were one group, while the Montreal men, or "pork-eaters," made up the second group. In late July, the north men set out from Grand Portage to spend the winter at remote trading posts, their canoes laden with European goods. These goods, including beads, blankets, and liquor, were traded with Indians for beaver pelts, which became the currency of the Northwest. Following ice-out in mid-May, the north men paddled back to Grand Portage to connect with the Montreal men, who were returning from their trek east across the Great Lakes to Montreal.

The paddling season climaxed during this great summer rendezvous, when the voyageurs received wages for the past year's labor. Hundreds of these men spent the better part of July camped outside the stockade, trading pelts and stories from the trail. The rendezvous was noted for its raucous atmosphere. Liquor flowed freely, and fists flew frequently.

The business was moved from American to Canadian soil in 1803, so that the British-owned North West Company could avoid the complications of citizenship, licensing, and high import duties.

Today the reconstructed stockade offers visitors a chance to relive the days of the voyageurs by touring the grounds and climbing the fort's lookout tower for a view of Lake Superior.

The actual portage bisects the reservation of the Grand Portage Band of Chippewa (Ojibwa) Indians, who donated the land that became the national monument. For voyageurs, the nine-mile trail was a 2 1/2-hour trek to the company's storage depot at Fort Charlotte, while carrying a pair of 90-pound packs. Those wishing to experience the same trek are welcome to hike the trail in summer or ski it in winter. Backpackers will find a primitive campsite at Fort Charlotte, but campers must register before pitching a tent on the site. Meanwhile, a second trail begins across the road from the stockade, ascending the 300-foot-high Mount Rose.

SUPERIOR HIKING TRAIL
Superior Hiking Trail Association
P.O. Box 4
Two Harbors, MN 55616
218/834-4556

The Superior Hiking Trail is a ribbon of access through the wilderness of Minnesota's Lake Superior North Shore, skirting the bluffs and crossing the rivers of the Sawtooth Mountains.

Over 150 miles of the 250-mile route have been completed to date, including an almost-complete footpath from Castle Dander to the Kadunce River north of Grand Marais. The trail is open to both day hikers and overnight backpackers. It will eventually lead from Duluth, Minnesota, to the Canadian border, linking eight state parks along the Minnesota North Shore through country previously inaccessible to all but the most ardent explorers.

The 18-inch wide trail passes through a northern transition forest of oak, maple, basswood, and second-growth birch and spruce into the boreal forest of fir, pine, spruce, and tamarack. Lake Superior is never far from view, and its influence is felt in the rapidly changing weather patterns you'll experience.

The trail crosses both public and private land, thanks to construction easements granted by both individual property owners and corporations. You'll be sharing the path with moose, wolves, black bears, and deer, as eagles and even peregrine falcons soar overhead. Although the trail is rugged, it is well-suited for even short day hikes, as easy access is provided from many points along Highway 61 identified by the Trail Association. The trail intersects roads and state parks, creating sections that average five to eight miles in length.

SUPERIOR HIKING TRAIL

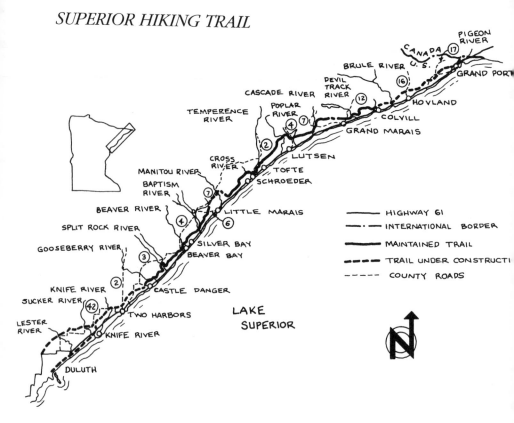

Shuttling from trailhead to trailhead is a popular means of exploring, and many resorts on the North Shore will be happy to provide this service for their guests. Loop hikes are also possible, especially in areas where the trail crosses state park and national forest trails.

Backpackers will find overnight treks rewarding, because the trail affords panoramic overlooks of Lake Superior and intimate encounters with the wild rivers of the North Shore. Backcountry campsites, complete with fire ring, tent pad, and privy are found every five to six miles along the trail. These campsites are available on a first-come, first-served basis, and most offer access to water. The trail intersects small communities along the route, allowing campers to restock their supplies or enjoy a hot shower and a warm bed before they hit the trail again.

Hikers are advised to plan on cool nights and wet weather. Insects, including ticks, can be bothersome to those who don't bring a head net, long-sleeve shirts, and bug spray. Drinking water should be purified, and sturdy footwear is necessary. Due to its rugged character, the trail is inappropriate for mechanized uses, and SHTA policy prohibits use of mountain bikes. Since many sections of the path are steep and narrow, it's ill-suited for cross-country skiing in most places, although travel by snowshoe is possible on many sections. Completed segments of the trail have been mapped by the Trail Association, and a trail guide is available offering further insight into the geology, flora, fauna, and cultural history of this unique area.

The Superior Hiking Trail became a reality thanks to the vision and labor of the Superior Hiking Trail Association. Founded in 1986, the Minnesota non-profit corporation was established to "link people with nature by footpath along the North Shore of Lake Superior." Construction of the trail, campsites, and bridges has been financed largely through state funds, coupled with Forest Service funding and private donations. Ongoing trail maintenance and upkeep will depend on volunteers who work under the guidance of the Trail Association.

The Superior Hiking Trail Association can use your help. Volunteers offer both their financial resources and their time to assist in trail maintenance, campsite construction, and bridge building. Volunteering is a way of leaving a positive imprint on the North Shore. Another way to help is by treating the trail and surrounding areas with respect and appreciation when you visit.

SUPERIOR NATIONAL FOREST
Forest Supervisor
P.O. Box 338
Duluth MN 55801
218/720-5322

Superior National Forest stands between the waves of Lake Superior and the wilds of the Canadian North. Here you can paddle for miles and hike for days with only your thoughts and dreams to accompany you. Or you can roll into a campground, pitch a tent, and never leave the comfort of your campsite. It's a land of both perspiration and inspiration, as a glowing fire signals the end of a hard day on the trail. It's also a land of opportunity, where hard-working loggers carve out a living from the area's timber resources.

Long before Europeans arrived in the New World, native Americans explored this region, gathering wild rice and hunting caribou, moose, and deer. Evidence of these settlements continues to be discovered, including a camp in the Laurentian District that dates back to the birth of Christ. The Ojibwa were among the last Indian cultures to settle the region, driving the once-dominant Sioux from the region in the mid-1800s. Today, sharp-eyed visitors will discover Indian pictographs on rock outcroppings.

Jacques de Noyons, who passed this way in 1688, is believed to have been the first white man to visit what would become the Superior National Forest. Driven by a European demand for fashionable beaver hats, de Noyons explored a vast forest that provided a seemingly endless supply of valuable pelts. To transport these pelts, fur traders depended upon the stout French-Canadians known as voyageurs, and these voyageurs have become synonymous with the Superior wilderness experience. Many of the portages we travel today were traveled by the voyageurs, and before them by the native hunters and gatherers.

As demand dwindled and the beaver felt the stress of harvest, the fur trade disappeared, only to be replaced by legions of axe-wielding loggers. Railroads penetrating the Minnesota wilderness opened vast timber stands, and today only isolated pockets of virgin white pine remain between blankets of spruce, aspen, birch, cedar, and tamarack in the Superior National Forest. Many of the white pine stands are now preserved in remote areas of the BWCAW. They serve as a tribute to the virgin forest that once covered this magnificent land.

But the Superior National Forest is much more than trees. It is also thousands of acres of clean, clear, inviting water, surrounded by soggy swamps and spongy bogs. Access to the region's lakes is available via 162 boat landings, over 1,500 miles of canoe trails, and endless motorboat routes.

Administered by the U.S. Forest Service and headquartered in Duluth, the 3.9 million-acre Superior National Forest is the largest federally managed forest in the continental United States. Moose, black bears, timber wolves, white-tailed deer, eagles, and osprey find refuge within its vast confines. Visitors find refuge as well, whether by casting a lure into a clear forest lake or by driving down a logging road at sunset in search of a moose.

Although the famous motor-free Boundary Waters Canoe Area Wilderness is perhaps the most renowned component of the Superior National Forest, it's by no means the only reason to visit. In fact, over one-half of the visitors to the Superior National Forest never spend a night in the BWCAW. These folks are quite content to explore the

SUPERIOR NATIONAL FOREST

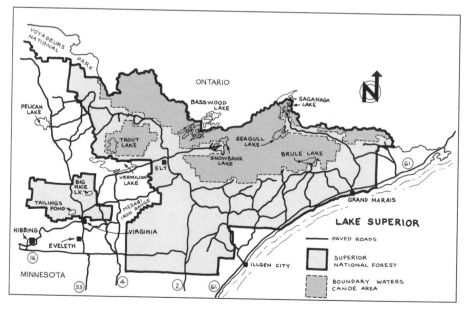

many surrounding lakes and campgrounds of the forest. This "fringe" area, although similar in topography, offers the conveniences of modern life coupled with accessibility via motorboat, automobile, or mountain bike.

Hiking trails are located throughout the forest. They vary in length and difficulty, affording opportunites to wander for an hour or a week. Specific trail maps and information on trail conditions are available at Forest Service offices located in nearby communities.

CAMPING

A campsite is an excellent base from which to launch your exploration of the Superior National Forest. Those seeking the comfort of a cleared campsite, fire grate, hand-pumped water and parking spurs able to accommodate trailers will find 27 developed campgrounds and seven less-developed camping areas maintained by the Forest Service. These campgrounds provide easy access to some of the forest's best fishing and swimming lakes. The campgrounds vary in size from less than ten to over fifty sites, and each is adjacent to a lake or stream. Fall Lake Campground offers cold running water, flush toilets, and a trailer dumping station, but all other campgrounds are more rustic in nature, providing hand pumps and pit toilets.

Most campgrounds are open from spring through late fall, and at least one campground in each area is generally open during the off-season. During winter, however, roads to these campgrounds are often unplowed, limiting access.

Swimming beaches are available at eight of the campgrounds, and most offer boat ramps to access forest lakes or rivers. There is usually plenty of room to wheel an RV into a campsite, but you won't find electricity. Camp units are usually limited to one family only, and pets are allowed if kept on a leash.

If you're seeking a more solitary experience, the Forest Service also maintains over 200 individual primitive campsites, each located within Superior National Forest but outside the boundaries of the BWCAW. Unlike overnight visitors to the BWCAW, campers in Superior National Forest are not required to secure a special permit. Many of these primitive campsites are accessible by water only, but others can be reached on foot or by car. These campsites offer a tent pad, fire grate, and latrine. They're ideal for fishermen who seek a wilderness experience but don't want to leave their motorboats behind. Contact the ranger district nearest the area you wish to visit for help in planning your adventure and locating these campsites.

Finally, Superior National Forest offers what rangers call "dispersed" camping opportunities. This means you are free to pitch your tent anywhere in the Superior National Forest backcountry without a permit, as long as you remain out of the designated BWCAW. You must, however, make your camp at least one hundred feet from any lake or stream, and practice minimum-impact camping etiquette. This will ensure that the party following you will be able to enjoy the same wilderness you've encountered.

The state of Minnesota also operates six state forest campgrounds and three state parks within Superior National Forest boundaries. All told, there are over 800 developed campsites available to forest visitors.

While camping in the Superior National Forest, you won't need a permit to make day trips into the BWCAW. But you are required to abide by BWCAW rules, which means you must leave your motor, cans, and bottles behind. You are perfectly free to fish, swim, hike, and paddle, as long as you don't plan an overnight visit.

SUPERIOR NATIONAL FOREST CAMPGROUNDS

AURORA RANGER DISTRICT
P.O. Box 391
Aurora, MN 55705
218/229-3371

Cadotte Lake Campground
27 campsites
Open mid-May through October
Fee charged, reservations accepted
800/283-CAMP

Summer visitors should consider making a reservation to secure a site. To reach the campground from Brimson, take County Highway 44 eight miles north to County Highway 16. Head 1 1/2 miles west on Highway 16 to Forest Road 425. Proceed one-half mile down F.R. 425, then one mile southwest down Forest Road 778 to Cadotte Lake Campground.

Whiteface Reservoir Campground
58 campsites
Open mid-May through October
Fee charged

The campsites of the Whiteface Reservoir Campground are very popular during the summer, so plan to arrive midweek and early in the day to secure one. To reach the campground from Aurora, head south 5 1/2 miles on County Highway 100 to County Highway 99. Go 6 1/2 miles south on Highway 99 to County Highway 16, and head east five miles to Forest Road 417. Take F.R. 417 three miles south to the Whiteface Reservoir Campground.

GUNFLINT RANGER DISTRICT
P.O. Box 308
Grand Marais, MN 55604
218/387-1750

Cascade River Campground
3 campsites
Open June through mid-September
No fee
   The campground provides access to Minnesota's highest peak, Eagle Mountain. To reach it from Grand Marais, head one-half mile north on County Highway 12 to County Highway 7. Take County Highway 7 four miles west to Forest Road 158. Take F.R. 158 nine miles northwest to the Cascade River Campground.

Devil's Track Lake Campground
19 campsites
Open June through mid-September
Fee charged
   An airport is located at the eastern end of busy Devil's Track Lake. To reach the campground from Grand Marais, head north four miles on County Highway 12 to County Highway 6. Take Highway 6 west one mile to County Highway 8, and proceed northwest eight miles to Devil's Track Lake Campground.

East Bearskin Lake Campground
47 campsites
Open June through mid-September
Fee charged
   Paddlers will enjoy direct access to the BWCAW from the campground. To get there from Grand Marais, head northwest 27 miles on County Highway 12 to Forest Road 146. East Bearskin Lake Campground is located 1 1/2 miles northeast on F.R. 146.

Flour Lake Campground
46 campsites
Open June through mid-September
Fee charged
   A vacant campsite can usually be found at the Flour Lake Campground. To get there from Grand Marais, head 27 miles northwest on County Highway 12 to Forest Road 147. Take F.R. 147 2 1/2 miles northeast to the Flour Lake Campground.

Iron Lake Campground
7 campsites
Open June through mid-September
Fee charged, reservations accepted,800/283-CAMP
   Iron Lake offers direct access to the BWCAW, and it's popular with paddlers seeking to avoid the better-known entry points. To get there from Grand Marais, head 38 miles northwest on County Highway 12.

Kimball Lake Campground
7 campsites
Open June through mid-September
Fee charged

The campground is popular with fishermen hoping to land a lake trout. To reach it from Grand Marais, head northeast 11 miles on County Highway 12 to Forest Road 140. A two-mile jaunt east on F.R. 140 brings you to Kimball Lake Campground.

Trail's End Campground
36 campsites
Open mid-May through mid-September
Fee charged, reservations accepted
800/283-CAMP
   Trail's End Campground is popular with paddlers preparing for their trek into the wilderness, because it provides access to two popular BWCAW entry points. To reach the campground from Grand Marais, head 58 miles northwest on County Highway 12 to the end of the Gunflint Trail.

Two Island Lake Campground
39 campsites
Open mid-May through September
Fee charged
   Campers looking for a vacancy are likely to find an open site here. To reach Two Island Lake from Grand Marais, take Highway 12 four miles north to County Highway 6. Take Highway 6 one mile west to County Highway 8. Head northwest five miles on Highway 8 to County Highway 27, and go northwest five miles to the campground.

ISABELLA RANGER DISTRICT
2759 Highway 1
Isabella, MN 55607
218/323-7722

Divide Lake Campground
3 campsites
Open May through October
No fee
   To reach tiny Divide Lake Campground, head out of Isabella one mile northwest on Highway 1 to Forest Road 172. Proceed five miles east on F.R. 172 to Divide Lake Campground.

Isabella River Campground
11 campsites
Open May through October
Fee charged
   Campers can usually find an open site at the Isabella River Campground. To reach the campground from Isabella, head west on Highway 1 four miles to the campground.

McDougal Lake Campground
21 campsites
Open May through October
Fee charged
   The McDougal Lake Campground is popular among mountain bikers roaming the nearby forest roads and trails. To get there from Isabella, head 12 miles west on Highway 1 to Forest Road 106. Take F.R. 106 to McDougal Lake.

KAWISHIWI RANGER DISTRICT
118 S. 4th AVE E.
Ely, MN 55731
218/365-6185

Birch Lake Campground
16 campsites
Open mid-May through September
Fee charged
   The Birch Lake Campground sees moderate use, so the chances of securing a campsite are good except during the busiest summer weekends. To reach Birch Lake from Ely, head nine miles south on Highway 1 to Forest Road 429. Take F.R. 429 south 4 1/2 miles to Birch Lake.

Fall Lake Campground
69 campsites
Open mid-May through September
Fee charged, reservations accepted
800/283-CAMP
   The campground at Fall Lake is one of the busiest in the Superior National Forest, so it's wise to make reservations if you're planning a visit during July or August. To reach Fall Lake from Ely, take Highway 169 east 5 1/2 miles to County Highway 18 and head five miles east to Forest Road 551. Take F.R. 551 two miles northeast to Fall Lake.

Fenske Lake Campground
16 campsites
Open mid-May through September
Fee charged
   When other campgrounds within the ranger district are full, try the Fenske Lake Campground. To get there from Ely, head east two miles on Highway 169 to County Highway 88. Go 2 1/2 miles north on Highway 88 to County Highway 16. Head north 8 1/2 miles on Highway 16 to the campground.

South Kawishiwi River Campground
32 campsites
Open mid-May through September
Fee charged

The South Kawishiwi River Campground offers paddlers direct access to the BWCAW. To reach it from Ely, head 12 miles south on Highway 1 to the Kawishiwi River.

LaCROIX RANGER DISTRICT
P.O. Box 1085
Cook, MN 55723
218/666-5251

Echo Lake Campground
26 campsites
Open mid-May through October 5
Fee charged, group camping available
    A group campsite at Echo Lake Campground is available to accommodate parties of up to 20 campers. To reach the campground from Buyck, head north four miles on County Highway 23 to County Highway 116. Go one mile east on Highway 116 to Forest Road 841. Take F.R. 841 one mile north to the campground.

Lake Jeanette Campground
9 campsites
Open mid-May through October 5
No fee
    The campground at Lake Jeanette is busy, especially on weekends, so plan to arrive mid-week to find an empty campsite. To reach Jeanette Lake from Buyck, head four miles north on County Highway 24 to County Highway 116. Go 12 miles east on Highway 116 to Jeanette Lake.

TOFTE RANGER DISTRICT
Tofte, Minnesota 55615
218/663-7981

Baker Lake Campground
5 campsites
Open mid-May to October
Fee charged
    Baker Lake provides direct access to the BWCAW, so it's popular with paddlers preparing for their trips. To reach the campground exit Highway 61 one-half mile north of the Tofte Ranger Station at Highway 2, and head north 17 miles. Take Forest Road 165 northeast five miles to Forest Road 1272 and proceed west one-half mile to Baker Lake.

Clara Lake Campground
2 campsites
Open mid-May through October
No fee
    Clara Lake Campground is located on Forest Road 339. To get there, exit Highway 61 one mile north of Lutsen at County Highway 4, and

proceed eight miles north to Forest Road 339. Clara Lake is four miles northwest on F.R. 339.

Crescent Lake Campground
35 campsites
Open mid-May through October
Fee charged, group campsites available
    Exit Highway 61 one-half mile north of the Tofte Ranger Station, and proceed 17 miles north on Highway 2. Then head 7 miles northeast on Forest Road 165 to Cresent Lake Campground.

Kawishiwi Lake Campground
5 campsites
Open mid-May through October
No fee
    The Kawishiwi Lake Campground provides direct access to the BWCAW. To get there, exit Highway 61 at Highway 2, one-half mile past the Tofte Ranger Station. Take Highway 2 north 17 1/2 miles to County Highway 3. Head west 10 miles on Highway 3 to Forest Road 354. Take F.R. 354 four miles northwest to Kawishiwi Lake Campground.

Nine Mile Lake Campground
24 campsites
Open mid-May through October
Fee charged
    Nine Mile Lake Campground is typically one of the last drive-in campgrounds to fill in the Tofte Ranger District. To reach it from Schroeder, head west ten miles on County Highway 1, then go four miles north on County Highway 7.

Poplar River Campground
4 campsites
Open mid-May through October
No fee
    The Poplar River Campground is often full in summer, so you may wish to plan an off-season visit. To get there, exit Highway 61 one-half mile north of the Tofte Ranger Station at Highway 2, and head north 11 miles to Forest Road 164. Head east six miles down F.R. 164 to the campground.

Sawbill Lake Campground
50 campsites
Open mid-May through October
Fee charged
    Sawbill Lake is one of the most popular entry points to the BWCAW, so consider yourself lucky if you find an open campsite during the busy summer months. To reach Sawbill Lake, exit Highway 61 one-half mile north of the Tofte Ranger Station at Highway 2 and head 24 miles north to Sawbill Lake.

Temperance River Campground
9 campsites
Open mid-May through October
Fee charged

The Temperance River Campground is busy in summer, so arrive early if you hope to land a campsite. It's located 11 miles up Highway 2 from Highway 61, just north of the Tofte Ranger Station.

VIRGINIA RANGER DISTRICT
505-12th Ave W.
Virginia, MN 55792
218/741-5736

Pfeiffer Lake Campground
21 campsites
Open May through September
Fee charged

There's a good chance you'll find an open campsite at the Pfeiffer Lake Campground. To reach Pfeiffer Lake from Virginia, head northeast 22 miles on Highway 169 to Highway 1. Take Highway 1 west five miles to Forest Road 256. Head two miles south on Forest Road 256 to the campground.

MOUNTAIN BIKING

Miles of logging roads cross the Superior National Forest, winding along streams, skirting lakes, and climbing hills. Mountain biking in this area provides a challenging, scenic ride. Campgrounds, cabins and lodges dot the surrounding forest, offering a number of bases from which to begin your excursion.

Please keep in mind that the BWCAW Wilderness Act of 1978 outlawed mechanized vehicles—including mountain bikes—in the Boundary Waters Canoe Area Wilderness. Use of mountain bikes in the surrounding Superior National Forest is encouraged, however, as long as riders tread lightly. Hills and wet sections of the trail are easily damaged by the fat-tired mountain bikes, especially given the thin topsoil found in northern Minnesota. Many miles of trails throughout the country, once open to mountain bikers, have been closed because of irresponsible riding by a handful of bikers. The Superior National Forest offers the following guidelines to assure that your impact on the trails is minimal:

- Yield to all trail users, motorized and non-motorized.
- Maintain a speed that is safe for you and for others.
- Respect wildlife, vegetation,the environment, and private property.
- Ride only on designated trails, and obey local ordinances.
- Take appropriate personal safety measures, such as wearing a helmet, informing someone of your plans, and carrying adequate supplies, including first aid and repair kits.

A good map and compass is essential for those who strike off on their own, as logging roads may be unmarked and numerous. Further, the logging roads and snowmobile and ski trails are often muddy, rocky, and rugged.

A number of routes have been mapped by the Lutsen-Tofte Tourism Association and the Grand Marais Chamber of Commerce in cooperation with the U.S. Forest Service. They are by no means the only routes available, but they will certainly give many miles of enjoyment. Tread lightly and have fun!

BEAR HEAD LAKE STATE PARK
Star Route 2
Box 5700
Ely, MN 55731
218/365-4253

A sand beach circled by immense white pines offers a grand view of the lake to visitors at Bear Head Lake State Park.

Located just 19 miles west of Ely off Highway 169, or 16 miles east of Tower off the same highway, Bear Head Lake State Park is popular with campers vying for sites within the park's 73-unit modern campground. Those seeking a more secluded camping experience have access to six remote lakeshore campsites, including two boat-in sites on the lake.

Ten clear lakes are protected within park boundaries, and four of these are stocked with walleyes or trout. Boat access is available on both Eagle's Nest and Bear Head lakes, and canoes are available for rent from the park's concession operation.

A hike along the park's trails reveals many pine stumps amid the second-growth forest. At the turn of the century, a huge white and red pine forest surrounded the lakes here. Then, as rail lines penetrated the wilderness, these forests fell before the logger's axe. As the logs were cut, they were dumped into Bear Head Lake and floated to the lake's south shore, where a steam-powered sawmill trimmed the virgin timber. The worthless slab wood was dumped into the lake, and today that same water-logged slab wood provides welcome cover for fish.

Remnants of the miles of narrow gauge railroad grades are found throughout the park, and in some places the park's hiking trails follow these routes. A jaunt along the west side of Norberg Lake and the beginning of the Becky Lake Trail indicates the area's logging past, while a hike through the second-growth will give you a glimpse of the park's bright future.

SUPERIOR-QUETICO
Boundary Waters Wilderness

The border lakes of Minnesota and Ontario perpetually sing with the laughter of loons and the soothing rhythm of a paddle gliding through a liquid paradise. It's no wonder that the Superior-Quetico ecosystem is considered America's favorite wilderness.

Perhaps nowhere else can you feel such intimacy with the wild. Swimming beneath an emerald lake or paddling through a pristine riverway, you're one with the beauty that surrounds you. Even portages where canoes and equipment must be carried overland seem enjoyable when the blue horizon of the trail's end reveals a new lake awaiting exploration.

This is rugged country. Travelers must be prepared to weather severe storms, endure pesky insects, or survive chilling winter temperatures. Here, a high degree of independence has always been

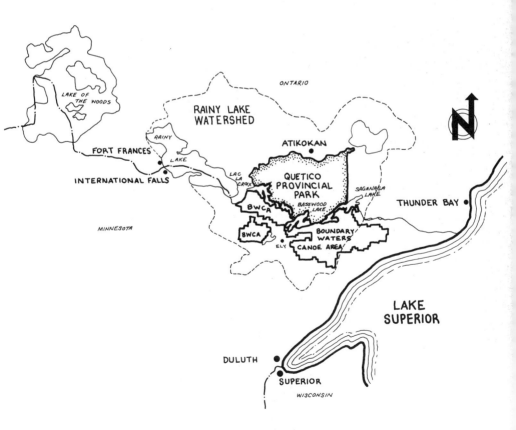

required. In 1688, Frenchman Jacques de Noyon pioneered a route from Lake Superior to Lake of the Woods, passing through the Quetico-Superior wilderness. This demanding route, called the "Voyageur Highway," opened the region to the fur trade. Modern canoeists traveling Saganaga, Basswood, and Lac la Croix still dip their paddles in the liquid highway and, like those who traveled before them, face the challenges of a wild and beautiful land.

The modern history of border country began in the 19th century, long after the glaciers had left their mark and retreated northward. When the frenzied European demand for beaver pelts that fueled exploration of the Superior-Quetico wilderness had slackened, voyageurs and settlers exchanged their paddles for hand saws. About 100 of these homesteaders settled border country, hoping to carve farms out of the forest. But the thin soil of the wilderness proved unable to support agriculture, and most of the homesteaders moved on.

Picks and shovels followed the plow, as gold fever swept the border lakes following discovery of the precious metal at Lake Vermilion in the 1870s. Even though prospectors rushed to the area and some gold was found at Saganaga and Clearwater lakes, most returned home with empty pans and deflated dreams. Ultimately, it was iron, not gold, that left its mark on border country. Minnesota's first iron mine opened at Soudan in 1882 and, five years later, Ely was incorporated around an iron mine. By 1911 the "Iron Range" was producing more iron ore than all other regions of the U.S. combined. Today mining remains an important part of the area's economy, and much of the development of the Iron Range can be traced to this industry.

In 1878, as Minnesota's Timberland Stone Act opened the border lakes to private ownership, Canada was attempting to nationalize its holdings in the Quetico. Nine years earlier, French-Indian homesteaders had rebelled after losing their land to the Canadian government. The uprising ended when the government sent 1200 troops to the Quetico from Toronto. The troops traveled through the rugged wilderness, following the old Voyageur Highway.

At the turn of the 20th century, the axe arrived in the Superior-Quetico wilderness, forever changing the complexion of the ecosystem. In just over one decade, a single lumber company established more than 50 logging camps, each camp housing over 100 men. The amount of lumber cut as a result was staggering. Between 1896 and 1923, the St. Croix Lumber Company harvested about one billion board feet of timber in what was to become the Boundary Waters Canoe Area Wilderness (BWCAW). By 1978, when logging finally ceased in the BWCAW, some 262,000 acres had been cleared. The Quetico side of the wilderness didn't fare much better. Logging began there in the 1860s and continued until 1971, when all commercial logging within the park was halted.

The scars of the logging axe are slow to heal. Even though roughly one-half of the BWCAW was untouched by loggers, only isolated stands of valuable virgin white and red pine forest remain. The white pine groves are a living memorial to the great forest that welcomed the voyageurs of days gone by.

The serenity and peace enjoyed by today's visitors to the Superior-Quetico Wilderness was hard-won. In 1909, thanks to President Theodore Roosevelt, the Superior National Forest (which includes the Boundary Waters Canoe Area Wilderness) was established. A legacy of the logging era, the new national forest was just over one million acres in size, including thousands of acres of seemingly worthless stumps.

Roads, or the access that they provide, soon became central to the conflicts involving the Superior-Quetico wilderness. As the automobile gained popularity, so did the notion that access roads should pierce the wilderness. However, this vision was not shared by everyone. In 1922, Forest Service landscape architect Arthur Carhart surveyed the Superior Wilderness while formulating a comprehensive recreational policy for the area. Struck by the area's canoeing opportunities, Carhart recommended that road-building cease in the northern half of the Superior Forest, suggesting that the area should serve as a "boat and canoe forest." Even though Carhart left the Forest Service shortly after submitting his proposal, he's credited with convincing his superiors to withdraw over $50,000 that had been allocated for road construction in 1923.

The battle was not over. In 1924, famed conservationist Aldo Leopold canoed from Basswood Lake into Canada. He returned from the journey a staunch defender of the border lakes, and joined the conservation-minded Izaak Walton League in its attempt to maintain the integrity of the wilderness. Leopold convinced League members that the border country was threatened not only by roads, but also by private land holdings. Taking Leopold's advice to heart, the league supported efforts at new public land acquisition and continued to lobby for wilderness protection.

By 1926, the Forest Service ended its ambitious road-building program, allowing only completion of the Seagull Lake extension of the Gunflint Trail, the Fernberg Road, and the Echo Trail. Even though many logging roads still crisscross the Superior National Forest, the wilderness character of the BWCAW remains intact.

The Boundary Waters Canoe Area Wilderness was given its current name in 1958. Twenty years later, following a sometimes heated conflict with logging and motorboat interests, the BWCA Wilderness Bill of 1978 was passed, establishing the area's current 1,075,000-acre boundaries. As part of its provisions, the bill prohibits logging and limits use of motorboats to one-third of the total water area until 1999, when motors will be restricted to one-quarter of the wilderness.

Today, with tents pitched beneath an endless BWCAW sky, we owe special thanks to those who paddled before us. They, too, heard the song of the wilderness, and were so moved that they preserved it on our behalf.

BWCAW PERMITS, PLANS, AND RESTRICTIONS

If you're one of the over 150,000 paddlers planning to spend a night in the BWCAW between May 1 and September 30, you'll need a permit. You won't need one if you're a day-use visitor planning to paddle, hike, or fish in the wilderness, unless you plan to use a motorboat. You can pick up the free permit no more than 24 hours in advance of your trip from any Superior National Forest office or from a cooperating business, such as an outfitter or resort. The permit allows up to ten people to enter the wilderness on a specified day and from a specific entry point.

Permits are required because there are simply too many campers competing for a limited number of established campsites on the border country's most popular lakes. In order to limit this competition, the Forest Service restricts the number of parties that can enter via any given entry point daily.

To assure that you have access to the entry point you desire, you may reserve a permit in advance by mail or by phone. Reservations are accepted for the upcoming season beginning each February 1. You can make one by mail by sending $5 and writing to: BWCA RESERVATIONS, SUPERIOR NATIONAL FOREST, P.O. Box 338, DULUTH, MN 55801. Telephone reservations are accepted if you charge the $5 fee on your VISA or MasterCard. Make them by calling 218/720-5440.

Reservation requests must include the name, address, and phone number of the party leader, an alternate leader, the party size, the date you wish to enter and exit, and the planned entry and exit point. You must also specify your method of travel (canoe, hiking, boat, or motorboat) and it's wise to list an alternative entry point in case your first choice is unavailable.

After receiving confirmation of your reservation in writing, you will still need to pick up your permit from a Forest Service district officer or a cooperating outfitter or resort. This requirement is intended to ensure that you're advised of the special regulations you'll be expected to abide by while you're visiting the wilderness. Among others, the restrictions include a ban on most cans and bottles (with the exception of insect aerosol cans and fuel containers) as well as special motorboat restrictions. Although a few BWCAW lakes allow unlimited motorboat use, motors are banned from all interior lakes, and motorboat size is restricted on many others. You must also camp only in designated campsites unless you're in specified remote sections of the wilderness.

BWCAW campsites are wonderful. You'll always enjoy a great view, and you'll usually find an excellent rock from which to swim, fish, or plot the next day's travels. The campsites include a massive steel fire grate, a cleared tent pad, and a box latrine. You'll find plenty of wood across the lake from your campsite, and the bugs won't find you if you choose a high, wind-swept site. Try to choose your campsite early in the day, so you have an empty site and plenty of time to prepare your dinner in daylight.

Fishing in the BWCAW can be very good. May and September are the best fishing months, but skilled and persistent fishermen can usually catch northern pike, smallmouth bass, walleye, or lake trout all season long. Packing in your own nightcrawlers is inconvenient, but very effective. Rapalas, daredevils, and silver or white spoons trolling behind a canoe have landed many BWCAW lunkers.

Fish aren't the only species that bite in border country. Blackflies, mosquitoes, and deerflies are also part of the wilderness experience from late May through mid-July. Head nets, cotton pants, and a long sleeve t-shirt will provide welcome protection.

July and August are the warmest and busiest months in the BWCAW. That's the time of the year to take long portages and camp in the back bays off the main paddle routes. May and September are peaceful months, but the unpredictable weather means you should pack a wool cap and gloves. Raingear, long underwear, and a fleece or wool sweater are musts for every wilderness visitor. Thunderstorms are common in the BWCAW, and when lightning strikes it's time to make camp, regardless of your planned itinerary.

Keep in mind that all watercraft on Minnesota waters, including canoes and sea kayaks, must be registered. Canoes and sea kayaks carrying registration from another state do not have to be registered in Minnesota, but even if your home state does not require registration, Minnesota does. Each year heavy fines are levied against many paddlers who fail to have their canoes registered. To register by mail, contact the Minnesota DNR License Center, 500 Lafayette Road, St. Paul, MN 55155-4026.

Black bears can be a nuisance in the BWCAW. Even seasoned, leave-no-trace campers are occasionally bothered by bears, because the party before them may have left scraps in the latrine or unburned leftovers in the fire ring. Always hang your food at least ten feet off the ground and six feet from any tree limb, even if you're fishing for northern pike within sight of your camp.

In 1987 a bear attacked two campers in two separate incidents before it was killed by Forest Service rangers. Fortunately, the hapless victims were left scared but not severely injured. This was the first verified bear attack in the BWCAW, but each summer campers lose their food packs to visiting bruins. And it's a long hike out of the wilderness on an empty stomach.

Choosing routes is fun, and looking at a map of the border lakes will get you excited about your adventure. To penetrate the area, you'll need high-quality maps. The best are available from local outfitters, or through the mail directly from suppliers. Contact W.A.Fisher Company, Box 1107, Virginia, MN 55792 or McKenzie Maps. When planning your trip, keep in mind that portages—the overland treks you'll make carrying your canoe and equipment between lakes—are measured in rods. A rod is 16 1/2 feet, roughly the length of a canoe. Some portages are steep, short, and difficult. Others are long, flat, and easy. Any portage over 100 rods is tough, but taking a few long portages is a great way to evade the August crowds.

The former Voyageur Visitor Center, once the headquarters for paddlers visiting the area, has now been incorporated into the new International Wolf Center. The Center is a great place to learn about the wilderness, plan your route, and prepare for your trip.

Many backcountry canoe trips begin in Ely, the "Canoe Capital of America." This modern Iron Range community has all the supplies you'll need for your trip, and a host of commercial operators can provide you with specialized equipment, including specialized food.

Ely lies at the crossroads of two major access points to the wilderness—Echo Trail and Fernberg Road. Moose Lake, the BWCAW's most popular put-in, is accessible from Fernberg Road. You may want to avoid it due to its popularity. The BWCAW offers 73 entry points, but unfortunately over two-thirds of the paddlers enter from the top fifteen lakes. The daily quota system prevents unreasonable congestion, but avoiding popular entries like Moose Lake, Lake One, Trout Lake, and Fall Lake will help you beat the summer crowds and will enhance your sense of solitude.

Author Robert Beymer provides detailed route information in a pair of guides called *Boundary Waters Canoe Area Vol.1, The Western Region* and *Vol. 2, The Eastern Region.* It's also useful to talk to rangers and outfitters regarding your interests, experience, and time limitations. Tailoring your trip to your skills and interests will make the experience more satisfying.

The tiny Lake Superior community of Tofte is also a popular spot from which to launch your trek into canoe country. Cook County Road 2, known as Sawbill Trail, originates at Tofte and leads to Sawbill and Brule lakes, two of the BWCAW's most popular entry points. Those seeking solitude will find Baker and Homer lakes, also accessible via the Sawbill Trail, less busy and more secluded.

On the northeastern corner of the BWCAW, you'll find the famous Gunflint Trail. The Gunflint, actually Cook County Road 12, begins in the bustling lakeshore community of Grand Marais. Paddlers will find the municipal indoor swimming pool at Grand Marais a welcome relief after time spent in the backcountry.

On the Gunflint Trail, you'll travel over 75 miles to its terminus at Sea Gull Lake, gateway to Canada and the eastern half of the BWCAW. Public campgrounds and outfitters can be found along the trail, ready to outfit your trip or supply you with last-minute items. Saganaga Lake, accessible off the Gunflint, is the most popular entry point in this part of the BWCAW. Inexperienced paddlers may wish to avoid the lake, however, as it's large and wind-swept. Experienced paddlers have been known to hoist a tarp and sail across, but the lake commands respect.

Like any wilderness, the BWCAW is a living, growing, changing entity. Fire plays a role in this process. Since 1987 fires started by lightning have been left to burn, providing they don't endanger life or property. Fire has always shaped the land, and many species of wildlife depend on the openings that fire creates and the new growth it inspires. If the sky begins to blacken and the smell of fire is in the air, it's prudent to move away from the area into the safety of large waterways with a direct escape route.

To protect the solitude and peace of the wilderness, we must paddle quietly and tread lightly. Only then will the traces of our visit vanish in a ripple and our noises be rightfully replaced by the song of loons.

QUETICO PROVINCIAL PARK
Ministry of Natural Resources
Atikokan, Ontario P0T 1C0
807/597-2735

According to an Objibwa legend, the word "Quetico" was derived from a Cree term relating to the presence of a benevolent spirit in places of awesome natural beauty. Quetico Provincial Park lives up to its name.

The park's island-studded lakes are rimmed by granite cliffs, and majestic waterfalls bathe all who visit them in a mist of clear, cold water. Loons wail their haunting cries, while black bear, deer, wolves and foxes scamper into the bush when caught off guard by an approaching paddler.

Quetico Provincial Park preserves an awesome waterway through a roadless wilderness, where packs and paddles provide the only means of transportation to all visitors except members of the Lac La Croix Guides Association. These Ojibwa people inhabited Quetico during the fur trade era and today are allowed to operate small motorboats when pursuing their livelihood as fishing guides.

The motor that may interrupt the tranquility of your visit to the Quetico is the sound of the native community earning a living on its ancestral lands.

The Quetico is indeed a spiritual place, but traversing the preserve is not always easy. In the Quetico, it seems the thunderstorms are more fierce, the blackflies are more ferocious, and the portage trails always seem to lead uphill. The Quetico is ill-suited for novices. Even if you're an extremely adventurous canoer, you should consult an experienced outfitter. First-time visitors to the border lakes are generally better off staying in the American BWCAW, where mistakes in navigation and lack of skill are more easily overcome.

Experienced paddlers with a thirst for adventure will love the Quetico. For those with the proper equipment and the necessary skill, the Quetico offers pristine lakes filled with hungry fish, isolated campsites, and long stretches of wilderness waterway.

In 1973 Canada classified the Quetico as a wilderness park, and today the park looks much as it did when Jacques de Noyon arrived in 1688. You won't find the lakes signed or the portages marked; instead you must use your map and compass for navigation. Backpacking stoves are mandatory, because there are no steel fire grates on which

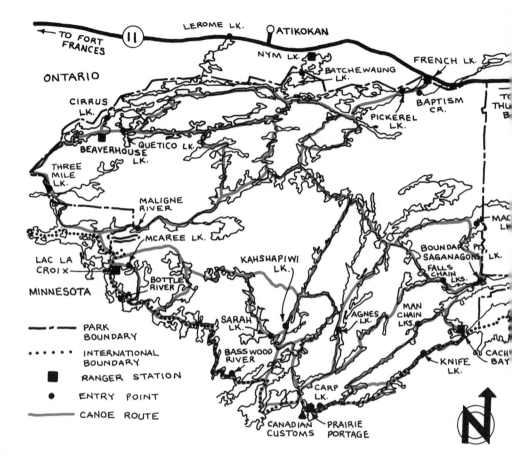

to rest your cooking pots and fires may be banned during dry periods. You won't find marked campsites or box latrines in the Quetico. This is true wilderness, where the intrusions of man are minimal.

Insects, weather, and, to a lesser extent, wildlife present the other hazards of travel in the Quetico. Mosquitoes reach their peak in late May through June, and they're often joined by biting flies. July is the month of the black flies. These annoying pests torment campers caught without long sleeve shirts, headnets, and long pants. You're advised to carry insect repellent throughout the season.

Black bears are an important part of the Quetico landscape. In southeastern Canada, about 90 percent of the bears' diet is plant material, but they'll eat anything. To avoid an unpleasant encounter with bears in the Quetico, keep your campsite clean at all times, avoid cooking in your tent, and store everything edible—even toothpaste—in a food cache suspended between two trees. Fish entrails should be left for the gulls on a high rock in the water, and garbage should be packed out, not buried.

Those who have learned to accept the Quetico on its own terms enjoy world-class adventure that inspires paddlers to return year after year. Campers who arrive unskilled and ill-prepared, however, quickly discover that the Quetico wilderness can be harsh and unforgiving.

DRIVE-IN CAMPGROUNDS

The Dawson Trail Campground offers those without a surplus of time, skill, or experience the opportunity to enjoy the Quetico from the comfort of a drive-in campground.

Located on the northeast shore of French Lake, the campground also serves as an interior entry point, offering hot showers to those departing for or returning from a long trip in the Quetico backcountry.

The campground features two large camp units, a public beach, and an information center. It's busy and hectic during the brief summer in the north, but those who venture out for a day trip up the French River will enjoy a taste of the wilderness. A motor vehicle permit is required to enter the campground. For reservations and information, call 807/597-2735.

INTERIOR TRIP PLANNING

Planning your route is one of the most important aspects of a trip to the Quetico. A waterproof map of the park showing entry points, customs stations, portages, and other information is published by the Quetico Foundation, and is available at entry stations upon arrival. The map can also be obtained from the park by mail. Call the park office at 807/597-2735 for current price information.

If you're an experienced paddler but this is your first trip to the region, consider utilizing the services of an experienced outfitter. A good outfitter can supply the maps, advice, specialized food, and equipment you'll need to make your trip memorable, safe, and fun.

There are six entry points to Quetico Provincial Park where visitors must secure their reserved permits. Cache Bay, Prairie Portage, and Lac La Croix serve as entry points from the United States, while French Lake, Nym Lake, and Beaverhouse Lake provide Canadian access. A quota system is in effect at each entry point, in order to limit the number of paddlers entering the Quetico. Americans entering the park from the U.S. side of the border must first pay a visit to Canadian customs, where they're asked to declare their citizenship and pay a duty on their food.

In planning your route, keep in mind that portages and campsites are not signed. Details about portage conditions and water levels should be discussed with rangers at your point of entry into the park.

BACKCOUNTRY PERMITS

Interior camping permits are required for all overnight adventures into the Quetico. From February 1 through August 30, interior permits can be reserved by calling the park at 807/597-2735 weekdays during normal business hours. A nominal reservation fee is charged, and MasterCard and VISA are accepted for payment. Permit reservations are available for visits between May 17 and Sept 2.

When making your interior permit reservation, you must specify the entry point you plan to use, as this is where you'll pick up your reserved permit and pay your daily camping fees. Day visitors to the park must pay a small fee for a vehicle permit.

You must check in at your entry point between 8 a.m. and 5 p.m. Central Daylight Time unless you're using the French Lake access, which is open from 7 a.m. to 9 p.m. daily. The stations— especially the popular Prairie Portage entry station—can be busy, so your patience may be tested as you await a permit.

Off-season visitors arriving between Labor Day and Thanksgiving are served by a self-registration system. Services are not offered during the winter months.

No-shows are charged the permit reservation fee plus one night's camping fee for each member of the party. You're considered a no-show if you don't arrive on the day your reservation specifies. Allowances are made, however, for paddlers held up by high wind on Saganaga and Beaverhouse lakes. It's unwise to challenge a wind-swept lake, and your permit will be waiting for you after the tempest has passed.

Americans entering the Quetico from Moose Lake or Saganaga Lake must first pass through the Boundary Waters Canoe Area Wilderness. If you're a paddler who's simply passing through the BWCAW en route to the Quetico, you won't need a permit unless you plan to camp. An overnight visit to the BWCAW requires a separate permit. Refer to the BWCAW section for details.

CANADIAN CUSTOMS

Visitors to the Quetico must pass through customs if entering the park from outside of Canada. Canadian customs stations require that you have identification proving your citizenship and funds to pay a duty on your food. VISA and MasterCard are accepted. A vaccination certificate is required of pets brought into Canada, and neither firearms nor fireworks are allowed. Be sure to check the location of the nearest Canadian customs station on your map prior to embarking on your trip. They are as follows:

Cache Bay. Located on Government Island on the southeastern shore of Saganaga Lake, 7 1/2 long miles from the Cache Bay Entry Station.

Prairie Portage. Adjacent to the Prairie Portage entry station on Basswood Lake.

Lac La Croix. Located on Sand Point Lake, north of Crane Lake, 40 miles from the Lac La Croix entry station.

FISHING

The fish of the Quetico bite best when the mosquitoes and black flies are at their peak, from mid-May through June. Most visiting fishermen target the park's highly prized walleye, lake trout, northern pike, and bass. Panfish are also found in abundance, and just about every lake offers opportunities to catch a fresh-fish dinner. Northern pike are active all summer long, and fishermen who seek out back bays and isolated campsites will improve their chances.

A fishing license, available at any of the park's entry stations, is required of all park visitors who plan to cast a line. You will be issued tags appropriate for the species you plan to pursue. The use of live bait fish is prohibited, in order to protect the waters from the intrusion of non-native species.

CANADA'S NORTH SHORE
Home of the Sleeping Giant
and the Forest of the North Wind

Through the Windshield

The Greeks called the North Wind "Boreas," regarding it as a spirit from a cold and vast land. So it is that the northern forest of Canada surrounding Lake Superior is called the "boreal forest." This forest of the north wind is a land of striking extremes—rugged yet fragile, harsh yet delicate.

The Canadian Province of Ontario lays claim to over six hundred miles of Lake Superior shoreline, but it is home to only one-sixth of the lake's 750,000 residents. Most of Canada's Lake Superior residents are clustered in two cities: Thunder Bay, with a population of 120,000, and Sault Ste. Marie, with a population of 83,000. Much of the remaining shore is wild. Moose, wolves, black bears, deer and even caribou outnumber residents in many areas of Canada's Superior shore, adding to the joy of a visit.

Lake Superior's rock cliffs once served as a canvas for native Americans, who used red ochre to paint fascinating pictographs. Even though the meaning of some paintings remains a mystery, a journey to these walls of history brings visitors back to a time when man and nature lived in close harmony. The ancestors of these painters arrived following the meltwater of the region's last glacier, and Chippewa names like Michipicoten, Wawa, and Obatanga remain familiar to today's travelers.

French voyageurs were the first Europeans to explore the region. Paddling their canoes along Lake Superior's north shore, these hardy men pioneered fur trade routes to the border country of northern Minnesota and Ontario in the 17th century. French culture continues to influence Canadian life, and visitors will find public signs and publications written in both French and English.

Timber from Ontario's vast forest and ore from the mineral-rich rock of the Canadian Shield now provide the base of the region's economy. Shipping continues to play an important role, and it's interesting to note that more commodities pass through the locks of Sault Ste. Marie than through the Suez Canal. Thunder Bay, meanwhile, is the world's largest grain port.

Travel along Lake Superior's northern shore follows the two-lane Trans-Canadian Highway 17. Lake Superior is accessible along much of the route for sea kayakers anxious to pull a paddle, and there are plenty of opportunities for campers to roll out a sleeping bag. At

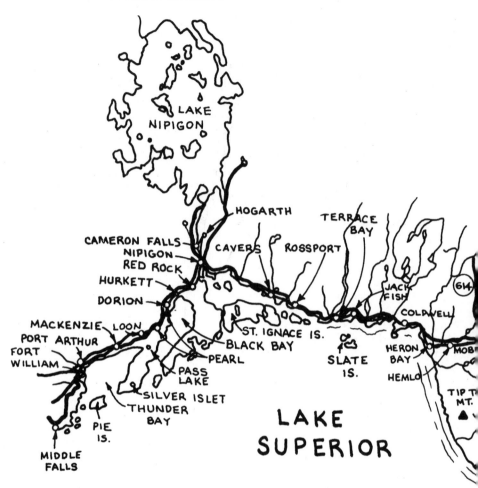

LAKE
NIPIGON

HOGARTH

TERRACE
BAY

CAMERON FALLS
NIPIGON
RED ROCK

CAVERS

ROSSPORT

HURKETT

DORION

JACK
FISH

614

COLDWELL

MACKENZIE LOON
PORT ARTHUR
FORT
WILLIAM

ST. IGNACE IS.
BLACK BAY

PEARL

PASS
LAKE

SILVER ISLET
THUNDER
BAY

SLATE
IS.

HERON
BAY

MOB

HEMLO

TIP T
MT.

PIE
IS.

MIDDLE
FALLS

LAKE
SUPERIOR

MICHIPICOTEN
IS.

TRANS-CANADIAN HIGHWAY

HIGHWAY 17

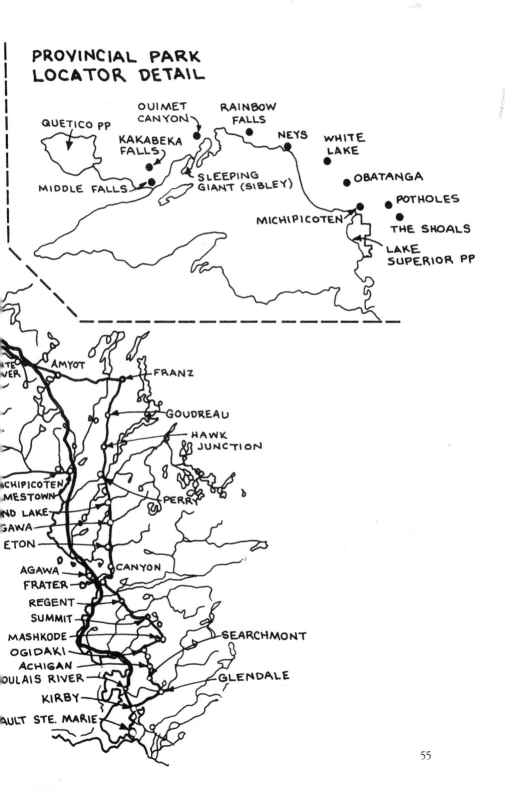

PROVINCIAL PARK LOCATOR DETAIL

QUETICO PP

OUIMET CANYON

RAINBOW FALLS

KAKABEKA FALLS

NEYS

WHITE LAKE

MIDDLE FALLS

SLEEPING GIANT (SIBLEY)

OBATANGA

POTHOLES

MICHIPICOTEN

THE SHOALS

LAKE SUPERIOR PP

AMYOT

FRANZ

GOUDREAU

HAWK JUNCTION

CHIPICOTEN
MESTOWN

ND LAKE

GAWA

ETON

PERRY

AGAWA

CANYON

FRATER

REGENT

SUMMIT

MASHKODE

SEARCHMONT

OGIDAKI

ACHIGAN

OULAIS RIVER

GLENDALE

KIRBY

AULT STE. MARIE

Marathon, a spur road leads to the Lake Superior headquarters of Pukaskwa National Park, but Highway 17 skirts the boundary of the remote park and continues overland to Wawa and the Michipicoten River.

En route to the Canadian border, a viewing area atop Mt. Emma provides a panoramic view of the Susie Islands. Once exploited for copper and silver, Susie Island, the largest of the chain, has been acquired by the Nature Conservancy to preserve the rare plants harbored there.

BORDER CROSSING

Americans crossing the U.S./Canadian border at the Pigeon River will usually find the process quick and effortless. You will be questioned concerning the nature of your visit and the amount of time you plan to spend in Canada, and you may be asked to provide proof of citizenship. A passport, driver's license, or birth certificate will suffice.

If you're traveling with a dog or cat that's over three months old, you'll have to provide a signed affidavit from your veterinarian that the animal has been vaccinated against rabies. Bear in mind also that radar warning devices are prohibited in Canada, even if stored in your trunk.

As a visitor to Ontario, you're allowed to bring in any reasonable amount of personal effects, food, and a full tank of gas. Gifts valued at up to $40 Canadian each are duty-free, provided they don't contain alcohol, tobacco, or advertising material. Visitors may also import up to 40 ounces of liquor or one case of beer.

A license is required to fish or hunt in Ontario. You'll find licenses available from most sporting goods stores and many hunting and fishing lodges. Contact the Ministry of Natural Resources for specific information on seasons, regulations, and license fees by calling 416/965-2000. Visiting hunters can bring a rifle or shotgun and up to 200 rounds of ammunition into Ontario, but handguns are not allowed.

Ontario's weather is much like that of the northern United States. Visitors will encounter warm days and cool nights during June, July, and August. Seasoned travelers always pack along an extra sweater, rain gear, and plenty of insect repellent when visiting in summer. Medium to heavyweight clothing is the rule from mid-September to mid-November, and down-filled parkas are advised for Canada's long, cold winters.

Within Canada, you'll find prices quoted in Canadian currency. Although most merchants are glad to accept U.S. monies, it's quick and easy to exchange currency at one of the shops near the border. Traveling with credit cards is convenient, since MasterCard and VISA are widely accepted, even for campground fees at Ontario provincial parks. The currency exchange rate will be computed on the date that the purchase is posted.

Ontario's provincial parks are clean, comfortable, and well-maintained. Camping is an excellent means of enjoying Canada, and visitors will find campsites reasonably priced and beautifully located amídst the best natural areas that can be found in Ontario. Campsite reservations can be made by mail, in person, or by phone using a MasterCard or VISA. If you don't have a reservation, you'll usually find a campsite available along the Lake Superior Circle Tour, because the parks reserve a number of sites that are filled on a first-come, first-served basis.

Daily quotas on the number of people entering the interior of Quetico Provincial Park have been established. Those venturing into the Quetico are advised to reserve an interior permit in advance if a specific route is desired. Reserving an interior permit is not required, but it ensures that you'll be able to enter the park at your chosen spot.

Some provincial parks accommodate motorhomes and provide electricity. Pets are allowed in provincial parks if they are on a six-foot leash. Cans and bottles are allowed at drive-in campgrounds, but not within the Quetico interior or the interior backcountry of Lake Superior parks.

Just across the Canadian border, Highway 593 leads to Middle Falls Provincial Park (listed separately). This park shares a border with Minnesota's Grand Portage State Park, providing a quaint spot for a picnic along the shores of the lovely Pigeon River. The river cascades over Middle and High Falls before making an impressive 30-foot drop at the Pigeon River Gorge.

Highway 61 continues through Ontario to the bustling community of Thunder Bay. The spectacular Sibley Pensinsula guards the entrance to this port city at the head of Lake Superior. The unique shape of the peninsula's awesome labyrinth of cliffs and hills led to its Ojibwa designation as "Sleeping Giant." Much of the Sibley Peninsula is free of development and is protected as Sleeping Giant Provincial Park (listed separately), formerly known as Sibley Provincial Park. The peninsula is laced with hiking trails that allow you to climb the Sleeping Giant and offer a pleasant relief from the metropolitan hustle of Thunder Bay.

Located about halfway across Canada, Thunder Bay is the largest city along the shore of Lake Superior. Until 1970, the city was actually made up of two towns, Port Arthur and Fort William, both competing for the same industrial base. After merging into one community, Thunder Bay has maintained its significance as a grain port and industrial center.

Since 1717, a French fort has stood along the mouth of the Kaministiquia River in Thunder Bay. When the North West Company moved its fur trading operations from Grand Portage, Minnesota, to the site in 1814, the fort became host to the voyageurs' annual rendezvous. During this raucous event, furs from the northern wilderness were traded for goods from Montreal, amidst a festive atmosphere. Old Fort William recreates these historic days by allowing visitors to mingle with costumed staff members who play the roles of tradesmen and voyageurs. The fort is open year-round, and you can obtain information by calling 807/577-8461.

If you're looking for a place to camp while enjoying Old Fort William, consider Chippewa Park, located on the city's south end off of Highway 61B. Chippewa Park is a modern 150-site municipal campground on the shore of Lake Superior, at the base of 1,000-foot Mount McKay. For camping information, call 807/623-3912. Mount McKay is located within the NorWester Mountain Range, and for a small fee you can drive to a ledge at the 600-foot level to enjoy an impressive view of Thunder Bay Harbor.

The Thunder Bay region is quickly becoming the rock-climbing center of the Canadian North Shore. Local climbers have put up over 100 routes at the city's Centennial Park, and a short 20-minute drive brings you to the cliffs of Squaw Bay, where climbers reaching the summit are treated to a wonderful view of the Sibley Peninsula and Isle Royale.

Meanwhile, those interested in fishing Lake Superior will find charter fishermen operating from Thunder Bay who are anxious to take anglers on excursions in search of lake trout and Chinook salmon, the latter a species recently introduced to the area.

At Thunder Bay, you'll find Highway 61 intersecting with Trans Canadian Highways 11 and 17. These highways across the wilderness often follow Canada's rail lines, and travelers are amazed at the engineering skill and human toil required to build the roads. Canadians refer to the northland as "the bush," and in this area travel is often restricted to sea plane or canoe. Those making the effort, however, will usually be rewarded with a stringer full of fish.

Just 19 miles west of Thunder Bay, the Kamanistiquia River tumbles 128 feet over cliffs of slate at Kakabeka Falls Provincial Park (listed separately). Walkways offer viewing platforms on both sides of the river gorge, and visitors are often bathed in the mist of the thunderous falls. A modern campground is available for those who wish to spend the night, and children will enjoy the park's sand swimming beach.

Meanwhile, exiting the Circle Tour, canoeists anxious to pull a paddle through the border lakes of the Quetico will find Highway 11 leading west to Atikokan, Ontario. This city of 4,400 is the headquarters of Quetico Provincial Park (listed separately). Outfitters in Atikokan can supply the specialized equipment you'll need to paddle the Quetico, but be advised that this is a true wilderness park. Your camping skills will be tested against the weather, the insects, and the often difficult portages. A permit is required to penetrate the interior. Campgrounds, hiking trails, and picnic areas are also available.

If you continue west on Highway 11, you'll reach the popular Canadian fishing cities of Fort Frances on Rainy Lake and Kenora on Lake of the Woods. Fort Frances, with a population of over 8,500, is located right across the U.S. border from International Falls, Minnesota.

Rolling out of Thunder Bay, Circle Tour drivers will be heading down Highway 17 en route to Pass Lake and the Sibley Peninsula. An archaelogical discovery at Pass Lake offers an interesting insight concerning the importance of the area to prehistoric Paleo-Indian cultures. The site was revealed when Danish immigrant Jorgen Brohm, a Pass Lake farmer, began turning up stone artifacts with his plow. Archaeologists have since discovered that the narrow isthmus of the peninsula was used by early hunters. Apparently, the hunters would ambush migrating caribou as the animals passed through the narrow neck of the Sibley Peninsula, relying on the natural funnel created by the borders of Lake Superior and Pass Lake.

Scenic Highway 587 winds down the 24-mile-long Sibley Peninsula, passing many inland lakes. These lakes are noted for their importance to Sibley's declining moose population, members of which feed on the tender aquatic plants that line the shores.

En route to the boomtown mining community of Silver Islet, located at the tip of the peninsula, be sure to bear left as the road branches past the entrance to Sleeping Giant Provincial Park, since it's a one-way route when you reach the narrow streets of Silver Islet. Originally, the tiny outcropping of rock at the tip of the Sibley Peninsula was called Skull Island. In 1868, a mining survey party led by Thomas MacFarlane discovered silver on the island and renamed the outcropping after the mineral.

The Ojibwa legend of the Sleeping Giant tells how a silver mine brought the white man, and indeed it happened just that way. During the 1870s miners, housed in what are now used as cottages at Silver Islet, removed $3 million worth of silver from the site. Extracting the precious metal was extremely difficult, as the silver vein stretching to Silver Islet reached below the surface of Lake Superior.

Today, silver remains beneath the chill of Lake Superior, and the original underwater mine shaft is visible to sea kayakers paddling around the island. Don't plan to set foot on Silver Islet itself, however, since it is privately owned and is off-limits to visitors.

Before leaving the Sibley Peninsula, pull into the Sleeping Giant Campground and pause at the dock on pastoral Lake Marie Louise. As the Sleeping Giant rests before your eyes, you may wish to recall the wonderful Objiwa legend that accounts for the creation of this rock outcropping, and you might ponder the white man's impact on this peninsula of silver, blue, and green.

MIDDLE FALLS PROVINCIAL PARK
**Ministry of Natural Resources
P.O. Box 5000
James Street South
Thunder Bay, Ontario P7C 5G6
Seasonal Telephone 807/964-2097
Off Season 807/475-1531**

The Middle Falls of the Pigeon River was one of the obstacles that canoe-paddling voyageurs encountered on their journeys from Lake Superior to the fur-rich border lakes of the Superior wilderness.

Seeking an overland route from Lake Superior to Lake of the Woods, these travelers found the Pigeon River impossible to run. Undaunted, they hoisted their canoes and 90-pound packs on their shoulders and made the "Grand Portage" along the Pigeon River.

The Pigeon River Route was predominantly used between 1722 and 1797 as the shortest way west. Today, as you're wandering along the Pigeon River Gorge exploring Middle and High Falls, it's easy to understand the necessity for this portage.

MIDDLE FALLS PROVINCIAL PARK

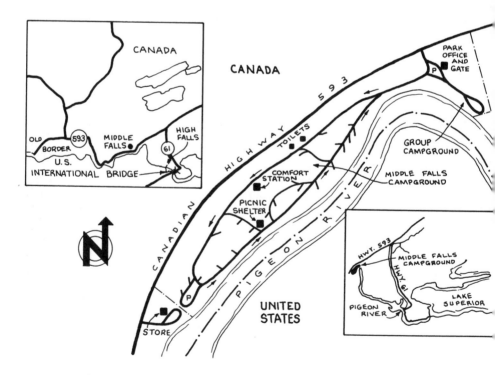

Middle Falls Provincial Park offers an excellent resting spot for picnickers. A shelter affords protection from foul weather and a view of the Pigeon River. Campers are welcome to pitch their tents in one of the park's 25 campsites, and 12 of the sites can accommodate large travel trailers. There are no electrical sites in the park, but a comfort station offers flush toilets and hot and cold running water.

The spectacular scenery found in the Middle Falls area is due to the geology of the region, and you'll want to witness High Falls as it cascades 31 feet into the Pigeon River Gorge.

In the 1930s, the Pigeon River Lumber Company harvested huge white and red pine trees, using the river to drive the logs downstream to Lake Superior. A wooden chute, known as a sluiceway, can still be seen on the trail to High Falls. The chute allowed logs to be safely transported down the drop at High Falls to the Pigeon River Gorge and on to Lake Superior. Once in the lake, huge boom logs created floating timber rafts, and these were towed to sawmills in Thunder Bay and the United States.

Visitors to High Falls will find that it makes an excellent subject for a photograph. Exercise caution, though, because the sides of the gorge are unprotected. While hiking the trail to the falls, it's entertaining to remember the days of the voyageur and imagine the challenge of portaging the Pigeon River.

KAKABEKA FALLS PROVINCIAL PARK
Ministry of Natural Resources
P.O. Box 5000
Thunder Bay, Ontario P7C 5G6
Seasonal Telephone 807/964-2097
Off Season 807/475-1531

Early explorers described feeling "the earth quaking under us" as they portaged their canoes in order to bypass the thunderous treachery of Kakabeka Falls on the Kamanistiquia River.

Today, visitors to Kakabeka Falls Provincial Park can bathe in the same mist that greeted voyageurs over 150 years ago as the Kamanistiquia River tumbles 163 feet over ancient slate cliffs into the gorge below.

Kakabeka Falls, christened "The Niagara of the North," proved a barrier to voyageurs paddling down the Kamanistiquia River from the fur-rich hinterlands of the northwest to the mouth of the river at Thunder Bay. Hiking along the historic one-mile Mountain Portage Trail, you can retrace the footprints of these voyageurs as they made their way past the falls en route to the annual Great Rendezvous at Old Fort William in Thunder Bay. It was during the Great Rendezvous that voyageurs exchanged their furs for ironware, cloth, and trinkets brought from Montreal.

Walkways and viewing platforms on both sides of the river gorge allow you to investigate the powerful forces that have shaped the region. The gorge was carved from the Precambrian Shield by meltwater from the last glaciers that covered the area. Amidst the ancient exposed rock layers, scientists have discovered fossils that are 1.6 billion years old, among the oldest found anywhere on earth. Erosion continues to shape the gorge, as the falls creeps ever so slowly upriver.

Since 1904 a hydroelectric power station has harnessed the power of the falls, providing electricity for the park and the surrounding area. Campers can take advantage of this electricity at the park's two campgrounds, which are served by a modern comfort station complete with showers. The park offers a total of 166 campsites, including 50 that provide electricity.

Children will enjoy the park's playground, and families will have fun joining the park staff on guided hikes or taking advantage of the special children's programs and campfire talks. Winter visitors will find a seven-mile groomed cross-country ski trail tracked for both diagonal and skate skiing.

Swimmers can take a dip in the roped area above the falls, where a sandy beach greets summer-lovers ready to shake off a long, cold winter. Swimming outside the designated area should be avoided, since a dam upstream may cause rising water levels and treacherous currents.

SLEEPING GIANT PROVINCIAL PARK
(Formerly Sibley Provincial Park)
Pass Lake, Ontario P0T 2M0
807/933-4332

Sleeping Giant Provincial Park is a delightful place to wander amidst ferns, bogs, cliffs, and forests. Flanked on each side by the endless horizons of Lake Superior, Sleeping Giant rests on a peninsula where you can climb atop a rugged cliff made sacred by Objibwa legend or admire the delicate beauty of an orchid in bloom. The park is expansive, and within its boundaries you'll find plenty of room to camp, hike, swim, and fish.

Sleeping Giant occupies much of the 24-mile-long, six-mile-wide Sibley Peninsula, which stretches into Lake Superior's northern shore near the city of Thunder Bay. The eastern lowlands of the peninsula rise gently from the lake, while the western shore features the highest vertical cliffs in Ontario. Much of the summer activity at the park centers around the clear water, sand beaches, and drive-in campground of spectacular Lake Marie Louise.

The park takes its name from the immense cliffs, highlands, and forested valleys that tower above the peninsula. In geologic terms, the "giant" is a series of mesas, composed of sedimentary rock and capped with erosion-resistant igneous rock, but the Ojibwa have a more colorful explanation for this forested ridge of rock. According to legend, Nanabijou, the giant who was son of the West Wind, was the special protector of the Ojibwa people. He lived among his people for thousands of years, helping them reach great heights of glory. To save the Ojibwa from their traditional enemies, the Sioux, and a newly arrived threat, the white man, Nanabijou led his people to the north shore of Lake Superior.

One day while sitting by the lake, Nanabijou scratched a rock and discovered silver. Frightened for his people, he made them bury the silver in the tiny islet at the end of the Sibley Peninsula, and had them swear never to reveal the location of the precious metal. The silver was worthless to the Ojibwa, but wise Nanabijou knew that if white men found out about it, they would take his people's land.

The secret was kept until vanity got the best of an Objibwa chieftain, who made himself weapons of silver. Soon afterward, he was killed in a battle with the Sioux, and the secret of the silver was revealed.

A few days later, Nanabijou witnessed a party of Sioux paddling canoes across Lake Superior, leading two white men to the silver on the Sibley Peninsula. To save his people, Nanabijou disobeyed Manitou the Great Spirit and raised a fierce storm on Lake Superior, which sank the canoes and drowned both the white men and their Sioux guides. As punishment, Nanabijou was turned to stone and, to this day, Nanabijou the Giant rests in the place where the Great Spirit struck him, majestic in his silent slumber.

The awesome Sleeping Giant, so beautifully explained by the Objibwa legend, remains the park's most impressive feature. From Thunder Bay, the giant looms dramatically over the eastern horizon, protecting the mouth of the harbor. From the shores of inland Lake Marie Louise, it offers more subtle protection.

The silver featured in the Ojibwa legend did, in fact, bring the white man. In 1868 a mining survey party under the supervision of Mr. Thomas MacFarlane discovered a vein of silver ore on what he called Skull Island, less than one mile off the tip of Sibley Peninsula.

MacFarlane's men became hysterical when the silver vein widened from a few inches to some 20 feet. MacFarlane renamed the island Silver Islet, and during the 1870s the mine became the center of economic activity on the peninsula. Today the buildings that once housed miners at the tip of the peninsula serve as summer homes. The old general store, however, remains in business, and a trip to the Sibley Peninsula is not complete without a visit to this historic structure.

Protection of the Sibley Peninsula began in 1944, fueled by the concerns and efforts of local residents. Years of logging on the peninsula had taken a heavy toll, and the once-vast stands of white and red pine had nearly vanished. Sibley Provincial Park was created to protect these last stands of virgin timber.

At the time, the park did not occupy the entire peninsula, so timber was harvested until the boundaries of the park were expanded. Today the park encompasses nearly 150 square miles, including over 40 miles of hiking trails.

Sleeping Giant Provincial Park lies within the Superior section of Canada's boreal forest. Due to past logging and the lack of forest fires on the peninsula over the past several decades, balsam fir is widespread in the park. White birch deciduous forests are also common, especially where logging has occurred. Cedar swamps are extensive on lowland areas of the peninsula, and on the Sleeping Giant itself.

Sibley is justifiably noted for its orchids and ferns. Some 24 species of orchids have been found within the park, including two of North America's rarest species. Bog adder's-mouth and a striped variety of the small, round-leaved orchids are found in bogs near the southern end of the park. Other beautiful orchids in the park include arethusa, calypso, and the more common but exquisite pink lady's slipper. Braun's holly fern, fragrant fern, and alsine woodsia are among over 40 species of ferns that have been noted in the park.

Wildlife tends to congregate on the peninsula, and white-tailed deer are a common sight along park roads, especially at sunset. A glance at a map reveals the reason that wildlife prefer the peninsula. Pass Lake forms a narrow inland isthmus on the Sibley Peninsula, which acts as a funnel for wildlife. Free-roaming animals make their way down the peninsula, but find themselves surrounded by water on three sides at the "neck" of the peninsula on their journey north. Reluctant to pass through this funnel, animals stay in the park, putting pressure on the available food resources.

Until the 1900s, the woodland caribou was the most abundant large mammal on the peninsula. Around the turn of the century, loggers began cutting the mature coniferous stands and removing the associated lichens, which provided critical habitat for caribou. The result was the virtual disappearance of the caribou. Moose and white-tailed deer, once scarce on the peninsula, replaced the caribou, finding the new growth of small trees and shrubs particularly inviting. In fact, moose numbers increased to such a level that, in the summer of 1971, 21 moose were spotted feeding simultaneously at Joeboy Lake.

As the forest has matured, the moose population has declined. White-tailed deer continue to thrive, though, and are more numerous now than at any other time in the park's history.

Timber wolves have always been present on the Sibley Peninsula, and backpackers camping in remote sections of the park may hear them howling in the moonlight.

Anglers will find northern pike, perch, and smallmouth bass in lakes throughout the park, and fisherman often try their luck off the dock at Lake Marie Louise. Lizard Lake, located off the Rita Lake Road, is noted for its shoreline pike fishing at the picnic area.

Paddlers will enjoy dropping a canoe in lovely Lake Marie Louise or one of the park's many inland lakes. Joeboy Lake is off limits to all boaters including paddlers, to ensure that the park's remaining moose

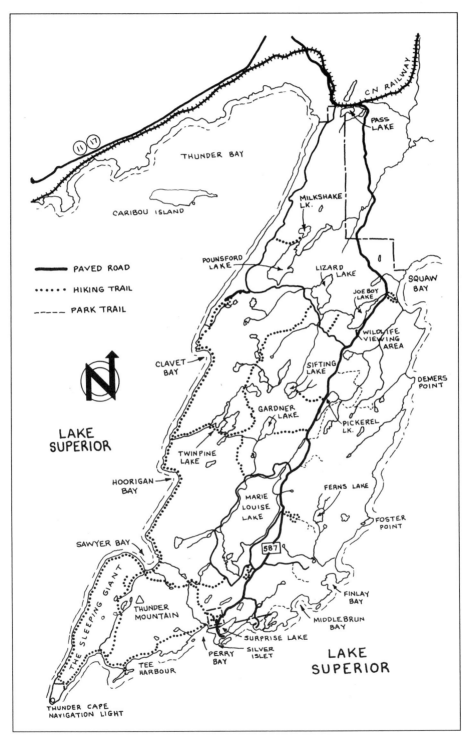

can dine in peace. Canoes are available for rent and motorboats are restricted to ten-horsepower on lakes.

The scenic roads of the Sibley Peninsula provide a wonderful means of enjoying the beauty of Sleeping Giant for those who find park trails too challenging.

If you're driving, head south from the park's gatehouse on Highway 587, bearing left at the first intersection. This road leads to the end of the peninsula and to the shore of Lake Superior. During the 1870s this was the base of operations for the famous Silver Islet Mine. Summer homes found here once housed miners, and residents have retained the area's original character.

Tiny Silver Islet is located less than a mile from the mainland. As you proceed along the lakeshore drive, the island disappears behind Burnt Island as the road reaches the former general store. The store offers a resting place with a turn of the century flavor.

Mountain bikers and motorists alike will enjoy the park's gravel spur roads, which branch off Highway 587. Beginning at the campground, the 12-mile Lake Louise Scenic Drive makes a delightful mountain bike ride, with heart-pounding hills and views of Lake Marie Louise beneath a canopy of green. The ride ends at Highway 587, just a quick trip down the road from the campground. Those looking for a longer route, either by mountain bike or auto, will enjoy the Rita Lake Road. Be advised that this is a rough road. Drivers of cars towing trailers will find the hills steep and the potholes deep.

Rita Lake, on the east side of Highway 587, was named after the daughter of Alexander Sibley. Sibley, the namesake of the entire peninsula, was the director of the company that developed the Silver Islet Mine.

The road continues to Lizard and Poundsford lakes before a short spur road branches to the Thunder Bay Lookout. The lookout rests on erosion-resistant cliffs rising some 400 feet above Lake Superior.

Returning to the Rita Lake Road and continuing north, you'll pass a pair of lookouts en route to the park exit and Highway 17. Near Highway 17, a tablet commemorates the first Paleo-Indian archaeological site found in Ontario. Native hunter-gatherers were the park's first campers, visiting the peninsula over 7,000 years ago and following the caribou on its western migration route. These hunters ambushed migrating caribou along the narrow isthmus created by Pass Lake and ancient Lake Minong (Superior), using stone-tipped spears fashioned from jasper taconite, a rock found locally. Today the spot is known to archaeologists as the Brohm site, and it offers an interesting glimpse of the area's history.

Driving the peninsula is a pleasant means to enjoy the park's grandeur, but the Sleeping Giant also demands exploration on foot. Those who venture into the backcountry will meet the giant on even more peaceful terms, departing with a sense of renewal and respect for the land and its people.

CAMPING

In the shadow of the Sleeping Giant, there are 200 drive-in campsites at the Lake Marie Louise Campground. This is a busy place during Canada's national holidays, but if you arrive mid-week there's a chance you'll be able to pitch your tent or park your RV along the shore of the spectacular lake. Each of the campsites is equipped with a picnic table and fire ring, and the park has modern comfort stations with warm showers.

While staying in the campground, you'll find plenty of things to do. The park staff offers evening campfire presentations and daily children's programs. Guided hikes up the Sleeping Giant are scheduled from mid-June through August, and the park's museum is open daily in the summer from 10 a.m. to noon and 1 to 3 p.m. Canoes are available for rent, and rangers often guide canoe excursions on Lake Marie Louise.

HIKING

If you enjoy an invigorating hike, climbing the Sleeping Giant could well be the highlight of your trip to the Sibley Peninsula. Once atop the formation, you'll be perched 750 feet above Lake Superior, enjoying a panoramic view from Ontario's highest vertical cliff. As the landscape unfolds before you, it's interesting to ponder the legend of the Sleeping Giant and the white man's impact on this land of beauty.

There are two principal routes up the giant, one leading to the Nanabijou Lookout and the other leading to the Chimney Lookout. The Nanabijou Lookout is the most accessible, but it nonetheless requires a heart-pounding climb up a spiny ridge. The trail to the Nanabijou Lookout begins at the base of the cliff at Sawyer Bay.

Climbing the Sleeping Giant is demanding. Both routes up require that you hike overland to the giant's base, where your climb will begin. Park officials suggest that you bring along a day pack containing a map, food, water, matches, rainwear, and a first-aid kit. If you encounter rain, be especially careful. The rocks, particularly those on the talus slopes, become slippery when their surface lichens are drenched in rain water.

To reach Sawyer Bay, take the Sawyer Bay Trail via the Sawbill Lake Trail, accessible off the park's scenic drive around Lake Marie Louise, a 3.5-mile hike. Alternatively, you can approach Sawyer Bay via the Sawyer Lake trailhead located just south of the park, a 3.6-mile trek. From Sawyer Bay, it's a climb of less than one mile up the giant's chest to the Nanabijou Lookout. Your efforts will be rewarded as Sawyer Bay, Black Bay, and the entire Sibley Peninsula unfold before you.

The Sleeping Giant is also accessible from Lehtinen's Bay on the south shore of the park. This spectacular route takes you over a talus slope of huge boulders, further up the cavernous chimney, and on to the giant's knees. From the east side of the knees, you'll be treated to views of Tee Harbour and Silver Islet at the tip of the peninsula. Isle Royale National Park is visible in the distance, rising from the depths of Lake Superior.

The Kabeyun Trail, accessible off Highway 587 just south of the park, leads to the base of the Chimney Lookout, a hike of 4.5 miles. Mountain bikes can take you to Tee Harbour along the logging road that marks the beginning of the Kabeyun Trail, but exercise caution, because hikers are using the trail. From Tee Harbour you'll have to proceed on foot. The last mile up the giant is steep and rugged, so it's best to wear sturdy footwear.

NATURE TRAILS

There are eight nature trails in Sleeping Giant Provincial Park, all relatively short. Many offer interpretive stations along the way to help you understand the park's unique resources. Park officials ask that you sign the registers at the trailheads.

JOE CREEK TRAIL

The Joe Creek Trail is just over one mile long, and follows Joe Creek through a series of small cascades from Highway 587 to Lake Superior. The trail is noted for its many varieties of woodland flowers, and 19 interpretive stations along its length will help you determine where the flowers grow. After crossing a small footbridge, the trail returns to its starting point.

MILKSHAKE LAKE TRAIL

The one-way, two-mile Milkshake Lake Trail travels though a quiet corner of the park to the pine-forested shores of Poundsford and Milkshake lakes.

PINEY WOOD HILLS TRAIL

The 3/4-mile Piney Wood Hills Trail is appropriately named, since it passes through a pine-forested hilly area before ending at a lookout over Joeboy Lake. Interpretive stations along the trail provide information about the area's moose and white pine populations. Try this trail near sunset and perhaps you'll see a moose in Joeboy Lake.

PLANTAIN LANE

Plantain Lane is a 1/4-mile section of the abandoned old Silver Islet Road, taking you to a small bridge over Sibley Creek. This trail is suitable for wheelchair traffic, and the view from the bridge is wonderful.

RAVINE LAKE TRAIL

The one-mile Ravine Lake Trail climbs to a pair of lookouts over Grassy Lake and the peninsula's southern shore. It then takes you down to the shore of Ravine Lake, returning via a shaded cedar grove. Care should be exercised on the steep descent to the lake.

SIBLEY CREEK TRAIL
If you enjoy wetlands, don't miss the one-mile Sibley Creek Trail. The trail leads through a mixed forest to a marshy section of Sibley Creek that harbors waterfowl, beavers, and moose.

THUNDER BAY BOGS TRAIL
Interpretive stations along the 1/2-mile Thunder Bay Bogs Trail will help you understand the impact that glaciers have had on this rugged landscape. The trail traverses a rocky section of the park to a tiny lake before looping back.

WILDLIFE HABITAT TRAIL
The 1 1/4-mile Wildlife Habitat Trail will help you understand man's impact on wildlife. Some of the areas along the trail have been cleared to create moose habitat, and studies are in progress to determine the eating habits of park wildlife.

BACKPACKING

Sibley Provincial Park offers nearly 50 miles of backcountry hiking trails. Some routes follow the rugged shoreline of Lake Superior to the steep accents of the Sleeping Giant. Other trails lead to quiet lakes and streams in the park's interior.

Trips ranging from easy overnights to five-day excursions are possible on the Sibley Peninsula. Before lacing up your boots, however, be mindful of a few factors. First, anyone camping the park's interior must possess a valid interior camping permit. These are available from the gatehouse at the Lake Marie Louise Campground, and a fee is charged. Camping parties are limited to a maximum of nine, but consider camping in smaller groups to lessen your impact on the park. You must choose your route in advance and camp only at sites marked by a blue campsite sign.

Biting insects and flies are, of course, part of the wilderness experience on the Sibley Peninsula. Headnets, long sleeves, and insect repellent provide hikers with welcome protection during June and July.

The most popular campsites in the backcountry are those at Tee Harbour, Lehtinen's Bay, and Sawyer Bay. These sites usually fill early, especially on holiday weekends, so have an alternative destination in mind when you're registering.

To minimize your impact, it's best to use a pack stove, especially since fire restrictions may result in a ban on open fires during dry periods.

Everyone appreciates solitude in the backcountry. Traveling quietly and walking softly will increase your chances of viewing wildlife, and will ensure that you won't be the one to wake the Sleeping Giant.

INTERIOR TRAILS

THE KABEYUN TRAIL

Hugging the shores of Lake Superior, the 24-mile Kabeyun Trail is the most popular backpacking route on the Sibley Peninsula. From its start at the Thunder Bay Lookout off the Lake Marie Louise Scenic Drive, it follows the Sibley coast past Clavet and Horrigan points to Sawyer Bay. There, hikers can depart the Kabeyun for a climb up the Sleeping Giant to the Nanabijou Lookout.

From Sawyer Bay, the trail skirts the outside of the giant to its feet near Thunder Cape on the far southwest end of the peninsula. The trail then heads up the east side of the giant, twisting and turning through a talus slope en route to Lehtinen's Bay. Hikers should use extreme caution here, because the talus slope becomes slippery and dangerous in wet weather. The trail continues along Tee Harbour before reaching the trailhead at Highway 587.

The Kabeyun Trail can be hiked in either direction. It's a popular route for both overnight hikers and day trippers who are hiking short sections of the route, because Lake Superior is always within reach, offering the pleasure of a quiet beach or secluded cove.

THE BURMA TRAIL

Wildlife watchers will enjoy the six-mile Burma Trail, as the route passes through much wildlife habitat in the center of the peninsula. The trail winds through a virgin forest of red and white pine, situated on ridges so steep and rugged that it was inaccessible to loggers. Backpackers will find campsites on both ends of remote Holt Lake and on the south side of Norwegian Lake. For those who seek a longer excursion, the Burma Trail intersects the Twinpine Lake Trail, in turn offering access to the Kabeyun Trail.

Southern access to the Burma Trail is off the Lake Marie Louise Scenic Drive, while the northern trailhead is at the Lizard Lake Picnic Grounds.

GARDNER LAKE TRAIL

The 1.2-mile trail to Gardner Lake is popular with day hikers who hope to spot a moose. The trail follows an old logging road, and it can be quite wet. There are no campsites, and you must return down the same trail.

SAWBILL LAKE TRAIL

The Sawbill Trail is a 1.5-mile former logging trail that provides access to the Sawyer Bay Trail for those who wish to climb the Sleeping Giant. You can access the Sawbill from the Lake Marie Louise Scenic Drive. The trail climbs a moderately steep hill before intersecting with the Sawyer Bay Trail.

SAWYER BAY TRAIL

The 3.6-mile Sawyer Bay Trail is a popular route to the base of the Sleeping Giant. It follows an abandoned logging road, offering views of the giant from its many hills. In season, the Sawyer Bay Trail is noted for wild berries found along the route.

SIFTING LAKE TRAIL

Hikers can reach the quiet shores of Sifting Lake by taking the 1.2-mile Sifting Lake Trail. This is a dead-end trip, so you'll return on the same trail. No campsites are available.

TALUS LAKE TRAIL

Hikers traveling in wet weather should proceed with care down the rugged 3-mile Talus Lake Trail. Noted for its variety, the scenic trail follows a route between the Sleeping Giant and Thunder Mountain. Hikers will skirt three secluded lakes, travel through a sedge meadow, and walk below spectacular cliffs to a waterfall. Campsites are located at Talus Lake and further south on the trail near its intersection with the Kabeyun Trail.

TWINPINE LAKE TRAIL

Twinpine Lake Trail connects the Burma Trail with the Kabeyun Trail. Campsites are found along this 2.8-mile trail at picturesque Twinpine Lake and at the trail's intersection with the Kayeyun Trail. Use caution on the stretch between Twinpine Lake and Lake Superior, since this section is slick in wet weather.

PUKASKWA COUNTRY
Land of the Woodland Caribou

Through the Windshield

You'll be passing through a land born of fire and water, shaped by volcanic activity, erosion, and glaciation, as you roll toward Canada's roadless Pukaskwa (pronounced PUK-a-saw) National Park.

Precambrian rock, formed more than 600 million years ago and known as the Canadian Shield, is the rugged backbone of Pukaskwa Country. The waterfalls you admire, the beaches on which you bask, and the cliffs from which you dangle were all formed by the geologic forces that had an impact on the land and inland sea of the Canadian North Shore.

The same geologic forces that shaped the region's landscape brought amethyst, Ontario's official gemstone. Amethyst is a crystalline variety of quartz, made up of silicon dioxide and minute amounts of iron. Natural heat produces the gem's colors, which range from soft lavender to deep purple, making the amethyst of the Canadian North Shore among the finest in the world.

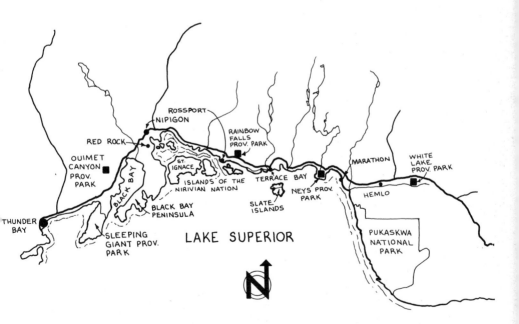

The stretch of Trans-Canada Highway 11-17 from Thunder Bay to Nipigon passes through the center of the amethyst region. Several mines near the town of Pearl are open to the public, and you can try your hand at prying the violet crystals from exposed rock outcropping. If it's a polished amethyst stone or jewelry you're seeking, you'll find merchants along the route who are happy to help you select the perfect shade to complement your color chart.

Exiting the Circle Tour briefly, you'll find sheer rock cliffs and incredible views awaiting you after a seven-mile drive to Ouimet Canyon Provincial Park. You won't find camping facilities at Ouimet, but the park's well-marked trails lead to viewing platforms that present you with vistas of Canada's miniature Grand Canyon. Formed by an immense rock fault in the diabase of the Canadian Shield, the canyon's massive 350-foot cliffs face each other from 500 feet apart. Rare arctic plants, sheltered from the heat of day, find refuge in the shadow of these cliffs. The park is open from mid-May through mid-October.

Continuing on to the land of Nipigon, you'll find the Nipigon River, noted for its speckled trout, spilling into Lake Superior near the town of Red Rock. The town takes its name from the exposed red cliffs of Red Rock Mountain, and you're welcome to climb the unmarked but well-worn trail up the ridge to a perch high atop the cliff.

Across from the cliffs, at the mouth of the Nipigon River, Objibwa pictographs adorn the sedimentary rock walls of Lake Superior. The pictographs, visible only by boat, are believed to depict Maymaygwayshi, a mischievous Objibwa spirit. Travelers have traditionally left gifts of tobacco on ledges or in the water while passing Maymaygwayshi as a plea for good luck.

Sunbathers looking for a unique beach will enjoy the black sand beach of Lake Nipigon Provincial Park (807/885-3181).

Located 35 miles north of Nipigon on Highway 11, the dark beach of Lake Nipigon is tinted when eroded basalt is transported by wave action to the shore. The park offers 60 modern campsites along the lakeshore. Open from early June through August, the park provides excellent fishing opportunities, boat launching, and docking facilities.

Between Nipigon and Rossport, the enchanting Lake Superior islands of the Nirivian nation (listed separately) will unfold before you if you visit one of the cliff-top waysides along the Trans-Canada Highway. Founded by declaration, the unique Nirivian nation is actually an environmental organization fostering the preservation and wise use of this 40-island archipelago. From its headquarters in Nipigon, the Nirivian Embassy can arrange water transportation to the islands for those wishing to enjoy the hiking trails, inland lakes, and pristine beaches. Overnight accommodations are available for both backpackers and cabin dwellers.

St. Ignace, the largest island in the Nirivian chain and the second largest in Lake Superior, shelters Nipigon Bay from the fury of Superior. Home to 1,865-foot Mount St. Ignace, the island offers inland lakes, waterfalls, beaches, and some 75 miles of hiking trails. The islands of the Nirivian nation are held largely in public ownership as "Crown

Land," and they provide a mecca for sea kayakers challenging the north shore of Lake Superior.

The tiny town of Rossport is a popular spot from which to launch fishing or sightseeing excursions to the scenic Rossport Islands. These islands shelter the Rossport Harbour and add a salty flavor to the village. For over 50 years, Rossport has hosted an annual July fishing derby, and prizes are awarded to anglers who reel in the largest lake trout and salmon.

Nearby, travelers will find campsites at Rainbow Falls Provincial Park and at the Rossport Campground (listed separately). There are five campgrounds within the two units, providing a total of 161 campsites. Both campground units offer showers, and 28 campsites at Rainbow Falls provide electricity. Rainbow Falls is a nice place to pause and enjoy the sparkling cascades of the Whitesand River as it tumbles over the park's rocky ledges.

The route between Rossport and Terrace Bay can be traversed not only by highway, but also by footpath. Accessible from the Rainbow Falls Trail in Rainbow Falls Provincial Park, the 15.5-mile North Superior Hiking Trail, a segment of the Voyageur Trail (listed separately), meanders along cobble beaches, raging seas, and lakeshore cliffs inscribed with Indian pictographs. Now under construction, the 660-mile Voyageur Trail will eventually stretch from Manitoulin Island in Lake Huron to Thunder Bay, linking many North Shore communities along the way.

Situated off Terrace Bay, you'll find the remote but alluring Slate Islands. Preserved for wildlife as Slate Islands Provincial Park, this 14-square-mile archipelago of eight islands is noted for its critical importance to the rare woodland caribou. Once common on Canada's Superior North Shore, woodland caribou are now confined to remote pockets where they roam undisturbed. They often seek the isolation of offshore islands, where they can rear their young in an environment free of man and predators, especially wolves. During the summer months, caribou feed on nutrient-rich green plants, accumulating fat that will help them survive through the long winter months. In winter, lichens found on the rocky ground and the limbs of mature trees are the caribou's primary food source.

Terrace Bay takes its name from glacial deposits in the area that drop in a series some 325 feet to Lake Superior. The town's golf course is a major summer attraction, as is the 100-foot Aguasabon Falls, accessible by hiking through a deep gorge at the west end of the city.

From Terrace Bay, it's just a short drive to the beach of Neys Provincial Park (listed separately). During July and August, water in the sheltered bay at Neys is sometimes warm enough for swimmers unwilling to endure the chill of Lake Superior. Neys occupies the Coldwell Peninsula, which juts into Lake Superior east of Terrace Bay. Artists have found inspiration for paintings in the mighty rocks and unique landscape of this shoreside park.

Woodland caribou still visit the isolated Coldwell Peninsula, swimming from offshore islands in search of food. Because of the peninsula's natural isolation, it was utilized as a prisoner of war camp during World War II. Today there is little evidence of the camp, and most visitors are escaping *to* the peninsula, rather than planning their escape from the area. As they roll into one of Neys' 144 campsites, they immediately sense the peace found in abundance on the Coldwell Peninsula.

Departing Neys en route to Pukaskwa National Park, you'll reach Marathon, where the glitter of gold is fueling the local economy. Long noted as a pulp mill town, Marathon is enjoying a mining boom thanks to the discovery of gold in the nearby Hemlo area. Mining interests have made Marathon their headquarters, and three veins are currently yielding the precious metal.

Marathon boasts all the conveniences of a modern city, making it a great place to stock up on supplies for your trips to outlying areas. At an information center on the outskirts of town, a chairlift offers you a scenic view in summer and a downhill ski run in winter. When rain is falling or the fish aren't biting, you can take a dip in Marathon's indoor pool and beat the chill of Lake Superior. This is truly a town on the edge of the wilderness, where a tasty pizza and an ice cold beer will soothe the bug bites of backpackers and cement the memories of a rugged hike along the Canadian North Shore.

Miles of shoreline wilderness—a carpet of green and a sea of deep blue—is waiting for you at Pukaskwa National Park (listed separately). This is big country, where adventurous travelers rely on wits and wisdom to access the backcountry, but where day trippers will find marked trails, courteous rangers, and a developed campground to aid them in their exploration of the region.

Hattie Cove, located just southeast of Marathon on Highway 627 in the northwest corner of Pukaskwa, is the center of the park's activities and services. Here you'll find a 67-site campground with 29 sites that offer electricity. Central comfort stations with heated showers add a degree of comfort on chilly mornings. The cove also provides access to three sand beaches on Lake Superior, and it serves as the trailhead of the Coastal Hiking Trail. A primitive boat launch at the park allows access to skilled canoeists and sea kayakers who are anxious to confront the power of Lake Superior. Motorboaters will find a small boat launch on the Pic River just north of the park entrance, but there are no docking or marine facilities provided within Pukaskwa National Park, so self-sufficiency is necessary. To protect sensitive wildlife breeding areas, boaters are barred from using motors beyond the Hattie Cove visitor center. Canoeists, however, will enjoy pleasant paddling within the protection offered by the cove.

Hattie Cove is the center of the park's interpretive program, and visitors are encouraged to quiz the park staff regarding the natural history of Pukaskwa. Evening programs in summer are a treat for both young and old, and you'll find a posting of scheduled activities at the visitor center. In the center you'll also discover a nature gift shop called Wildshores, operated by Friends of Pukaskwa. This non-profit volunteer organization supports the park's philosophy and offers books, maps, and guides for sale to visitors.

White Lake Provincial Park (listed separately) marks the last stop for visitors to Pukaskwa Country. The 187-campsite park sits on the bay of White Lake, and offers some of the finest walleye and northern pike fishing in northern Ontario.

Years before the Hudson's Bay Company established a fur trading post here, the Cree and Ojibwa tribes battled for control of the fish-and-game-rich region. White Lake marks the last outpost of civilization for paddlers challenging the White River on an ambitious trip to Lake Superior. Paddlers without the energy needed to conquer the White River will find plenty of casual paddling opportunities elsewhere in the park, notably on Deer and Clearwater Lakes. Before departing Pukaskwa Country, hikers will enjoy walking the 1.2-mile Clearwater Trail and may want to take a dip in spring-fed Clearwater Lake at trail's end.

ST. IGNACE ISLAND
The Nirivian Nation
c/o The Nirivian Embassy
P.O. Box 508
Nipigon, Ontario P0T 2JP
807/887-2438
After Hours: 807/983-2671

Buddhists describe Nirvana as a state of perfect blessedness. In 1979, with this notion of complete natural harmony in mind, a group of conservation-minded Canadians christened an archipelago off Lake Superior's North Shore the "Nirivian Islands." Located in Nipigon Bay off the shores of Nipigon, Ontario, this island chain is so divine that its natural grandeur can only be described as Nirvana.

Formed in 1978 by citizen proclamation, the island nation of Nirivia is not actually a sovereign country. Rather, it's an attempt by caring citizens to protect and preserve the outstanding resources of St. Ignace Island and its 58 surrounding islets.

Thirty miles offshore from the town of Nipigon, the Nirivian Islands are clean, uncrowded, and unspoiled. They're also open to the adventurous. Amidst the mountainous terrain of the islands, hikers will find developed trails winding past some 50 inland lakes and beneath 80-foot waterfalls. Sea kayakers can slide their boats up pristine beaches, and photographers may catch a woodland caribou beating a hasty retreat.

St. Ignace Island, the largest and best known of the Nirivian chain, was named to honor Saint Ignatius, the founder of an order of Jesuit priests. The island is indeed a spiritual place. Its 75 miles of hiking trails penetrate black spruce forests, winding through spectacular ravines and along shoreside cliffs. Varying in difficulty from very easy to challenging, many of these trails pass the chain's 50-plus lakes, which range in size from beaver ponds to an inland lake over four miles long. Fishermen will enjoy a stroll down the north trail, leading to Williamson and Muir lakes before offering access to the hungry pike of Burnt Point Lake. Those who appreciate a challenge will enjoy climbing the Precambrian rock summit of Mount St. Ignace. At 1285 feet, it's the third-highest point in Superior.

Protected to the north by 25 miles of open water on Nipigon Bay and to the south by dangerous reefs and shoals, Nirivia has been overlooked by many. Only recently have sea kayakers begun discovering the joys of Nirivia as they paddle beneath gravity-defying Rooster's Rock and past ancient cobblestone covered with nutrient-rich lichens.

Wildlife finds refuge in Nirivia as well. The islands are noted for an unusually large population of warblers, and the birds provide a soundtrack for hikers rambling down the island trails. There are no permanent residents, with the exception of woodland caribou, wolves, black bear, white-tailed deer, mink, and pine martens, which roam free of disturbance. The island's larger inland lakes are home to bass, northern pike, and walleye, but you'll need an Ontario fishing license to pursue these species.

Divine Nirivian Law dictates that domesticated pets and radios with external speakers are barred from entering Nirivia. You are also required to pack out whatever you pack in, and you're advised that everything you find on Nirivia must remain on Nirvia.

GETTING THERE

The Nirivian Islands Expeditions Company (807/887-2438) offers backpackers and adventurers access to the Nirivian Islands via an 80-mile roundtrip boat ride from Nipigon. A limited number of cabins are available, but the number of visitors admitted to Nirivia is monitored closely, to avoid overcrowding. Reservations are accepted through the Nirivian Embassy, P.O. Box 508, Nipigon, Ontario, Canada P0T 2J0. Your party must consist of at least two people. Budget about $125 U.S. per person to make the roundtrip crossing. Sea kayakers with necessary skills and the equipment required to paddle from the mainland are free to camp on the islands, but the Nirivian Embassy asks that you refrain from leaving fire rings on the pristine beaches of the archipelago. You're urged to use camp stoves instead.

Dubbed the only new nation to be formed in North America in the 20th Century, Nirivia has no army, and its borders are open to all who wish to leave the asphalt and streetlights of the modern world behind. As a visitor to this magical realm, you'll receive honorary citizenship papers, thereby becoming part of a nation in which man is but a guest, and the natural world reigns supreme.

RAINBOW FALLS PROVINCIAL PARK
District Manager
Ministry of Natural Resources
P.O. Box 280
Terrace Bay, Ontario P0T 2W0
807/825-3205

Rainbow Falls Provincial Park takes its name from the flashing, sparkling cascade that tumbles over the ledges of the Whitesand River. A colorful rainbow can sometimes be seen from the timber bridge spanning the falls, suspended in the misty spray.

The park consists of two geographically distinct units, each with its own unique appeal. The campground at Rainbow Falls surrounds clear Whitesand Lake. The beach of this inland lake is popular among swimmers, and canoeists will enjoy dipping a paddle in the crystal Canadian jewel. Meanwhile, three miles away on the shore of Lake Superior, you'll find the forty-unit Rossport Campground. From the beach here, you'll enjoy watching the morning fog of Lake Superior gradually burn away in the afternoon sunshine.

The history of the Whitesand River, which drains Whitesand Lake through the park, remains a mystery. It was once known as Maggot River, and there are several stories that attempt to explain the origin of the river's gruesome namesake. One story contends that, during the winter of 1870-71, a group of Indians raided a trading post at the mouth of the river, killing the manager and his wife.

A second story maintains that the trading post was raided due to a battle between rival fur trading operations, the North West Company and the Hudson's Bay Company. According to this version, paid assassins posing as Indians actually committed the atrocity.

A third tale claims that a group of Ojibwa were massacred by the Sioux at the same trading post.

The common thread uniting all of these tales is that the remains of the victims were left unburied at the riverside. When the bodies were discovered, the river was given its name.

Another mystery remains off the shores of Rossport. It was here in 1911 that the ship *Gunilda* struck a reef and sank in 240 feet of water. Some folks believe the Standard Oil Company ship was laden with treasure, and that it still rests on the floor of Lake Superior. Others insist that the ship was stripped of its valuables as it rested on a shallow ledge before making its final plunge into the depths.

Meanwhile, the mysteries of Rainbow Falls are discussed along a self-guided nature trail that crosses the Whitesand River. This is a popular hike for families interested in discovering the park's floral marvels. Other short hiking trails in the park lead to lookouts that offer vistas of the surrounding countryside.

Fishing is popular in Whitesand Lake, in the Whitesand River, and in McLean's Creek at Rossport Campground. Smallmouth bass and limited populations of lake and speckled trout are hauled out of Whitesand

Lake, while the river contains speckled and rainbow trout during the spring and fall steelhead runs.

Campers will find 121 tent and trailer sites at Rainbow Falls, and an additional 40 sites at Rossport Campground. Both campgrounds offer showers, and 28 of the sites at Rossport provide electricity.

Although the park is gated during the winter and facilities are not provided, you'll often find a groomed cross-country ski trail open for public use.

NEYS PROVINCIAL PARK
District Manager
Ministry of Natural Resources
P.O. Box 280
Terrace Bay, Ontario P0T 2W0
807/229-1624

Woodland caribou join weary travelers who find refuge on the isolated Coldwell Peninsula, home of Neys Provincial Park.

Until the 1880s caribou were relatively common along the Canadian North Shore of Lake Superior, but railway construction and subsequent timber-cutting changed the complexion of the old-growth forest. As mature white and red pine forests disappeared, so did the nutrient-rich lichens that draped the branches of the mature trees. These lichens had provided a critical food source for the caribou.

About 40 caribou still inhabit Lake Superior's Pic Island just south of Neys, and a smaller herd occasionally wanders on the Coldwell Peninsula. Today these caribou share the territory with moose, wolves, foxes, deer and even sub-arctic plants. Normally found further north, the plants survive due to the cooling influence of Lake Superior on the Canadian North Shore.

The trees within Neys' boreal forest are typical of those found along the cold North Shore. White spruce, balsam fir, white birch, and trembling aspen dominate the dry regions of the forest, while black spruce and white cedar are found in the park's damp lowland areas.

Man has played a role on the Coldwell Peninsula since at least 4,000 years ago, when prehistoric cultures fished and hunted here. On the southern shores of the peninsula, examples of "Pukaskwa Pits" are found. Named after similar finds on the cobblestone beaches of Pukaskwa National Park, the stone enclosures are believed to be the legacy of ancient Indian cultures.

Trappers and traders followed Indian inhabitation of the region. In the 17th century the French built a fur trading post at the mouth of the Pic River east of Neys, and later the Hudson's Bay Company erected a fort at the same location.

When the Canadian Pacific Railroad reached the peninsula in 1885, the village of Coldwell served fishermen who relied on the rail to ship their catch to market. In recent times, as the lake trout population diminished due to overfishing and the invasion of the sea lamprey via the St. Lawrence Seaway, the village of Coldwell all but disappeared.

During World War II, the government found the isolated shores of the Coldwell Peninsula well-suited for housing German prisoners of war. Today few signs remain of the German officers' barracks that stood where campers now pitch their tents.

The same isolation that made Neys so useful as a prison draws campers to the Coldwell Peninsula today. Now easily accessible from the Trans-Canada Highway, the park's four modern campgrounds offer travelers hot showers and a 1.5-mile beach on which to enjoy the crashing waves of Lake Superior. Of the park's 144 campsites, 27 offer electricity. A visitor center, interpretive presentation, and evening programs help visitors enjoy the park's unique resources.

Canada's famed "Group of Seven" artists captured many scenes from the park on canvas. Fascinated by the rocky landscape and the island views from the park's shore, these artists found inspiration in the ancient beauty of the Coldwell Peninsula. The landscape's character can be traced to geologic events that occurred deep within the earth about one billion years ago, when granite-hard rock was thrust to the surface in concentric bands. As glaciers crept over the region, the rock was scoured smooth in some areas but remained immovable, creating formations that today stand in stark contrast to the surrounding forest.

Neys' expansive Lake Superior shoreline and its beach are the park's focal points. Campers frolic in the cool whitecaps of Lake Superior, while children take advantage of the park's playground.

A boat launch is located on the Little Pic River, offering access to Lake Superior. Pic and Detention islands are popular destinations for sea kayakers confident of their skills, but canoeists should hug the shore in case the changeable weather of Lake Superior takes a turn for the worst.

Families enjoy the short stroll along the half-mile self-guided Dunes Trail, which begins near the visitor center. At the opposite end of the park, off the campground four-loop, a trail leads to the CBC Tower Lookout, which affords a rewarding view of Lake Superior and the interior peninsula. The park's Point Hiking Trail begins at the Prisoner Cove Picnic Area, traversing a rocky cove before it terminates at a headland. From this perch, you'll see vistas of Superior and the peninsula. It's a great place to end your visit to Neys Park, because the trail ends where the sky, the land, the lake, and the forest are one.

PUKASKWA NATIONAL PARK
Highway 627
Hattie Cove
Heron Bay, Ontario P0T 1R0
807/229-0801

A wilderness song echoes through the boreal forest of Canada's harsh, intriguing Pukaskwa (pronounced PUK-a-saw) National Park. It's a chorus consisting of the laughter of loons, the howl of wolves, and the eerie cries of nesting great blue herons.

Lying between the Pic and Pukaskwa rivers, Pukaskwa National Park stretches 48 miles along Lake Superior's shore, encompassing ancient, rocky headlands, thundering waterfalls, and sand beaches along the untamed coast of the Canadian Shield. Perhaps no section of Lake Superior's shore is as remote, harsh, and spectacular as this one. Fortunately, thanks to the Canadian Parks Service, much of the rugged beauty is accessible. A campground, hiking trails, and a staffed interpretive center bring the pleasures of Pukaskwa within reach, even

PUKASKWA NATIONAL PARK

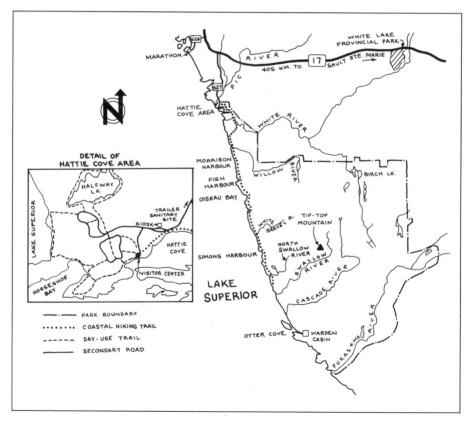

to those without the skill or stamina to explore the park's extensive backcountry.

The story of Pukaskwa begins with the birth of the Canadian Shield over two billion years ago. Massive fissures, or fault valleys, split the earth's crust, unveiling huge volcanic cauldrons. As these cauldrons began erupting, molten lava crept over the huge volcanic chamber below. Today, the flows of ancient lava can be traced in the white ribbons of quartz and the green beds of lava we see slicing through the Pukaskwa bedrock.

As the lava cooled and hardened to form valleys, ridges, and cliffs, the weight of the newly formed rock collapsed the roof of the hollow volcanic chamber below, forming a basin occupied by a much different lake than the one we now call Superior.

Eons later the glaciers arrived, scouring the rocks and again altering the landscape. Glacial meltwater flooded the Superior basin, and terraced sand and boulder beaches are still found high above the present levels of Lake Superior. When the glaciers finally retreated, Pukaskwa's rocky headlands, sandy beaches, and ancient bedrock remained as a tribute to the forces of nature.

Man's role in shaping Pukaskwa has been less dramatic, but perhaps no less important. Long before European explorers touched these shores, Objibwa Indians erected stone rock structures now known as Pukaskwa Pits along the pebble beaches of Lake Superior's northern and eastern shores. Named because they were initially discovered near the mouth of the Pukaskwa River, these structures were erected of round stones of various sizes, placed within circular, oblong, or rectangular shapes. In some cases, the stones were stacked to encircle a fire ring. In others, elaborate structures with partitions, entrances, and split-level interiors were erected.

Much speculation and mystery surrounds these pits. Some believe they were used by Objibwa youth who sought the Great Spirit's guidance on their journey to manhood. Others speculate that the pits were more utilitarian in nature, serving as either a place in which to store food or a spot from which to ambush prey.

To date, over 300 Pukaskwa Pits have been located along the shores of Lake Superior. We may never know why these sanctuaries of stone were created, but there's little doubt that the Great Spirit can still be found on the isolated beaches of Pukaskwa, hovering within these stone oracles.

The 16th century brought European explorers to the area, seeking an inland route to the exotic riches of the Orient. The riches they found were not the silks and spices of China, but rather a trade route to the fur-rich country of the northwest. Paddling from Montreal, their canoes laden with European treasures and trinkets, voyageurs passed the shores of Pukaskwa en route to trading posts further west.

Railroads arrived with a roar in the 1880s, opening Pukaskwa's boreal forest to the logger's axe. The Pukaskwa River became the center of the area's logging activity, but even the axe couldn't tame this rugged country. Few remnants of this era remain, mostly consisting of decaying cabins along the river's banks and at Imogene Cove, which is near the park's southern border.

The Pukaskwa area was initially considered for national parkland in the late 1960s, but it wasn't until February of 1978 that a land transfer agreement was signed between the province of Ontario and the Canadian government, creating Pukaskwa National Park. Established to protect and preserve the region's outstanding boreal forest and its pristine Superior coast, Pukaskwa National Park was opened to the public in 1983. Within its environment, the park shelters a herd of less than 30 woodland caribou that still roam wild, while the Superior coast remains home to the sensitive rookeries of the great blue heron.

Today Pukaskwa's black spruce and jack pine stretch for 145 square miles across the park's interior. Below this canopy, a thick, fragrant carpet of moss blankets the forest floor. Above the forested interior sits Tip Top Mountain which, pending official verification, is the highest point in Ontario.

Along the coast, stunted spruce trees extend their roots into the cracks of seemingly barren rock, securing a fragile hold in a hostile environment. Rare arctic plants, including pearlwort and encrusted saxifrage, cling to a narrow band of Superior's shore. These remnants of the last Ice Age include the carnivorous butterwort, which relies on its sticky leaves to trap and devour unsuspecting insects.

With the exception of a single road leading to Hattie Cove in the far northwest corner of the park, Pukaskwa is a roadless wilderness. Those setting forth on foot or by paddle will encounter Pukaskwa Country just as the earliest explorers did, finding serenity and challenge along the wild shore of an inland sea.

HATTIE COVE

A carpet of moss and a sea of wildflowers blanket the forest floor at the Hattie Cove Campground. Located in the northwest corner of Pukaskwa, Hattie Cove is the center of the park's activity and the launching point for excursions to the Pukaskwa backcountry.

Creature comforts, including comfort stations complete with heated showers, will make your stay a pleasant one at the 67-unit campground. Electricity is available at 29 campsites within the two-loop campground, and three walk-in units are available to those seeking more privacy. The campground is open from the third week in May through mid-October, but showers and hot water are available only from mid-June through mid-September. Leashed pets are permitted in the campground.

Overlooking the cove, the visitor center serves as the information hub for visitors seeking backcountry permits, topographic maps, or expertise from the well-trained staff. Exhibits and interpretive programs are scheduled throughout the summer to help you broaden your understanding of the Pukaskwa's unique environment.

BEACHES

The sands of Pukaskwa will warm both the hearts and the toes of July visitors to Hattie Cove. Hearty swimmers will enjoy taking a dip in this protected bay where the water is often warmer than it is off the beaches of Superior. Nearby picnic tables and a changing station make this beach popular with families.

Those wishing to roll out their beach blankets in a more secluded setting will enjoy the short hike down the Beach Trail. The interpretive nature trail leads to the sands of sheltered Horseshoe Bay and the exposed beaches of Lake Superior. Driftwood is scattered along these quiet beaches, and delicate plants reach into the dunes to find a home in the desert-like setting.

DAY HIKES

Pukaskwa's varied trails allow virtually anyone to explore the park, regardless of age or stamina. From Hattie Cove, the 1.25-mile Southern Headland Trail traces the Pukaskwa's past, encompassing the volcanic rocks and ancient sea beds of the Canadian Shield before circling back at Horseshoe Bay.

Those with a penchant for the beach life enjoy the one-mile hike on the Beach Trail, accessible from either of the two campground loops in Hattie Cove. Boardwalks on the Beach Trail protect the fragile dune communities from hikers' footsteps. Visitors are reminded that stepping off the planked trail, even for a quick photograph, could destroy rare and delicate plants.

Sunset is the best time to embark upon the 1.25-mile Halfway Lake Trail. Located half the distance between Lake Superior and Hattie Cove, Halfway Lake is a scenic, rock-rimmed lake cradled in the boreal forest of Pukaskwa.

BACKCOUNTRY

Currently, there is no charge for entering Pukaskwa National Park or for using backcountry facilities. Nor is there a trip preregistration or backcountry campsite reservation system.

The park does, however, require backcountry self-registration of day hikers, paddlers, and backpackers. This allows the park to monitor your interests and to assist you if you find yourself in trouble. It also helps the staff plan and design park facilities, based on your comments and experience.

There are four self-registration booths: one at the mouth of the Pic River; one at the Hattie Cove visitor center (trailhead of the Coastal Hiking Trail); another at White Lake Provincial Park (listed separately), the last bastion of civilization for white water boaters planning to run the White River from White Lake to Lake Superior; and a fourth at the Husky Service Station on Highway 17 at Saniga Lake, just east of the town of White River. Pukaskwa River runners should register at this station and at the checkpoint booth at Schist Falls, near the river's mouth. The booth is open from May through July.

If you're entering or leaving the park via a route without a registration booth, you may register immediately before you depart and again immediately upon your return by calling 807/229-0801, extension 223 or 224.

HAZARDS

Pukaskwa's biting insects are truly legendary. Louis Agassiz, a 19th-century naturalist, is quoted as saying, "Neither love of the picturesque nor the interest of science could tempt us into the woods, so terrible were the black flies." This remains true. The blackflies of Pukaskwa are a force to contend with. Fortunately, relief from these tiny vampires can often be found along the wind-swept coast of Lake Superior, but all visitors are advised that a headnet, long sleeves, long pants and plenty of insect repellent are mandatory equipment for your daypack.

Backpackers should realize that black bears are common and should take necessary precautions to protect food. Garbage should not be buried, as the black bears will find it. Pack out what you pack in.

If you follow the well-marked trails, you will not get lost. If you get turned around while hiking off-trail, use your map and compass to determine where you are. To the west, the setting sun leads to the coastline, as do the streams that flow from the park's interior.

Be prepared for weather extremes, from hot, humid daytime conditions and cool nights to fog, rain, and cold weather. Even in July and August, seasoned veterans pack a wool cap and gloves along with their pile (fleece) and rain gear.

PICKUP SERVICE

It is possible, albeit expensive, to hire a marine or aircraft charter to drop you off or pick you up in the Pukaskwa backcountry. This is a means for paddlers and hikers to avoid returning via the same route taken down the Pukaskwa coast. For boat charter service on the Coastal Hiking Trail, try Pic Repair and Marine in Marathon (807/229-0677) or Buck Fisheries and Marina in Wawa (705/856-4488). For airplane charter service, contact White River Air (807/822-2222).

DAY TRIPPING THE COASTAL HIKING TRAIL

The day hike to the White River down the Coastal Hiking Trail is a rigorous, rewarding trip to the spectacular cable suspension footbridge over Chigamiwinigam Falls. Upon your arrival, your heart may skip a beat as the wooden planks of the cable bridge sway beneath your feet while you pass across Chigamiwinigam Falls in order to enjoy lunch on the opposite side.

Before setting out on this ten-mile round trip, register your itinerary at the Hattie Cove Visitor Center. Sturdy boots are mandatory, as sections of the trail are rocky and often wet. To aid hikers, bridges and planks are provided over wetlands at the south end of Hattie Cove and along many sections of the trail. A day pack with water, rain gear, bug repellent, lunch, and a first-aid kit is standard equipment, even if the sky is blue and the temperature warm.

The trail begins near the beach at the visitor center and winds south along Hattie Ccve to a ridge that separates the cove from Pulpwood Harbor. The ridge provides a scenic overlook of Pulpwood Harbor, so named because timber companies once used the bay as a giant storage bin for timber.

The trail continues to Playter Harbor before heading inland through a low section along the hillsides that flank the harbor to the south. After a mile and a half, the trail reaches high ground and levels out en route to the White River.

The White River Bridge is as intimate as it is intimidating. The massive, spun-steel cable supports on each side of the suspension bridge will help instill confidence, but it's still a white-knuckled, hand-over-hand experience to cross the tumultuous White River Gorge.

The last log drive down the powerful White River happened in 1960. In April of that year, logs came tumbling down the river from a cut near White Lake, some forty miles upstream. Passing over Chigamiwinigam Falls, the logs were driven to the mouth of the White River at Lake Superior, where a rafting crew and tugboats were waiting to tow the logs to Sault Ste. Marie.

For many, the White River Bridge marks the end of the trail. Day hikers enjoy lunch on the south side of the river before heading back to Hattie Cove via the same trail. Backpackers will find campsites on the south side of the river by following the trail to the right after crossing the bridge. Be sure to check back in at the Hattie Cove visitor center, so the park staff knows you have returned safely. You're also encouraged to leave comments regarding your trip and your crossing of the White River.

BACKPACKING THE COASTAL HIKING TRAIL

The Coastal Hiking Trail is a demanding, 36-mile (one-way) trek from Hattie Cove to the remote North Swallow River. The trail follows the obstinate terrain of the Canadian Shield, where your skill and stamina will often be tested, but the rewards are many. The northern section of the trail from Hattie Cove to Oiseau Bay is well-used and well-maintained. South of Oiseau Bay, you'll be entering a remote section of Pukaskwa where your map-reading skills and backcountry savvy will be tested, since in some spots the trail may be challenging to follow.

Park wardens suggest that you allow at least five days to hike the length of the trail, but six would be better, considering the unpredictable weather of Lake Superior. To allow time for leisure, consider hiking a shorter section of the trail and spending time enjoying the Superior coast and the rivers that feed it.

There's no charge for hiking the trail, but you must advise park officials of your plans by filing a backcountry self-registration plan. You'll return via the same route, and Circle Tours are not possible without chartering a boat, plane, or helicopter.

The Coastal Hiking Trail is not blazed or flagged, so a well-worn path is the only indication you'll have that you're on the route. Rock cairns indicate direction on rocky promontories, and large rivers are bridged. Nevertheless, expect to encounter wet sections of trail, steep inclines, and loose boulders. Exercise special caution along the slippery rocks of the Lake Superior shore and along rivers, since it's a long walk out with a sprained ankle. Surface water should be filtered or boiled. You'll find campsites spaced approximately one-half day apart, and hikers are required to use the designated campsites. These offer a fire ring and, in some cases, privies. The sites are accessible to groups of not more than six members.

Thanks to a volunteer support group called Friends of Pukaskwa, an excellent waterproof map is available. Backpackers venturing beyond the White River should carry it with them on the trail. It's available at the Hattie Cove visitor center. A trail guide is also available through Friends of Pukaskwa (807/229-0801), providing an overview of the route's natural history. Those trekking the 17 miles beyond Oiseau Bay to the North Swallow River should also pick up the topographic maps of the route available at Hattie Cove. The primitive campsites along this stretch are marked on the map, but they have not been developed.

Many feel that August is the best month to tackle the Coastal Hiking Trail, as you can often plan on warm days, cool nights, and fewer insects. August can also be wet, however, so add rain gear, a wool hat, and mittens to your packing list.

As you head south past the well-traveled route to the suspension bridge over Chiwamiwinigam Falls, you'll leave the day hikers behind and enter the hinterlands of Pukaskwa. Here, the song of the Pukaskwa wilderness can best be heard. Your duty is only to listen.

PUKASKWA BY PADDLE

A canoe or sea kayak can open the door to great adventures along the Pukaskwa coastline and down its inland rivers. With the exception of the Hattie Cove day trip, these are not excursions for beginning paddlers, but those with the necessary skill and proper equipment will find clear water, crashing surf, and challenging rapids as they paddle through Pukaskwa.

DAY PADDLING HATTIE COVE

The sand beach at Hattie Cove cushions the feet of paddlers as they gently nudge their boats into the protected harbor and discover its wonders.

The day trip here is a great one for families or beginning paddlers who are rightfully intimidated by the open water of the Superior coast. You can spend an hour or a day on Hattie Cove, paddling the far reaches of the harbor.

Hattie Cove was once known as Mud Bay, and a glance down while paddling amidst the bulrushes and sweet gale in the eastern reaches of the cove will reveal the mud that gave the bay its name. The sweet gale and marsh cinquefoil that thrive in the mud are important food sources for the waterfowl that feed here.

If you're ambitious, you'll enjoy paddling out of the cove into Pulpwood Harbor. You'll still be well-protected from the open water of Lake Superior, but a gentle swell may occasionally roll beneath your canoe. Look closely and you may spot a deadhead in the water. A deadhead is a log with one end in the bottom of the lake and the other at or just below the surface of the water.

After completing your exploration of Pulpwood Harbor and Hattie Cove, be sure to inform the staff at the visitor center of your safe return by completing the self-registration return form.

COASTAL TRAVEL

During your voyage down the Pukaskwa coast, scattered sand beaches, crystal clear water, and granite headlands will be your companions as time is measured not in hours but in sunsets.

The one-way, 108-mile trip from the Pic River, north of Hattie Cove to Michipicoten Harbor south of Pukaskwa National Park, would take the hard-paddling voyageurs of the fur trade era less than two days. However, you're undoubtedly on vacation, so relax. Today most paddlers allocate ten days or more for completion of the journey, allowing time for exploration and for *degrade*, an old voyageur term meaning "waiting out the wind."

Canoeists should plan on being wind-stranded one of every three days, while aerodynamic sea kayakers will fare somewhat better. Since this is a one-way trip, many paddlers simply complete a portion of the route and return via the same route. Boat charter pick-up or drop-off service is available, and car shuttles or hitchhiking remain options. Campsites are spaced along the coast in many areas, and paddlers are required to camp in designated sites wherever such sites are available, using the existing fire rings. In the event of bad weather, however, don't hesitate to retreat to the safety of a protected cove where you can pitch your tent and wait out the storm.

Most paddlers venturing along the Pukaskwa coast put in at the park's canoe launch, adjacent to the visitor center in Hattie Cove. This is convenient, because you can discuss your trip with the park staff and pick up the latest marine forecast information. All backcountry visitors must self-register, and it's easy to do so while you're at the visitor center. A small boat launch is also located on the north side of the Pic River, just outside the boundary of Pukaskwa National Park, and you may park your vehicle there at your own risk. Backcountry registration is also available at the Pic River, but there are no marine facilities such as docks, gasoline, etc., for motorboaters who wish to travel the coast.

A boat launch is located outside the park's southern boundary at Michipicoten Harbor. Upon arrival at Michipicoten, contact the park office (807/229-0801) or the Ontario Provincial Police in Marathon (807/229-0220) to notify them that you have arrived safely. If you're paddling from Michipicoten to Hattie Cove, the reverse is true. If you require assistance during your trip, you'll find a warden station located at Otter Cove.

Canoe-paddling voyageurs called the wind in this area La Vieille—the Old Woman Wind. It can torture paddlers and whip the waves of Lake Superior into a nightmarish frenzy. While many paddlers still choose a canoe to make the coastal journey, sea kayaks are much better-suited to withstand Old Woman Wind. Sitting close to the water and snapped securely in a spray skirt, you'll be able to ride the waves and winds of Lake Superior when other craft are better left on shore.

If you're lucky, you may awake to spot the tail of a woodland caribou as it scampers into the bush. A small remnant herd of these animals still roams the park's shoreline, but catching a glimpse of one is a rare treat. Black bears, deer, moose, and timber wolves are more common, and as you reach remote sections of the Pukaskwa coast your chances of encountering these animals increase.

While exploring the remote boulder beaches of the Pukaskwa, you may happen upon one of the park's many mysterious Pukaskwa Pits. These man-made stone enclosures could be up to 7000 years old, and they represent one of the mysteries of Pukaskwa that paddlers ponder and only La Vielle can resolve.

PADDLING THE WHITE RIVER

Flowing through the boreal forest and surrounded by the Canadian Shield, the White River slices through a wilderness rich in beauty and history.

Archaeological finds indicate that Ojibwa once followed the White River on their nomadic search for fish and game. Fur traders followed, paving the way for lumberjacks and log drives.

The White River canoe route begins at Negawazu Lake, the river's source, and continues for 192 kilometers to Hattie Cove, near the mouth of the Pic River. Dropping 765 feet from its source, the White River plunges through 68 rapids and waterfalls before spilling into Lake Superior. Portages have been established at all falls and rapids on the White, and they should be taken, especially in the spring.

Although the White can be run from its source all the way to Hattie Cove, trying to do so may present a logistical nightmare, as access to roadless Negawazu Lake is difficult at best. The Trans-Canada Highway crosses the river at several points, but most paddlers shave days off the route by beginning their journey at White Lake Provincial Park. From the park it's a four to five-day paddle down the White.

There is a visitor self-registration station at White Lake Provincial Park, and you are required to register because your excursion will take you through Pukaskwa National Park.

If approached with the respect it deserves, the White River can be run all season long. You'll see few if any paddlers on the river, and fishing for northern pike, yellow pickerel, and brook trout can be satisfying. Established campsites are spaced approximately four miles apart along the river.

Ojibwa Indians believed that Mishipishew, a dragon-like mythical monster, lived in the deep waterways and tipped canoes over as they passed by on the White River. Modern paddlers would be wise to heed this warning and portage their canoes past the river's dangerous rapids and waterfalls. From the mouth of the White River at Lake Superior, it's an easy half-day paddle along the coast to civilization at Hattie Cove, but always be prepared for Le Vielle, the old woman wind of Lake Superior.

For a detailed planning guide, information on obtaining the necessary topographic maps, and current river conditions, contact the Ministry of Natural Resources in Wawa (705/856-2396).

PADDLING THE PUKASKWA RIVER

One translation defines Pukaskwa as "something evil." Perhaps the phrase was coined as an old-timer trudged his canoe over the Two Pants portage, a tedious hike that bypasses Ringham's Gorge on the Pukaskwa River.

Paddling the Pukaskwa River is hard work! There are 52 miles of boulder bed, gorges, ledges, and falls along the Pukaskwa as it drops

850 feet from Gibson Lake to the river mouth at Lake Superior. From Superior, it's a 55-mile paddle along the coast to Michipicoten Harbor to the east or Hattie Cove to the northwest.

If you're interested in making the run, keep in mind that the Pukaskwa is only navigable from about the first week in May to the first or second week in June, depending on runoff and local conditions. You'll be navigating 57 negotiable rapids through a river that's narrow and strewn with boulders.

For those with the necessary wilderness paddling skills, running the Pukaskwa is a real adventure. National Park rangers suggest that you allow eight or nine days to run the Pukaskwa from Sagina Lake, or five days for the run from Beaver Lake to the river's mouth.

Getting to the put-in is equally difficult. There are two options. One is to fly in from the town of White River or Wawa to Gibson, Jarvey, or Beaver Lake. A less expensive option is to put in where Highway 17 crosses the White River near Sagina Lake, then paddle to Gibson Lake via Pokei Creek, Soulier Lake, and Pokei Lake. The park service suggests that you consider carefully before attempting the paddle route, because portages of Pokei Creek require almost an entire day to accomplish.

A boat charter service can pick you up when you reach the mouth of the Pukaskwa River at Lake Superior. By arranging pick up, you'll avoid the additional five days of coastal paddling necessary to bring you to Hattie Cove or Michipicoten Harbor.

Those with the stamina and skill to paddle the Pukaskwa will find themselves surrounded by true Canadian wilderness. It's said that once you run the Pukaskwa, the Pukaskwa runs through you.

For detailed maps and information on current river conditions, contact Pukaskwa National Park (807/227-0801).

PADDLING HAZARDS

The waters of Lake Superior are icy cold, even in summer. Survival is estimated at a mere 30 minutes for a swimmer clinging to his or her overturned craft. Therefore, it's imperative that you paddle close to shore and beat a hasty retreat to the mainland at the first sign of foul weather. The area's frequent fog means that all paddlers should carry a compass and navigation (hydrographic) charts. Topographic charts are also useful, and both can be purchased from Friends of Pukaskwa (807/229-0801).

The current forecast, or MAYFOR, is available from the visitor center at Hattie Cove or by monitoring VHF radio channels 21B (Thunder Bay) or 83B (Sault Ste. Marie).

Flies and mosquitoes won't bother you on Lake Superior, but once you reach the shore, insect repellent, long sleeves, long pants, and a headnet are mandatory all summer long. Paddlers on the White and Pukaskwa rivers will find relief within the mesh of their tents and under a loose-fitting headnet.

Black bears inhabit all areas of Pukaskwa National Park, and it's mandatory that you hang your food and keep a clean campsite. Cooking in your tent attracts bears, and should be avoided.

Drinking water should be filtered, and an extra supply of food should be packed in case the weather extends your trip. Don't forget to register before and after your journey, and don't be afraid to discuss your plans with park staff. Warm, dry clothes are necessary throughout the paddling season, as are flares, a strobe light and a bilge pump.

Bon Voyage!

WHITE LAKE PROVINCIAL PARK
P.O. Box 1160
Wawa, Ontario P0S 1K0
807/822-2257

Warm summer temperatures and fog-free days keep campers coming back to the sand beaches and clear waters of White Lake Provincial Park. Thanks to its inland location, White Lake is often much warmer than its larger shoreside neighbor, Pukaskwa National Park.

Europeans weren't the first visitors to discover the superb fishing and bountiful wildlife of White Lake. Long before Europeans arrived, the Cree and Objiwa battled for control of the rich hunting and fishing grounds surrounding Natamasagami, a name that means "first lake from Superior."

Fur traders from the Hudsons's Bay Company followed, taking advantage of the region's central location on an extensive river system to transport pelts down the White River to Lake Superior. These traders renamed the lake, due to the frequent whitecaps they encountered while crossing the northern reaches of the waterway.

Today White Lake provides a peaceful escape for campers rolling into one of the park's 187 tent and trailer sites, which include ten units with electricity. Families enjoy the sand beach setting of Sundew Campground, while RV owners appreciate the electrical hookups found at Woodlily Campground. Moccasin Flower Campground is the park's largest, offering comfort stations including showers, and it's open from late May through mid-September. In July and August, evening programs are presented in the park's amphitheater.

White Lake Provincial Park is noted for its excellent fishing and boating opportunities. Paddlers can enjoy a peaceful day retreat on Deer and Clearwater lakes, or a full-blown expedition down the White River. Sailboaters will find exhilaration in the winds of White Lake, and fishermen will encounter hungry walleyes and northern pike within park waters.

A stroll down the park trails will renew your senses and reveal a host of wildflowers, including 12 different orchids anchored to the moist forest floor. Not to be missed is the 1.2-mile Clearwater Trail, which culminates in a refreshing swim in spring-fed Clearwater Lake.

AGAWA COUNTRY

Stories in Stone

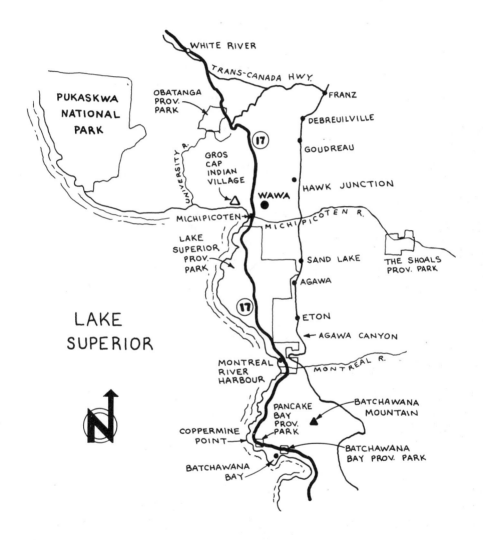

WHITE RIVER

TRANS-CANADA HWY.

PUKASKWA NATIONAL PARK

OBATANGA PROV. PARK

FRANZ

DEBREUILVILLE

17

GOUDREAU

GROS CAP INDIAN VILLAGE

WAWA

HAWK JUNCTION

MICHIPICOTEN

MICHIPICOTEN R.

LAKE SUPERIOR PROV. PARK

THE SHOALS PROV. PARK

SAND LAKE

AGAWA

LAKE SUPERIOR

17

ETON

AGAWA CANYON

MONTREAL RIVER HARBOUR

MONTREAL R.

BATCHAWANA MOUNTAIN

PANCAKE BAY PROV. PARK

COPPERMINE POINT

BATCHAWANA BAY PROV. PARK

BATCHAWANA BAY

Through the Windshield

Spinning into the White River, it's easy to forget that Lake Superior once provided the only means of travel through this mountainous countryside. Only recently did pickaxes and wheelbarrows pave the way for heavy machines to move mountains of rock and lay a ribbon of asphalt between the Circle Tour cities of Wawa and Sault Ste. Marie. Finally completed in 1960, this was the last link of the Trans-Canada Highway to cross the rugged terrain of the Canadian Shield.

Portions of the route were surveyed as early as 1924, but twenty years later conscientious objectors from World War II were still clearing the Montreal River Hill with wheelbarrows and iron wills. By 1952, the road was passable up to Speckled Trout Creek and, a million dollars later, the road crested the brutal Agawa hill—one of the most challenging sections of the link.

When the highway officially opened on September 17, 1960, over 4,000 vehicles motored into Wawa. The Lake Superior Circle Tour had become a reality.

Rimmed by grey granite and tall pines, White River has the kind of small town charm that rural Canada is noted for. It's also famous as the birthplace of Winnie the Pooh, the real-life bear that inspired A.A. Milne to begin writing his now-famous children's stories in 1926.

As the story goes, Captain Harry Colebourn, a soldier from Winnipeg, Manitoba, was aboard a World War I troop train bound for Quebec in 1914. When the train made a routine refueling stop in White River, Colebourn noticed a trapper carrying a black bear cub in his arms, and purchased the little orphan for $20. He named the cub Winnie, short for his hometown of Winnipeg, and continued the trip east with Winnie in tow. When Captain Colebourn's regiment was called to London, Winnie made the ocean crossing with the soldiers.

In December of 1914, Captain Colebourn's regiment was called to the front lines, and Winnie found a new home at the London Zoo. It was here that A.A. Milne's son Christopher Robin developed a special fondness for Winnie, his favorite bear. Allowing his imagination to wander, Milne chronicled his son's relationship with Winnie and penned the timeless adventures of Christopher Robin and Winnie the Pooh.

Skirting the northern border of Pukaskwa National Park, you'll reach Obatanga Provincial Park (listed separately). This is a pleasant park to roll into. The campground's tall pine trees and modern comfort stations are sure to provide you with a refreshing overnight break. Before driving out of the park, be sure to take a swim off the sand beach of Burnfield Lake.

If you're looking to leave the highway behind, you're sure to find peace among the backcountry campsites located along a canoe route that links 32 lakes within park boundaries. Motorboats are permitted within Obatanga Provincial Park, but most visitors prefer the simple beauty of a canoe.

When surveyors discovered thousands of migrating geese resting on a spring-fed inland lake in 1897, they christened the lake "Wawa" after an Objibwa name meaning wild goose. The town has since capitalized on its name by erecting a 28-foot, 4400-pound steel monument depicting a flying goose landing on water. Adjacent to the town's log information booth, the flying goose is perhaps the most famous feature of Wawa, but it certainly isn't the only reason to visit. Each year thousands of sportsmen "flock" to this town of 4,500 in the hope of landing a monster walleye or taking a record black bear. Wawa's airport provides bush plane access to the pristine lakes of the surrounding wilderness, while the town's business district caters to those with a taste for civilization.

The town's namesake, Lake Wawa, is located on Highway 101 just off Highway 17, and it offers swimming and picnicking. If you're staying in Wawa, you'll enjoy the 30-mile day trip down Highway 101 to Potholes Provincial Park. Opened as a day-use park in 1985, the park preserves unique eroded "potholes" left behind when the glaciers retreated. The park's self-guided trails are open from early June through early September.

It's wise to fill your gas tank before heading south from Wawa, because service service stations are scarce during the next leg of your journey.

The Magpie River drops 65 feet on its journey through a rocky gorge en route to Lake Superior just south of Wawa. You can stretch your legs on the short trail to Magpie High Falls by exiting Highway 17 one-half mile south of Wawa and taking the gravel road west to the trailhead. Magpie High Falls is visible from many angles along the trail, which continues on to Silver Falls further along the river valley.

Access to Lake Superior is available at the mouth of the Michipicoten River, three miles south of Superior. "Michipicoten" is an Objibwa word meaning high bluffs. To reach the river mouth, watch for the sign directing you to Buck's Marina off Highway 17 at the mouth of Michipicoten River Gorge. When you reach the Michipicoten River Village, a left turn on Harbour Road leads to the marina, headquarters for the Lake Superior Salmon Derby that's held during the fourth weekend of August each year. This is also the last harbor of civilization for those intent on paddling the wild shores of Pukaskwa National Park to the north.

A left turn on Harbour Road away from the marina at the Michipicoten River Village leads to the former site of an old Hudson's Bay Company Trading Post and a driftwood beach open to the public.

Off the shores of Michipicoten Harbor, separated from the harbor by 37 miles of open water, you'll find mysterious Michipicoten Island Provincial Park. Many Ojibwa legends speak of the mysteries of Michipicoten Island which, when viewed from the mainland, is said to float. Sometimes the island seems alluringly close to shore; at other times it seems impossibly distant. The island is accessible via float plane and large vessel, but many sea kayakers have dreamed of setting off in search of its distant shores. A small herd of woodland caribou lives on the island, as do a handful of cottage owners. A Coast Guard station is located on the island, but there are no campgrounds or other facilities.

Just south of Michipicoten Harbor, Highway 17 begins its 55-mile path through expansive Lake Superior Provincial Park (listed separately). At over 900 square miles, Lake Superior Provincial is one of the largest and most well-developed parks in Ontario. The park offers three modern campgrounds, including the popular 164-campsite Agawa Bay Campground. At Agawa Bay, campers can pitch their tents right on the sands of a Lake Superior driftwood beach. Competition for these shoreline sites can be intense, but those pulling in prior to the July-August rush have an excellent chance of gazing on the inland sea through their tent doors. The park's other two campgrounds are located at inland Crescent and Rabbit Blanket lakes.

The park offers eleven hiking trails, seven canoe routes, and 150 interior campsites. Both the hiking trails and the canoe routes vary in difficulty from hour-long meanders to overnight expeditions. You'll need an interior permit to access the wilderness, so be sure to consult with rangers at one of the developed campgrounds before beginning your trip.

The park's logo portrays Old Woman Bay, where sheer cliffs meet Lake Superior beside a sand beach. There's no charge to picnic at Old Woman Bay, so many visitors make this scenic spot the first stop on their travels south through the park. While at the bay, allow time to hike the 3.7-mile Nokomis Trail through the Old Woman River Valley. This trail will take you to some of the ancient, mysterious manmade rock depressions known as Pukaskwa Pits. Allow your imagination to wander as you approach Old Woman Bay Cliff, which rises from Lake Superior, and perhaps you'll recognize the Old Woman's face as she keeps vigil over all who visit.

If you're looking for a spot where you can pitch a tent or slide a canoe into the water, you'll find Rabbit Blanket Lake most accommodating. The campground is open from early May through October, and the recent addition of showers is sure to bolster the popularity of this 62-campsite unit.

The theme of Lake Superior Provincial Park is: "Human response to a rugged and wild shoreline and backcountry." Those venturing off Highway 17 to explore the backroads of the park are cautioned that the theme rings true. The roads that access the park's interior are usually passable, but are often better-suited to mountain bikes or high-clearance vehicles. Be especially cautious of the Gargantua Road past the Belanger Lake Canoe Route, since bridge washouts can make this route impossible to negotiate.

Meanwhile, back on Highway 17, you'll find a pair of short hiking trails worth considering before making a picnic stop at Katherine Cove. The one-mile Trapper's Trail follows the shoreline of Rustle Lake along an old trapline that was used until the mid-1970s. The seven-mile Orphan Lake Trail loop requires greater ambition, but provides a great deal of diversity as it passes through stands of sugar maple and yellow birch en route to lookouts over Orphan Lake and Lake Superior.

For those willing to brave the cold waters of Gitchi Gummi, Katherine Cove offers a fine place to take a swim. Even if you aren't up for a dip, it's tough to resist the warm sands of Superior on a hot August day.

Just south of Katherine Cove, you'll find the Sand River making its way to Lake Superior. The Ojibwa named this river "Pinguisibi," meaning river of fine white sand. Today it's a popular picnic spot for motorists. Speckled trout hide in the many small pools of the river, and fishermen can access these holes via the four-mile, one-way Pinguisibi Trail, which follows the river's bank.

A journey of history, inspiration, and mystery can be yours during a visit to the Agawa Rock Indian Pictographs. The ancient pictures on the stone canvas of Agawa Rock are located just off Highway 17 at the end of a narrow passage between huge split boulders. This is a spiritual place, a place in which to ponder the red ochre on the rocks and wonder what it signifies. During summer months, a park ranger is stationed at the site to answer your questions and to help you interpret the mysteries of these stories on stone.

South of the Agawa Rock Pictographs, you'll find the park's largest and most popular campground. Lucky campers at the Agawa Bay Campground can pitch their tents on the shores of a driftwood beach, enjoying the sound of crashing waves and the beauty of a setting northern sun. The campground is open from mid-May to late September, but July and August are the busy months when all park services are fully operational. Modern comfort stations offer running water and warm showers, and interpretive programs are given during July and August.

Rustic Crescent Lake Campground is located at the southern entrance to Lake Superior Provincial Park. Situated along the shore of Crescent Lake, the campground caters to those who don't require the modern facilities offered at Agawa Bay. The Crescent Lake facilities are open from late June to early September. Portages lead from Crescent Lake to nearby Kenny, MacGregor and Mudhole lakes. Canoeists will enjoy trying their luck fishing for brook trout, lake trout, and splake.

Highway 17 skirts the mouth of the Montreal River at Lake Superior just south of Lake Superior Provincial Park. A small settlement at the harbor offers lodging and snacks to visitors who stop to enjoy the Montreal River Gorge.

August travelers will undoubtedly want to break out their swimsuits for the next leg of the journey, which takes you to a pair of fine, warm water beaches on Lake Superior bays. In Superior Country, "warm" is a relative term, since Lake Superior is rarely warm enough for anything but a quick dip, even on the hottest days of summer.

Pancake Bay Provincial Park is your first stop. The bay was named by canoe-paddling voyageurs who were low on provisions. Since flour was often the only staple left in their food packs, these hungry canoeists often enjoyed pancakes for dinner, knowing that fresh supplies were just a day's paddle away at Sault Ste. Marie.

Today's visitors to Pancake Bay often plan an overnight stop at the park's 338-unit campground. Open from early May to early October, the park's two-mile-long beach is noted for its fine sand and crescent moon shape.

Not far away at Batchawana Bay Provincial Park, another beach attracts day trippers. This day-use park offers a fine view of Batchawana Island. Due to the calm water it offers, Batchawana Bay is popular with paddlers and motorboaters. Be advised that the shoreline of Batchawana Bay is privately owned with the exception of the parkland.

The Lake Superior Circle Tour crosses the Goulais River Valley 15 miles north of Sault Ste. Marie. In late September, the hills surrounding the Goulais River are alive with color, and the sky is filled with migrating waterfowl.

In winter, both downhill and cross-country skiers enjoy reliable snow and heart-pounding vertical descents just twenty miles north of Sault Ste. Marie. Miles of groomed trails await skiers at the Stokely Creek Ski Touring Center, while downhill skiers will find a 700-foot vertical drop at Searchmont, coupled with night skiing opportunities at Heyden. Those in search of a passive winter escape will enjoy boarding the Snow Train for a winter journey through the white wilderness of the Agawa Canyon. Operated by the Algoma Central Railways, the train awaits you during the next leg of your tour, which begins in Sault Ste. Marie.

OBATANGA PROVINCIAL PARK
District Manager
Ministry of Natural Resources
Wawa, Ontario P0S 1K0
705/856-2396

Located just a stone's throw off Highway 17, Obatanga Provincial Park provides a wonderful resting spot for weary travellers making the Lake Superior Circle Tour.

Early in the summer, you'll find mocassin wildflowers, also called pink lady slipper orchids, carpeting the floor of the park's attractive 132-unit campground. Towering above the tent pads, tall jack pine trees remind visitors of a forest fire that swept through the region some 45 years ago. Heat from the fire opened the cones of the old jack pine trees and as the old growth was destroyed a new generation was born.

Beyond the campground, another park unfolds. Here you'll discover a wilderness waterway linking 32 lakes by rivers and streams within nearly 60 square miles of Canadian wilderness. Paddlers will enjoy pitching a tent at backcountry campsites along the route, which park rangers say can be completed in five days.

Those without the energy to tackle the backcountry will enjoy curling up with a good book on the sands of Burnfield Lake, located adjacent to the campground. A marked swimming area and the lake's relatively warm, shallow waters combine to make this a popular place for an August dip.

Motorboats are permitted on Burnfield Lake, but canoes remain the favorite mode of transportation. The lake is noted for its pickerel, perch and northern pike fishing, but those venturing into the interior lakes are likely to heighten their odds of success.

The park has a pair of short hiking trails winding through the jack pine forest, and early risers may happen upon one of the many moose that frequent the park. Black bears are also common within the park, and campers are advised to leave their coolers within the confines of their cars or campers before retiring.

You won't be the only travellers depending on Obatanga Provincial Park for renewal. Great blue herons, loons, osprey and a host of ducks and geese all depend on the riches of Obatanga to restore energy as they make their migratory journeys.

LAKE SUPERIOR PROVINCIAL PARK
Box 1160
Wawa, Ontario P0S 1K0
705/856-2284

The river valleys, rocky shores, and sandy bays of Lake Superior Provincial Park have always held a spiritual meaning for those who cherish wild places. In days past, Objibwa youth would seek the solitude of this region by fasting and sleeping under the stars during their sacred vision quest, a rite of passage to adulthood. It was during this time of seclusion and deprivation that a dream or vision might reveal to them their Manitou—a guardian spirit who would accompany them through life.

Many of today's visitors to Lake Superior Provincial Park arrive seeking their own sense of renewal. For some it may be the chance to camp on the shores of a driftwood beach, with only the sun as an alarm clock and the waves keeping time. For others it may be the chance to embark upon an inland canoe trip that bonds father and son, portaging pack and fishing pole to remote lakes. And to still others it may be a train ride through the wilderness, where the rivers run free and the mountains pass unchallenged.

Spanning over 900 square miles, Lake Superior Provincial Park is immense in its grandeur. Within its boundaries you can hike among clouded hills, paddle remote inland lakes, or fish in clear, running rivers.

Lying within the southern section of the Canadian Shield, the park is composed of rocks over two billion years old. The landscape has been sculpted by volcanoes, earthquakes, and glaciers, leaving an awesome legacy of forested mountains and green valleys. Within the park steep

LAKE SUPERIOR PROVINCIAL PARK

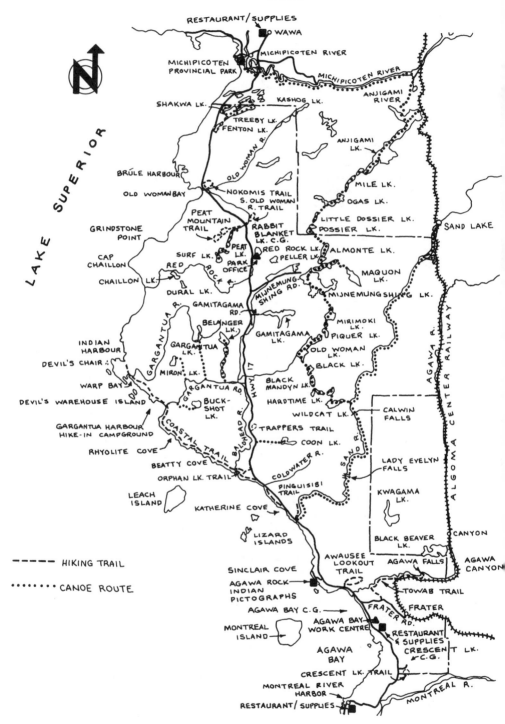

hills rise from the sand beaches of Lake Superior at Old Woman Bay, while the Agawa River tumbles through the spectacular floor of the Agawa Valley. Meanwhile, hikers traveling the demanding Coastal Trail will find themselves in the midst of a geology lesson as they stumble over, around, and through ancient bedrock dikes and faults, particularly at Fatman's Alley, where the route pierces an eroded chasm.

The park offers a unique combination of transitional southern hardwood forest intertwined with northern boreal forest. In autumn the park's high country is characterized by deciduous trees alive with color, including sugar maples and yellow birch. During the winter, the boreal forest of the park's lowlands and river valleys retains its evergreen cloak of fir, spruce, and pine. Spring finds the forest floor carpeted in wildflowers, while summer reveals shady swamps and verdant hillsides.

The park's diverse forest provides a wide variety of habitats for bird life. Over 250 species of birds have been counted at Lake Superior Provincial Park, making the preserve a haven for bird watchers. Resident species include ravens, ruffed grouse, woodpeckers, and chickadees, while spring brings the sweet songs of warblers and thrushes.

Moose are commonly sighted in the park, and can pose a threat to evening traffic on Highway 17. Woodland caribou are found on the offshore islands adjacent to the park, safely isolated from the wolves that roam the park's mainland interior. Black bears are found throughout the preserve, and campers are advised to leave a tidy campsite with all food safely stored in car trunks overnight.

Summer begins here in mid-June and lasts through August, and most travelers visit during this season. July tends to be the driest month of the year, but there are no guarantees, and seasoned travelers pack rain gear and pile or wool all summer long. Paddlers on Lake Superior should always have a compass close at hand, as fog is a frequent occurrence. It often blankets the coastline with an eerie, chilling mist until the winds of change or the heat of the sun dissipates the shroud.

Winter is the longest season at Lake Superior Provincial, lasting a brutal six months and sandwiched between a short spring and an only slightly longer fall. This doesn't deter an annual gathering of Great Lakes sea kayakers who make their annual pilgrimage to the park during the first weekend in November. The gathering takes place during the annual "Gales of November," and the kayakers sometimes meet freezing rain and pounding surf. Other years, they're treated to calm seas and blue skies.

Indian people, the area's earliest settlers, have always kept time by seasonal changes. Spring was celebrated when maple sugar provided the currency of barter, and fish could be caught in the Sault rapids. Summer would find Objibwa bands gathered at the mouths of the Sand and Michipicoten rivers, where fish and game were bountiful. As winter approached, the bands would disperse to their traditional hunting grounds, fearing the coming of "Windigo," the mythic god of winter who stalked the landscape, devouring all life and bringing starvation wherever he roamed.

In 1725 a trading post was opened by the French in Michipicoten, an Objiwa gathering spot. The arrival of French fur traders marked the beginning of the end of the traditional ways of the Objiwa. As the European appetite for fur increased, so did the number of trappers. At the peak of the fur trading era, trading outposts located at Agawa and Batchawana bays processed over 1500 beaver pelts in a single season. But the fur was not endless. By the 1840s, the beaver was almost extinct in the Lake Superior Basin. In 1894, the Agawa Bay trading post was closed, and most of the Indians left the region to farm at Goulais Bay.

AGAWA ROCK

The Indian people of Lake Superior were never separated from the often-harsh world in which they lived. Rising from the depths of Lake Superior, their pictographs at Agawa Rock depict their relationship with nature on a canvas of stone. Here, nomadic Ojibwa recorded their myths and travels, leaving a record of red ochre on a wall of granite they called *Wazhenaubikininguing Augawong*, or Inscription Rock.

Visiting Agawa Rock, you'll leave the present behind as you travel through time, passing between a steep walled chasm to the base of a stone shelf beneath the high cliffs. The most impressive rock paintings here are thought to commemorate the safe canoe crossing of Lake Superior by an Objibwa war party. The war party was led by a chief named Myeengun, the "wolf of the mermaid" whose band of Objibwa lived on the banks of Michigan's Carp River, which flows through the Porcupine Mountains. Myeengun made the successful crossing in order to join the Agawa band of Chippewa in battle against their enemies, the Iroquois. Depicted on the rocks are five canoe figures, believed to indicate the size of the war party. Also depicted is the clear figure of Misshepezhieu, the "great horned lynx" that calmed the seas during their crossing. This water spirit was of great importance to the Objibwa, as they believed that the lynx controlled the conditions on Lake Superior. If the spirit was content, the waters were calm; if enraged, a simple lash of the spirit's mighty tail would unleash a great storm.

Other pictographs at Agawa Rock may represent spirits revealed during dreams or vision quests. The quests were undertaken by Objibwa youth as a passage to adulthood. During these periods of prolonged isolation and deprivation, a link would be revealed between the harsh realities of everyday life and the mysterious spiritual world of the hereafter.

In July and August, a park naturalist is on duty at Agawa Rock to help you interpret the paintings and answer your questions. Visitors should be aware that the pictographs are extremely fragile. In 1958 a researcher visiting the site recorded 65 individual figures. Each year the waves and weather of Lake Superior take a toll on the granite, and today only half as many figures are clearly visible. Please avoid touching the paintings, so those who follow you may enjoy the mysteries of Agawa.

Visitors to Agawa Rock are advised that the trail to the pictograph site is short, but very rugged. If Misshepezhieu is upset, lake conditions may not allow you to step onto the precarious ledge of the rock. Perhaps it's fitting that today's visitors, like the Ojibwa, must be cautious when visiting this sacred site, and must beware the wrath of Misshepezhieu.

CAMPING

Lake Superior Provincial Park is served by three drive-in campgrounds as well as interior campsites (see Backcountry Camping).

Located on a Lake Superior driftwood beach, Agawa Bay Campground (fee charged) is the largest and most popular campground, offering modern comfort stations complete with showers. Reservations are accepted. The Agawa Bay Campground is open from mid-May through September, but facilities are limited prior to the third week in June and following Labor Day weekend. Interpretive programs are available from late June through Labor Day.

Rabbit Blanket Lake Campground (fee charged) offers campsites along Rabbit Blanket Lake. Modern comfort stations were scheduled for completion in time for the 1992 camping season. Reservations are not accepted here, and the campground is open from early May through October, with limited facilities available prior to late June and following Labor Day.

The only luxury offered by Crescent Lake Campground (fee charged) is hand-pumped water. The campground is open from late June through Labor Day.

WINTER

From late October to May 1, facilities and services are not available at Lake Superior Provincial Park. Campgrounds are closed and gated. Visitors are welcome to ski, snowshoe, and ice-fish (live bait not allowed), but snowmobiles are prohibited.

BACKCOUNTRY CAMPING AND REGISTRATION

All overnight travelers to the interior of Lake Superior Provincial Park must obtain an interior camping permit (fee charged). Interior permits are available at all park campgrounds, park offices, information centers, and self-registration stations at interior entry points. Interior permits are not required of visitors at day-use areas or campgrounds, but hikers should register at the trailheads.

You must camp only at campsites identified by diamond-shaped, blue-and-white tent symbols on trails, and by rectangular orange-and-black signs along canoe routes. Most campsites in the interior contain one designated fire pit. Your party is limited to nine people per campsite. Emergency or bad weather camping is allowed in non-designated sites, as long as no-trace camping is practiced. All plant life here is protected.

A can and bottle ban is in effect for all visitors to the backcountry. Snowmobiles, mountain bikes, and all-terrain vehicles are prohibited on all roads and trails that are closed to vehicular traffic.

FISHING

Ontario residents and non-residents alike are required to obtain a fishing license before dipping a line in park waters, including Lake Superior. Licenses are available at retail outlets in Wawa and at the park office.

The use of live baitfish is prohibited (worms are allowed) in park waters, except in Lake Superior. Outboard motors are prohibited on inland lakes with the exception of Sand Lake, where motors are restricted to ten horsepower or less.

Brook trout are found in lakes and streams throughout the park, while lake trout are found in Mijinemungshing and Old Woman lakes.

BEARS

Black bears are found throughout the backcountry. Never keep food in your tent overnight, as food odors attract bears, skunks, and raccoons. Keep a clean campsite and hang your food pack high off the ground in an airtight pack.

HAZARDS

Weather is the greatest hazard facing backcountry visitors. Be prepared to face extremes, even in summer. Serious rain gear is your first line of defense. A dry tent and a warm sleeping bag are necessities. Temperatures hovering around the freezing mark can occur even in summer, so you're advised to keep a wool cap and gloves in your pack along with your swimsuit. Fog is frequent in the park, especially along the coastline. Rain is common, averaging one or two days a week.

Biting insects are plentiful. Black flies are at their peak in June and early July, while mosquitoes, sand flies, deer flies and horse flies appear in July and early August. The best time for camping without encountering excessive insects is late July through October.

Hiking boots are recommended on demanding hikes, because the trails can become slippery due to rain, fog, or dew, especially near lookouts, cliffs, and ledges.

MAPS

A large-scale, waterproof map showing backcountry campsites, hiking trails, and canoe portages is available for a fee from the park office. It's worth the price. The reverse side of the map provides a topographic illustration of the Coastal Trail. To purchase a map call Lake Superior Provincial Park (705/856-2284). Off-season, contact the Wawa district office (705/856-2396).

HIKING TRAILS

THE COASTAL TRAIL
Length: 33 miles
Hiking Time: 5 to 7 days
The Coastal Trail forms an important link in the Lake Superior Voyageur Trail. Extending from Sinclair Cove to Chalfant Cove, the trail is the most challenging and scenic trail in Lake Superior Provincial Park. You'll travel along the high cliffs and rocky beaches of Lake Superior en route to many scenic coves and interior campsites. North and south of Sinclair and Chalfant coves, the trail is under development as a link in the Voyageur Trail. As part of this link, a three-mile section leading from Noisy Bay to the park boundary joins a nine-mile section of the Voyageur Trail ending at Wawa. Check with park rangers for current conditions.

Gargantua is the main access point for the Coastal Trail. The nine-mile gravel road from Highway 17 to the information kiosk and parking lot at Lake Superior is extremely rough. There is a self-registration station just off Highway 17. A high-clearance vehicle is recommended for the remainder of the 45-minute drive, but if the bridges are in good repair, any vehicle will suffice. Day hikers can mountain bike to the trailhead.

From the parking lot, it's an easy 45-minute hike to Gargantua Harbor, site of an abandoned fishing village. Here you'll find 11 campsites, a sand beach, a pit privy, and a short lookout trail above Lake Superior. A two-hour hike north from Gargantua leads to six campsites on wonderful and remote Warp Bay. This is a great three-day trip, as you can spend a full day exploring Warp Bay.

South of Gargantua and north of Warp Bay, the trail becomes extremely rugged. It ascends and descends over cliffs and rocky outcrops, and crosses beaches of boulders and driftwood. Use caution when hiking this difficult terrain, because the lichen-covered rocks can be extremely slippery. Wind-blown trees may obstruct the trail. Blue, diamond-shaped symbols mark spots where the trail enters forested areas, while rock cairns mark the exposed coastline sections. Generally, the trail hugs the coastline. If you lose it, continue along the shore and you'll eventually find the trail once again.

Experienced hikers with the proper gear will enjoy this remote section of the park, where campsites are found on sand and cobble beaches nestled in protected coves. Rhyolie and Beatty Coves are particularly inviting, and campsites are available to overnight visitors.

NOKOMIS TRAIL
Length: 1.8-mile loop
Hiking Time: 1 to 2 hours
Difficulty: Moderate

The Nokomis Trail leads through the Old Woman River Valley, past ancient and mysterious Pukaskwa Pits. Some of the manmade depressions in the rock are thought to be over 2,000 years old.

The trail climbs to a lookout that offers an expansive view of the Old Woman River Valley before leading across a granite ridge to other lookouts over Lake Superior. Looking to the west, you'll find Old Woman Bay Cliff rising from Lake Superior. Look closer and perhaps you'll see the old woman's face that gives the rock its name.

After descending past a series of lookouts, the trail passes through a red pine forest stunted by the harsh conditions of the region. The path then returns to the trailhead and the sandy beach of Old Woman Bay.

SOUTH OLD WOMAN RIVER TRAIL
Length: 2 miles
Time: 1 to 2 hours
Difficulty: Little

Brook trout inhabit the small pools of the Old Woman River, and fishermen will enjoy taking this trail equipped with a fly rod.

The trail follows the Old Woman River through a cedar forest along the river's banks, where ferns are found growing on the cool, moist forest floor.

PEAT MOUNTAIN TRAIL
Length: 6.2 miles
Time: 3 to 5 hours
Difficulty: Demanding

The heart-pounding trail to the top of Peat Mountain leads to an inspiring view of the glacial ridges and valleys of Lake Superior Provincial Park. To the north, Wawa is visible, while to the west you'll find Foam Lake, Lake Superior, and on a clear day even Michipicoten Island, some 30 miles distant.

The main trail continues to one backcountry campsite at Foam Lake, while a side trail takes a 45-minute jaunt to the Foam Lake Lookout before looping back to the main trail. Both trails meet for the return back to the trailhead.

TRAPPERS TRAIL
Length: 1 mile
Time: 1 1/2 hours
Difficulty: Easy

Occasionally closed due to flooding, the Trappers Trail is one of the most unique in the park. It follows the shoreline of Rustle Lake, which was just a wide spot in a stream until beavers created a dam that flooded the surrounding forest.

In the 1930s, the Renner brothers took advantage of this beaver activity and licensed a trapline to harvest the abundant fur bearers. The Trapper's Trail follows a portion of the former trapline, which was active until the mid-1970s.

The trail offers a pair of viewing platforms and a floating boardwalk. Along the path, you'll find the remains of a trapper's cabin, similar to the original cabin built by the Renners for use as a stopover while they ran their trapline from the Baldhead River to Lake Superior. The cabin's low roof allows snow to drift over the top of the structure, thereby providing much-needed insulation.

ORPHAN LAKE TRAIL
Length: 6.2 miles
Time: 2 to 4 hours
Difficulty: Moderate

The Orphan Lake Trail provides backpackers with access to the Coast Trail and day hikers with an introduction to the park's varied backcountry.

The trail passes through a transitional hardwood forest of sugar maple and yellow birch to a cliff overlooking Orphan Lake before climbing to picturesque lookouts above Lake Superior.

If you head down from here to a Lake Superior cobblestone beach, you'll have access to the demanding Coastal Trail. Follow the trail north to the Baldhead River, and you'll enjoy a series of rapids and drops as the trail winds upstream. It then climbs to the eastern shores of Orphan Lake before looping back to the original trail and heading back to the parking area.

AWAUSEE TRAIL
Length: 6 miles
Time: 4 to 6 hours
Difficulty: Demanding

You'll soar with the eagles on this hike to a series of lookouts above the Agawa River Valley.

The trail starts at the base of Agawa Mountain and follows an old logging road before veering up along a ravine to the first lookout. The lower Agawa River Valley and Agawa Mountain are visible from here, and those with stamina will enjoy continuing the climb. You'll pass through a maple forest en route to several lookouts until you reach the crest, high above the Agawa Valley. Upstream, the river valley narrows to the famous Agawa Canyon.

Descending, you'll join an old logging road that leads back to the trailhead.

TOWAB TRAIL
Length: 14.4 miles
Time: Two days
Difficulty: Demanding

Seasoned backpackers in good condition will enjoy this demanding overnight trip to Agawa Falls which, at 85 feet, is the highest in Lake Superior Provincial Park. Pack along your fly rod, because brook and rainbow trout can be found in the pool below the falls.

The Towab Trail takes its name from Towabanasay, an Objibwa Indian who once held hunting rights to the Agawa River Valley. At the turn of the century, Towab, as his guests called him, would guide visitors to the Agawa interior.

Today a guide isn't necessary to reach Agawa Falls, but sure footing is, since the trail makes several steep climbs and descents over cliff areas of the Agawa River Valley.

Day trippers who embark early will be able to make the hike to Burnt Rock Pool and back, but those continuing to Agawa Falls should possess an interior camping permit and backpacking equipment.

When you hear the thunder of the falls in the distance, you'll know your goal is within reach.

CRESCENT LAKE LOOP
Length: 3/4 mile
Time: 1 hour
Difficulty: Easy

Families will enjoy the short, scenic Crescent Lake Loop, which begins at the Crescent Lake Campground and leads through a forest of maple, birch, and white pine.

The area was logged in 1957, and the few remaining virgin white pine are over 100 years old. In an attempt to return this forest to its natural condition, thousands of seedlings were planted by the Ministry of Natural Resources.

PADDLING THE PARK

Lake Superior Provincial Park is a haven for paddlers. Sea kayakers trust their skills on the open water of Lake Superior, while whitewater paddlers challenge the foam of the Agawa River and flat water paddlers dip their blades in the park's inland lakes.

The topography of Lake Superior Provincial Park is rugged and demanding. Glacial meltwater sculpted the river valleys and lake systems found in the park. Many of the rivers and creeks that link the park's inland lakes drop through narrow, unnavigable channels that must be portaged. Canoeists planning to take these portages should be skilled and well-conditioned.

Meanwhile, the open water of Lake Superior beckons sea kayakers to explore. Each year competent paddlers with decked boats safely challenge the wind and waves of Lake Superior Provincial Park. The icy water of Lake Superior is much too cold to survive, and neoprene wetsuits provide the first line of defense. Experienced sea kayakers never depart the beach without a compass on board and an emergency plan in mind.

Whitewater paddlers will find themselves far from civilization should an accident occur. The Algoma Central Railway provides the only access to the whitewater of the Agawa River, and paddlers making the run should be prepared to portage.

MAPS

Lake Superior Provincial Park publishes a detailed canoeing guide, featuring maps and valuable tips to help you on your trip into the park's interior lakes and rivers. Before attempting any of the overnight routes described here, contact the park (705/856-2284) or the district office (705/856-2396) to request the free canoeing guide. Inquire regarding current portage conditions in the area you intend to visit.

Both canoeists and sea kayakers will find the park's hiking trail map extremely valuable, as it includes backcountry campsites. Before setting off on any overnight trip to the park's backcountry, you must first obtain an interior camping permit.

PADDLING THE COASTLINE

Distance: 60 miles
Time: 5 to 7 days
Difficulty: Intermediate to advanced

The coast of Lake Superior Provincial Park is a wonder to explore by paddle. Sea kayaks are the safest, most efficient means of paddling the coast, but open canoes will suffice if powered by experienced paddlers who remain close to the shore.

Motorboats have access to the coast at Sinclair Cove, while canoeists and sea kayakers can put in at Old Woman Bay, Gargantua Harbor, Katherine Cove, Agawa Bay Campground, and at the Agawa, Sand and Coldwater rivers. Lake Superior is calmest during June and July, while in August the brisk west winds may force paddlers to remain on shore.

The park's many coves, beaches, and harbors allow paddlers a chance to beat a hasty retreat and wait out bad weather. In the event of poor weather, paddlers are allowed to make camp at areas other than established campsites if no-trace camping is practiced.

Heavy fog is common along the shore, and may persist for several days in a row. Carry a compass and adequate rain gear. Be prepared to be wind-bound one out of every four days.

ALGOMA CENTRAL RAILWAY (FOR PADDLERS)
For the railway's Agawa Canyon schedule write:
Algoma Central Railway
129 Bay St.
Sault Ste. Marie, Ontario
Canada P6A 5P6
705/254-4331

The Algoma Central Railway (ACR) runs from Salt Ste. Marie to Hearst, passing the eastern boundary of Lake Superior Provincial Park. ACR trains are equipped to handle canoes and camping gear, and can be boarded at Sault Ste. Marie, Frater (near Agawa Bay), or Hawk Junction (12 miles east of Wawa). Paddlers should be at the train station at least 30 minutes before departure time to get passenger and freight tickets.

At Frater and Hawk Junction, tickets are often sold on the train. For up-to-date information about fares and train schedules, or to make arrangements for a special pick up at Sand Lake, call 705/254-4331 in Sault Ste. Marie or 705/889-2244 in Hawk Junction.

For paddlers dropped off at Sand Lake or those who decide later to return from this junction, the ACR passenger train can be flagged to a halt by waving your arms or a bright piece of cloth at the side of the tracks. The method can be employed elsewhere on the tracks in the event of an emergency.

CRESCENT LAKE CANOE ROUTE
Length: 1.7 miles
Time: 4 hours
Portages: 4
Difficulty: Easy

Canoeists can put in at Crescent Lake, or at Kenny Lake and Highway 17. The route is a loop trip via Kenny, MacGregor, Mudhole, and Crescent lakes. There are no campsites on this canoe route, but fishermen will enjoy trying their luck on the brook trout, lake trout, and splake that inhabit these waters.

FENTON-TREEBY ROUTE
Length: 9.6-miles
Time: Daytrip or overnight
Portages: 11
Difficulty: Easy

To take this route, put in at Fenton Lake and Highway 17. You'll return to Fenton Lake. The Fenton-Treeby loop is a nice trip for those getting introduced to overnight canoe camping. The portages are short, the lakes are relatively well-protected, and the scenery is pleasant. If you plan an overnight visit, be sure to secure an interior camping permit.

BELANGER LAKE ROUTE
Length: 8 miles
Portages: 4
Difficulty: Moderate

To begin this route, you'll need to portage to Belanger Lake, off the right side of Gargantua Road. Put in beside the second of two timber bridges on the road. The Belanger Lake Route is popular with families and fishermen pursuing the brook trout found in these lakes.

ANJIGAMI RIVER ROUTE
Length: 42 miles
Time: 5 days or more
Portages: 12
Difficulty: Advanced

Canoeists can put in at Mijinemunshing Lake. This canoe route follows the logger's spring river drive route of the 1920s. The route can be combined with the Sand River Route by using the Algoma Central Railway for access to the put-in at Sand Lake. Connections between Mijinemunshing Lake and the Old Woman Lake Route are also possible. These connections will add additional time and distance to your itinerary.

LOWER AGAWA RIVER ROUTE
Length: 18 miles
Time: 2 to 3 days
Portages: 4
Difficulty: Advanced

To take this route, plan to put in at the Algoma Central Railway Canyon Station (mile 114). The route is for experienced whitewater paddlers only. Water levels fluctuate from very low water in dry periods to very high water with treacherous rapids in spring run-off or after heavy rains. Ropes must be used to lower your canoe down the steep slope bypassing Agawa Falls. Below the falls, the route follows the fast-running, shallow water of the Agawa River. High canyon walls and Agawa Falls make this a spectacular route for those with the skill to make the run.

SAND RIVER CANOE ROUTE
Length: 35 miles
Portages: 29
Difficulty: Advanced

Skilled paddlers will enjoy the trip down the Sand River, but be prepared to endure many portages. The put-in is via the ACR train at one of two points: mile 138 at the north end of Sand Lake; or mile 136 1/4, on a bay on the southeast side of the lake. A short carry leads to Sand Lake from either stop.

The Sand River drops over 600 feet from Sand Lake to Lake Superior. The upper sections of the river offer calm water, while the lower reaches are characterized by fast water, boulder gardens, and scenic waterfalls.

AGAWA CANYON TOURS
Algoma Central Railway
129 Bay St.
Sault Ste. Marie 26
Ontario, Canada P6A 1W7
705/254-4331

SCHEDULE

Daily departures from early June through mid-October.
Depart Sault Ste. Marie: 8:00 a.m.
Arrival at Agawa Canyon: 11:30 a.m.
Departure from Agawa Canyon: 1:30 p.m.
Arrive back in Sault Ste. Marie: 5:00 p.m.
*All times are Eastern Daylight Time and subject to change. Call for schedule confirmation.

RESERVATIONS

Tickets are sold based on seat availability. Advance tickets may be ordered and paid for in advance using MasterCard or VISA (705/254-4331). You will receive written confirmation of your reservation by mail. Confirmation of advance booking must be presented at the sales counter to obtain your tickets upon arrival in Sault Ste. Marie, either one day prior to travel or between 7:00 and 7:30 a.m. on the morning of departure.

FARES

At this writing, the adult fare was approximately $40 Canadian, while the fare for children (through high school) was approximately $15 Canadian. Call for confirmation of fares.

ALL ABOARD!

The Algoma Central Railway rolls out of Canadian Sault Ste. Marie, then heads 114 miles through a vast and rugged expanse of forest, mountains, lakes, and streams, taking all passengers on a world-class adventure.

The one-day trip allows visitors to enjoy the harsh wildlands of the Canadian bush from the comfort and safety of an air-conditioned picture window on a passenger train. The trip terminates deep in Agawa Canyon, where a two-hour stopover allows you to explore nature trails and waterfalls.

A dining car offers a full-course breakfast, hot sandwiches, and box lunches, as well as snacks and cold drinks from the time of departure until 3:45 p.m. Travelers on a budget are welcome to pack their own picnic lunch, as snacking on the train is allowed. It's often a long trip for children. Games, coloring books, and drawing pads will help ease their restlessness until they have a chance to burn away some energy at the rest-stop playground.

During the two-hour stopover at Agawa Canyon Park, you can enjoy the picnicking facilities provided along the trout-inhabited waters of the Agawa River. Water pumps and benches are placed throughout the area, and lucky visitors may happen upon waterfowl, beavers, or even a river otter playing in the quiet pools of the Agawa.

Those wishing to stretch their legs will enjoy a hike down the wooden stairs that lead through the cool forest of the canyon floor to a pair of lookouts on the canyon wall. The trip to the intermediate lookout is fairly easy, but those who continue should be sure of their stamina, because the trail continues up a series of 372 wooden steps to the main lookout. Here, you'll stand 250 feet above the picnic grounds.

Nearby, the Edgar H. Foote self-guided nature trail leads hikers on a 20-minute stroll along the canyon floor. The trail has interpretive signs posted to assist you in understanding the beautiful surroundings.

Cascading streams and rivers that tumble down the Agawa Canyon to join the Agawa River provide a pleasant side-trip for canyon visitors. Otter Falls, the smallest of three waterfalls in the preserve, is easily accessible via a fifteen-minute hike down an established trail. Further down the canyon, a second 30-minute roundtrip trail leads to Black Beaver Falls and its two drops, which run year-round. Bridal Veil Falls is the most scenic of all, and was so named because its curtain of cascading water is said to resemble a bridal veil. Because a large volume of water spills over the falls during the spring runoff, early summer is the best time to visit Bridal Veil Falls. Budget forty minutes to make the roundtrip hike to the falls and back.

In autumn, the birch, maple, and elm trees are ablaze in color, and this is a popular time to board the train. Peak colors vary from year to year, but reserving a spot during the first week of October usually ensures that you'll see near-peak colors. It's wise to reserve early for this time of year, as the train fills quickly.

BACKCOUNTRY FLAGSTOPS

Those with the proper skill, equipment, and attitude are welcome to use the Algoma Central Railway as their ticket to adventure.

Since its inception, the Algoma has provided miners, trappers, and loggers living between Sault Ste. Marie and Hearst with a link to civilization. Now, explorers looking for a link with wilderness use the same tracks.

The 300 miles separating Sault Ste. Marie and Hearst encompass 16,000 square miles of wild Canadian backcountry.

115

Remote lakes and streams, teeming with speckled trout, walleye, and northern pike, are untouched by motorboats and battery-operated depth finders.

Nearly every lake along the route means a flagstop for fishermen, hunters, resort owners, and railroad workers. During the moose hunting season, the Algoma has earned the nickname, "The Moose-Meat Special," by collecting successful hunters along its tracks.

Trains operate year-round, but on a restricted schedule in winter. It's best to call for a scheduling update if you're considering off-season travel.

The railway publishes a guide, listing many free-of-charge wilderness camping areas. Self-sufficient travelers need only purchase a ticket to the nearest milepost or station stop indicated on the time schedule and board the train. The conductor will stop the train at the destination of your choice.

Backpacks are free baggage, but canoes travel at current freight rates. On the Algoma, wilderness is but a flagstop away.

SAULT STE. MARIE TO HEARST

Railroad buffs will enjoy traveling the entire length of the Algoma Central Railway, from Sault Ste. Marie to the French Canadian town of Hearst, Ontario. This tour requires an overnight stay in Hearst, and some travelers take extra time to explore the surroundings of this backcountry community. Because schedules and fares change frequently on this run, it's best to contact the Algoma for current rates and schedules.

THE SNOW TRAIN

On winter weekends from January through March, the Algoma Central snow train plows its way through a snow-filled wonderland.

From the comfort of the heated cabins, you'll watch winter in the northland pass by the window. Due to weather extremes, there is no stopover on the snow train. The brief pause at the end of the line only allows you enough time to hook up with a southbound engine for your return trip. Once back at the station in Sault Ste. Marie, many travelers pay a visit to the Whistle Stop Shop, where passengers purchase souvenirs of their railroad trip through Algoma Country.

PANCAKE BAY PROVINCIAL PARK
Ministry of Natural Resources
P.O. Box 130, 875 Queen St. East
Sault Ste. Marie, Ontario P6A 5L5
705/949-1231
705/882-2209 (park office)

Building castles of sand is a favorite pastime of visitors to Pancake Bay Provincial Park. Situated on a two-mile sand beach and sheltered by a pair of protective promontories, Pancake Bay holds a special appeal to visitors seeking respite along the eastern shores of Lake Superior.

Located some 40 miles from Sault Ste. Marie, Pancake Bay was named by hungry voyageurs en route to their homes in Montreal. These hungry travelers were often low on provisions following their long voyage down Lake Superior, and flour was typically the last of their remaining supplies. A pancake dinner often resulted at this location.

The name Pancake Bay has remained, and modern travelers, weary from a long day on the road, enjoy the same white sand beach and glorious northern sunsets that have always marked a resting spot on the shores of Superior.

Plant life in the park is diverse, due to the fact that the bay is located in a transitional zone between the northern boreal forest and the Great Lakes-St. Lawrence lowlands. Pine trees rise from the sand along the shore, while sugar maples and yellow birch dominate the landscape further inland. The park is noted for its seasonal wild berries, including raspberries, strawberries, and blueberries, which make a fine addition to anyone's pancake breakfast.

Pancake Bay offers 338 campsites, including 69 with electrical service (fee charged). Easy access off Highway 17 and large campsites make this a popular park with RV campers who are enjoying the Circle Tour. Despite its size, reservations are recommended during the peak summer season. Some of the campsites are wooded and private, while others are open, offering a pleasant view of Lake Superior and its fiery sunsets. Picnic tables and fire rings are provided. A comfort station with showers is provided for those who can't muster the courage to take a swim in Lake Superior.

The beach at Pancake Bay is the park's main attraction. Since the bay is relatively shallow, the sun's rays often warm the water to swimmable temperatures during late July and August.

The beach at Pancake Bay is a fine place at which to slide in a canoe or sea kayak for a day's outing on Lake Superior. The closest motorboat launch is located at the mouth of the Batchawana River, six miles to the south. All boaters should be wary of Lake Superior's sudden squalls and cold temperatures, and should plan their trips accordingly.

A two-mile nature trail at Pancake Bay explores a cedar swamp and its surrounding wetland. Along the route, the trail passes a huge boulder left behind by retreating glaciers some 10,000 years ago.

VOYAGEUR TRAIL
Voyageur Trail Association
Box 66
Sault Ste. Marie, Ontario P6A 5L2

The Voyageur Trail traverses the most rugged terrain of Ontario, taking hikers through long, isolated ribbons of Lake Superior shoreline, up steep hills, and down remote river valleys.

Thanks to the cooperation of both private landowners and public land managers, the 700-mile trail will eventually stretch from South Baymouth on Manitoulin Island along the north shore of Lake Huron to Gros Cap, west of Sault Ste. Marie, and north around the top of Lake Superior to Thunder Bay. An eastward extension south of Sudbury along the historic Voyageur Canoe Route following the French and Mattawa Rivers is envisioned, as is a westward extension to the Manitoba border.

The Voyageur Trail Association is a citizens' group organized in 1973 to develop and maintain the hiking trail for public use. The VTA produces a valuable guidebook including maps and descriptions of completed sections of trail, mandatory reading for hikers planning an extended trek.

The trail passes through Pukaskwa National Park and Lake Superior Provincial Park in long, unbroken segments. Other sections of the trail may be in poor condition due to fallen trees, logging debris, or vegetation overtaking the trail. Completed routes include the Saulteaux, Echo Ridges, Desbarats, Michipicoten, Casque Island, and Penewobikong sections. These sections are marked by white paint blazes on trees, rocks, and poles. A single blaze indicates the trail continues in the same direction; two blazes placed one above the other indicate a change of direction. Side trails are blazed in blue. The trail is also identified by diamond-shaped symbols posted at quarter-mile intervals. Green-and-white access signs are posted in appropriate locations. Within Lake Superior Provincial Park and Pukaskwa National Park, the trail is marked in accordance with park guidelines.

Camping is limited to designated sites. At Lake Superior Provincial Park and Pukaskawa National Park, interior permits are required of overnight travelers.

The Voyageur Hiking Trail is open to hikers, skiers, and snowshoers. Motorized vehicles of any kind are outlawed. Because the trail passes through remote territory, travelers must be completely self-reliant. An adequate first-aid kit and quality rain gear is mandatory. Flies are often a nuisance on the trail in May, June, and July, but are less of a problem along lakeshore sections when a wind is present.

Those with the necessary skill and proper attitude for tackling the Voyageur Trail will encounter the best that Ontario has to offer, from the sandy beaches of Superior to the shady swamps of the interior. The trail is both rugged and rewarding, offering a peaceful retreat and a challenging respite from the modern world.

COMPLETED SECTIONS OF THE VOYAGEUR TRAIL

1) Casque Isles section: A 15-mile section from Rossport to Terrace Bay. The trail was cleared and marked in 1991.
2) Pukaskwa National Park section: A 42-mile section. The park does not use white Voyageur Trail markers.
3) Michipicoten section: Begins near Wawa. A 12-mile section, cleared and marked. The trail was extended into Lake Superior Provincial Park in 1989, and now reaches Naomi Bay.
4) Lake Superior Provincial Park section: A 21-mile section of the Coastal Trail. Complete from Katherine Cove to Chalfont Cove. Striking in beauty, but very rugged. Overnight visitors must register (fee charged) with the park (705/856-2284).
5) Saulteaux section: A 42-mile, east-west section from Gros Cap, west of Sault Ste. Marie on Lake Superior, to a spot east of Kinsmen Park near Mable Lake, at the eastern edge of the Sault Ste. Marie city limits. The trail is generally in good condition, but crossing the Root River east of Old Goulais Bay Road can be a problem at high water. During low water, wading is possible.
6) Echo Ridges section: A 42-mile section, north of Echo Bay from Mabel Lake to Tower Lake. Completely cleared and marked except for a short, blue-flagged section.
7) Desbarats section: An 18-mile section, complete from Tower Lake to Rydal Bank. Cleared and marked.
8) Thessalon section: Cleared and marked from Rydal Bank to Melwel Lodge Road, extending about 45-miles. Parts are overgrown, and it's sometimes difficult to find trail markers on the rocky outcrops.
9) Iron Bridge section: Cleared and marked from Melwel Lodge Road to Iron Bridge. Distance included in the Thessalon section.
10) Penewobikong section: North of Blind River, 24 miles complete. The section begins in Iron Bridge and ends near Intersect Lake. Good condition.
11) Rainbow section: Located near Rainbow Falls on Manitoulin Island. A 12-mile loop, cleared and marked many years ago. Not recommended until recleared and marked.

VOYAGEUR TRAIL

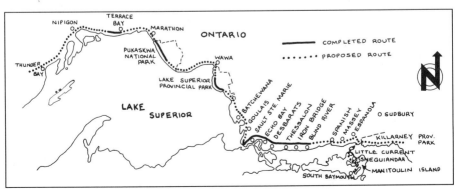

THE SOO

Where Superior Ends Its Reign

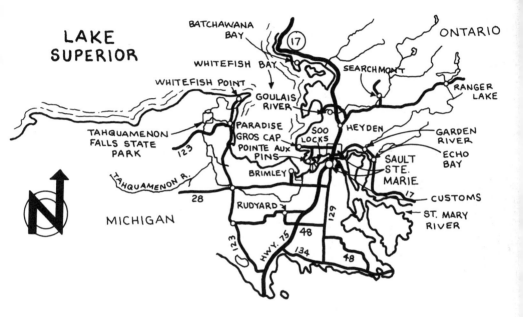

Through the Windshield

Just west of Canadian Sault Ste. Marie, Lake Superior surrenders its territorial reign to the St. Mary's River. The gradual transition from lake to river takes places along a massive, 650-foot-high outcropping known as Gros Cap. Translated from the French as "Big Cape," this massive point is accessible by foot trail at the end of the 16-mile Highway 550. Somehow it seems fitting that the queen of the Great Lakes should make her southeastern departure amidst such regal surroundings.

In generations past, Objibwa Indians staged an annual spring rendezvous downstream from Gros Cap, where the waters of Lake Superior join the other Great Lakes along the bountiful whitefish waters of a place they called "Bawating." Today, we know this place as Sault Ste. Marie, two cities divided by both the rapids of the St. Mary's River and an international boundary.

In 1668 Jesuit missionaries Louis Nicolas and Jacques Marquette established a mission at "Bawating," renaming it Sault de Sainte Marie. In 1783 the city of Sault Ste. Marie was divided by a treaty making the St. Mary's River the international boundary between Canada and the newly formed United States. During that period, the North West Fur Trading Company had founded a post at the site, and by the late 1790s a canal was begun that would bypass the tumultuous rapids of St. Mary's River.

The 38-foot lock was used to raise and lower large freighter canoes making the passage from Lake Superior to Lake Huron, eliminating the necessity of an overland carry past the St. Mary's rapids.

As the Lake Superior region developed, the Soo Locks, as they became known, expanded both in size and number. In 1895 completion of the Canadian Canal and Lock attracted the interest of Maine entrepreneur Francis Hector Clergue. Clergue planned to harness the hydroelectric power of the St. Mary's rapids by founding the Great Lakes Power Company. Unfortunately, his plans were bigger than his budget. The Maine businessman went bankrupt, but not before he had founded the successful Algoma Steel Corporation. Algoma Steel required dependable access to the iron ore mines of the untamed hinterland and, in 1901, the Algoma Central Railway began construction. Its rails pierced the rugged hills to link the iron mines of Michipicoten with Algoma Steel. Today the Algoma Central Railway is well-known for its Agawa Canyon tours (listed separately).

With a population of over 80,000, Canadian Sault Ste. Marie remains the larger of the two cities separated along the banks of the St. Mary's River. From April through December, visitors to the Canadian Sault waterfront can enjoy watching as Great Lakes freighters and ocean-going vessels gently ease into the locks, to rise or descend 21 feet before departing into a new waterway.

Constructed in 1895, the Canadian Lock lies within the over one-mile length of the Canadian Canal, located on the north side of the St. Mary's River. At 900 feet, the Canadian Lock is relatively short compared to its American counterparts, and therefore handles ships smaller than the massive iron ore freighters that make their way though American locks. Damage to the lock in 1987 has slowed traffic through the Canadian Lock, but you're welcome to walk along the structure and climb the observation platform, since it's surrounded by park land.

Those who would like to "lock through" the famous Soo Locks with sea-going vessels can do so by taking a two-hour cruise offered by Lock Tours Canada (705/253-9850). From mid-May through mid-October, tour ships depart daily from Norgoma Dock, located next to the Holiday Inn and just a five-minute walk from the Algoma Central Railway.

Norgoma Dock is named in honor of the *M.S. Norgoma*, the last passenger cruise ship built for cruising the Great Lakes. Berthed downtown near the civic center, the *Norgoma* was converted to a museum in 1982, and now offers a nostalgic look at the days of steamship travel. It's open to visitors from early June through mid-October.

Before crossing the border into the United States, you may enjoy a ride aboard the authentic, English-style double-decker tour buses that cruise through the sights of Canadian Sault Ste. Marie. The bus station is located on Foster Drive, next to the Holiday Inn. The moonlight bridge tour is a fitting way of ending your stay in the Canadian Sault.

BORDER CROSSING

Before the two-mile International Bridge opened in 1962, ferries provided the only transportation for passengers and automobiles crossing the St. Mary's River. Today the joint International Bridge Authority witnesses over three million vehicles make the crossing each year.

When traffic is light, crossing the bridge separating Canadian Saulte Ste. Marie from U.S. Sault Ste. Marie takes only about 15 minutes. During rush hours or holiday weekends, however, allow extra time.

Crossing the border is usually simple and painless, but there are restrictions regarding what you can take with you. United States citizens do not need passports or visas to enter Canada as visitors, but it's wise to carry identification such as a birth certificate or a voter's registration card. If in doubt concerning what you can take across the border, pay a visit to the information booth located at the foot of the bridge or call the nearest customs office.

In 1620, French explorer Etienne Brule became the first European to visit the rapids of the St. Mary's River, then a traditional Objibwa fishing and meeting place. Missionaries Gauche Marquette and Clause Dablon followed in 1668, christening the city in honor of the Virgin Mary.

With a population of less than 15,000, today's Sault Ste. Marie, Michigan, is dwarfed in size but not in notoriety by its Canadian neighbor. Each year thousands of travelers visit the famous Soo Locks of Sault Ste. Marie, making the city one of Michigan's most popular tourist destinations.

Navigational locks at the Sault are used to raise and lower vessels 21 feet between Lake Superior and Lake Huron. Each year more than 95 million tons of cargo pass through the locks, making the Soo Locks the busiest in the world.

Of the four navigational locks on the American side of the international border, the Poe Lock is the largest, measuring 1200 feet in length and 110 feet in width. Named after Colonel Orlando M. Poe, an engineer officer during the Civil War, the huge Poe Lock is the only one in the St. Lawrence Seaway capable of handling 1,000-foot-long super freighters.

Other locks within the American system include MacArthur Lock, Davis Lock, and Sabin Lock. Three observation platforms and the U.S. Corps of Engineer Information Center have been erected on the parkland that parallels the locks, allowing visitors to get a firsthand look at the operations. From the information center at Upper Locks

Park, a pleasant one-mile walk along the city's Historic Pathway leads along the waterfront through Brady Park and the Lower Locks Park. The interpretive path details the history of the St. Mary's River and passes many historic buildings en route to the *SS Valley Camp*, a 550-foot floating museum ship. The *SS Valley Camp* is a retired Great Lakes freighter, and a tour offers a taste of life aboard a cargo vessel. It's open daily from May 15 to October 15.

If you'd like to experience the Soo Locks personally, you can do so by taking a Soo Locks Boat Tour. The narrated, two-hour tour departs the docks at 500 and 1155 E. Portage Avenue daily from mid-May to October (906/632-2512).

You can also leave your car behind and board the Soo Locks Tour Train for a narrated, guided tour of Sault Ste. Marie followed by a trip across the International Bridge. Tours depart daily from Memorial Day through mid-October.

Departing Sault Ste. Marie on Interstate 75 south, the Lake Superior Circle Tour heads west at Michigan Highway 28 en route to Brimley, a fine state park along the shores of Gitchi Gummi once again.

BRIMLEY STATE PARK
Route 2, Box 202
Brimley, Michigan 49715
906/248-3422

Waves lap at the 2400-foot sand beach of Brimley State Park, slowly eroding the sandcastles built by visitors to this shoreline retreat.

Situated along the shore of Lake Superior's shallow and relatively warm Whitefish Bay, Brimley State Park often tempts swimmers into a mid-summer dip. Across the bay, huge ocean-going vessels can be seen en route to the locks at Sault Ste. Marie. Brimley serves as home base to many campers exploring the area's attractions and, despite its size, campsites can be at a premium during summer weekends, especially in July and August.

Brimley's modern campground offers 271 sites, but plan to arrive mid-week or off-season if you want to secure a site adjacent to the lakeshore. The park is frequently full on summer weekends, so it's best to plan ahead. Telephone or mail reservations are accepted.

When seas are calm, the protected waters of Whitefish Bay can be very productive if you're fishing for northern pike, walleye, or perch. The park offers a small boat launch, but offshore sandbars can prove a hazard to navigation.

PICTURED ROCKS
Sand Dunes and Inland Seashores

Through the Windshield

Michigan's wild Upper Peninsula is "paradise found" for those seeking outdoor adventure. Because it offers 1700 miles of shoreline on three of the Great Lakes, coastal travelers will never be far from the sand and surf of the inland seas. Paddlers could spend a lifetime exploring the U.P.'s 4300 inland lakes, and fishermen will find native trout hiding in many of the U.P.'s 12,000 miles of clear, fast-running streams.

Separated from lower Michigan by the Straits of Mackinac, the 384-mile-long Upper Peninsula was joined to its downstate brother in 1835, by a deal struck in the halls of Congress. The Michigan Territory was granted admission to the union in exchange for relinquishing to Ohio the rich Toledo strip and accepting the "barren waste of the Upper Peninsula." This wasteland would prove its worth when copper, iron, gold, and silver were discovered in the rocky hills and white pine forests of the U.P.

Today, many U.P. residents feel isolated from downstate government, and the isolation surfaces in occasional, halfhearted threats of forming the 51st state of Superior. Joined to their big brother by the Mackinac Bridge, residents jokingly refer to themselves as "Yoopers," proclaiming their pride on the back of pickup trucks and four-wheel drive vehicles.

The abundance of public land in the Upper Peninsula means travelers are always near an open campsite or a peaceful hiking trail. En route to your next destination, the cliffs and sand dunes of Picture Rocks National Lakeshore, you'll explore the magic of Michigan's wild and scenic Upper Peninsula.

The scenic Lake Shore Drive hugs the Lake Superior coast, entering the Hiawatha National Forest (listed separately) near Point Iroquois. Named in memory of Iroquois warriors massacred by rival Ojibwa Indians in 1662, Point Iroquois is home to a light station that towers over the waters of Lake Superior at the entry to the St. Mary's River. For 107 years, the lighthouse served passing ships by marking the narrow channel between Point Iroquois and the rocky reefs of Gros Cap on the Canadian side of Whitefish Bay.

In 1975, the Point Iroquois Lighthouse was placed on the National Register of Historic Places. Efforts are now underway to restore the lighthouse as an information center and museum. Visitors are welcome to climb a spiral staircase up to the top of the 65-foot light tower for a birds-eye view of ocean-going freighters en route to the Soo Locks.

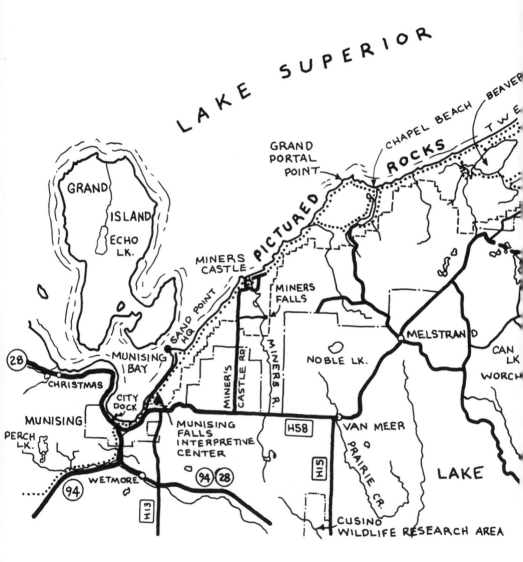

LAKESHORE TRAIL
NATIONAL LAKESHORE
INLAND BUFFER ZONE

N

LAKE SUPERIOR

PICTUAED ROCKS

CHAPEL BEACH

BEAVER

TWE

GRAND PORTAL POINT

GRAND ISLAND

ECHO LK.

MINERS CASTLE

MINERS FALLS

SAND HQ POINT

MELSTRAND

CAN LK

WORCH

NOBLE LK.

28

CHRISTMAS

MUNISING BAY

MINER'S CASTLE RD.

MINERS R.

VAN MEER

CITY DOCK

MUNISING

PERCH LK.

MUNISING FALLS INTERPRETIVE CENTER

H58

PRAIRIE CR.

LAKE

94

WETMORE

94 28

H15

H13

CUSINO WILDLIFE RESEARCH AREA

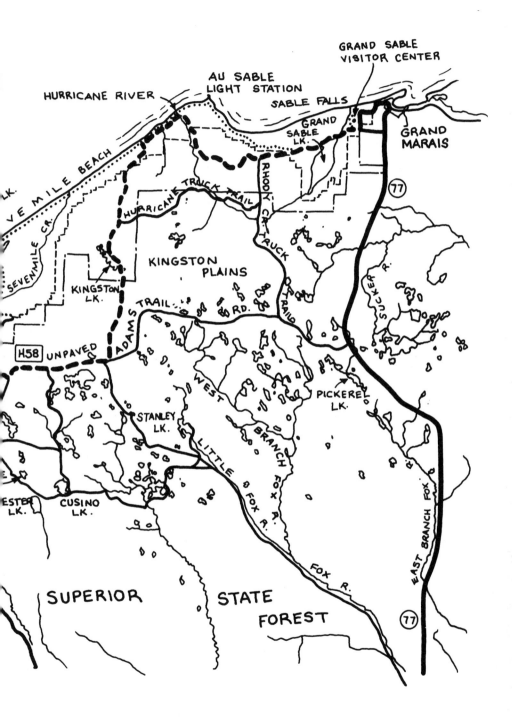

Just south of Iroquois Point off Forest Road 3699, Monocle Lake Campground offers 39 campsites (fee charged) along the hardwood-studded shores of the 172-acre lake. Families will enjoy catching rays on Monocle's sand beach, and fishermen will find the lake stocked with walleye.

Continuing on Lake Shore Drive, you'll pass a Forest Service picnic ground at Big Pine before reaching the 24-unit Bay View Campground, situated along the shores of Lake Superior. Pendills Creek Fish Hatchery is just west of the campground and is open to public tours.

En route to Tahquamenon Falls State Park, a scenic overlook atop Mission Road provides photo opportunities before you reach a sand beach on Whitefish Bay that's protected by Nodaway Point.

Just up the road, scuba divers often make the small community of Paradise their expedition base for exploration of the Whitefish Point Underwater Preserve. A national historic site and home to Lake Superior's first lighthouse, Whitefish Point is known as "The Graveyard of the Great Lakes." Off this point in 1975, a ferocious November storm sank the *Edmund Fitzgerald*, claiming the lives of all aboard. The incident was later remembered in a mournful ballad by Canadian folk singer Gordon Lightfoot.

The water clarity off Whitefish Point averages 50 feet, allowing for fine diving opportunities. Many shipwrecked steam freighters, wood schooners, and side wheelers lie in depths ranging from 20 to 100 feet, providing relatively easy access for those equipped to handle Lake Superior's icy depths.

Located 11 miles north of Paradise on M-123, the Great Lakes Shipwreck Historical Museum (free admission) pays tribute to the sailors and ships lost on the Great Lakes. The museum features a video presentation that offers a glimpse of Lake Superior's violent temper. Open daily from Memorial Day through mid-October, the museum also displays artifacts recovered from 11 ships that went down off the treacherous waters of Whitefish Point.

Modern campsites await travelers at the mouth of the Tahquamenon (pronounced Ta-KWAH-meh-non) River on the Lake Superior shore. The Tahquamenon River unit is one of two drive-in campgrounds situated within the massive, 35,733-acre Tahquamenon Falls State Park (listed separately). The impressive falls of the Tahquamenon River are located off Highway 123 west of Paradise, where camping is available within the park's 183-unit modern campground.

Tahquamenon is the largest waterfall in Michigan, and it's one of the Upper Peninsula's most popular attractions. Each year nearly 500,000 visitors take delight in Tahquamenon's golden curtain of water, which plunges over a 48-foot-high, 200-foot-wide sandstone cliff before dropping into a dark, bubbling pool. Natural tannic acid picked up by the river as it flows through tamarack swamps accounts for the water's amber shade. Just downstream from the falls, an island separates the river into a braided series of rapids and small drops known as the Lower Falls. Because Tahquamenon Falls is easy to access, it's a pleasant stop for travelers on a tight schedule.

If you'd like to take a more unusual approach to Tahquamenon Falls, consider a combination train ride and riverboat cruise aboard one of the two operations that cater to Circle Tour travelers. At Soo Junction, off M-28 east of Newberry, the Toonerville Trolley makes daily, half-day trips via a narrow gauge railroad to the Tahquamenon River, before joining a riverboat for the remainder of the journey to the falls. Just a few miles further northeast near Hulbert, Tom Sawyer Riverboats depart Slater's Landing for daily trips on the Tahquamenon River. Riverboat passengers board the Paul Bunyan Timber Train for the return journey.

The logging town of Newberry, 43 miles south of Tahquamenon Falls State Park, offers restaurants, lodging, and refueling opportunities. Sixteen Creek, a small, secluded 12-unit campground, is located within the Lake Superior State Forest (906/293-5131) and is on the Tahquamenon River, six miles northwest of Newberry via M-123 and Charcoal Grade.

The official Circle Tour continues west from Newberry on M-28 to McMillan and Seney, but travelers with time and a sense of adventure will enjoy the rugged roads accessible off County Highway 37, which penetrates Two Hearted River country. Ernest Hemingway immortalized the Two Hearted River in his writings, and it holds the same appeal for today's adventurers. Noted for its excellent trout fishing, the Two Hearted River spills into Lake Superior east of Deer Park at the end of County 37, where a 45-unit state forest campground (906/293-5131) is located. Rustic state forest campgrounds are located throughout the area, making it a mecca for fishermen. Note that many of the roads accessible from County 37 are not paved. Some routes may require high-clearance vehicles to assure safe passage. Mountain bikes provide an excellent alternative.

West of Deer Park, unpaved Highway 58 leads to Muskallonge State Park (listed separately) before continuing to Grand Marais. Agate hunting is popular along the shores of the park, which is situated between Muskallonge Lake and Lake Superior. The park offers 179 campsites within 217 acres.

Situated at the crossroads of highways M-77 and H-58 on a natural harbor, Grand Marais was christened by French explorers. Translated, its name means "shelter by."

Its strategic coastal location has always influenced the community's history, and in 1899 a lifesaving station was established to lend assistance to ships in distress on Lake Superior. The station has been closed since 1981, but plans are underway to restore the former Coast Guard headquarters and revive this slice of Lake Superior maritime history.

Today, Grand Marais bustles during the summer months, serving as the eastern gateway for Pictured Rocks National Lakeshore. During winter, snowmobilers and nordic skiers relish the community's 250-inch annual snowfall.

Campers looking for a place to pitch a tent are welcome to do so at Woodland Township Campgrounds (fee charged), and fishermen will enjoy dangling a line off the village pier.

Just west of Grand Marais, the massive sand dunes of Pictured Rocks National Lakeshore (listed separately) stretch to the shores of Lake Superior.

Pictured Rocks National Lakeshore is stunning. Along the western boundary of the 42-mile-long national park, sandstone cliffs carved by nature into castles and caves tower above the blue-green waters of Lake Superior. Along the eastern edge, giant sand dunes reach for the sky before giving way to the breaking waves of Superior. Sandwiched between, springs, rivers and streams crawl through the upland forest and dance over rock ledges en route to an outlet on the inland sea.

The Grand Sable visitor center (906-474-2660), near Sable Lake at the east end of H-58, should be the first stop for summer visitors exploring the eastern section of Pictured Rocks National Lakeshore. The center is closed in winter, but during the other seasons rangers offer advice on camping, driving, and exploring the lakeshore. County road H-58 provides access to the park through its entire length, but motorists planning to embark on the route should prepare themselves for a bone-rattling ride down an unpaved washboard road. H-58 is mostly gravel from the Grand Sable visitor center to the Little Beaver Campground, where pavement begins.

To avoid the gravel of H-58 en route to Pictured Rocks National Park headquarters at Munising, take highway 77 south of Grand Marais to M-28. Head west to Munising, passing through Seney.

Located 25 miles south of Grand Marais, the village of Seney is home to the 96,000-acre Seney National Wildlife Refuge (listed separately). The Seney preserve is the largest wildlife refuge east of the Mississippi River, providing undisturbed habitat to waterfowl and wildlife within the confines of the Great Manistique Swamp. A visitor center is located off highway 77, and rangers can direct you to outfitters that offer canoe trips through the refuge, or to a scenic drive within refuge boundaries.

Rolling toward the western entrance of Pictured Rocks National Lakeshore, you'll pass through Shingleton. Here you're welcome to take a weekday tour of the Iverson Snowshoe Factory before reaching Munising.

Munising's natural harbor is well-protected by the sandstone cliffs and sand beaches of historic Grand Island (listed separately). Grand Island was purchased by the federal government in 1990, and is now open to the public under management of the U.S. Forest Service. Passenger ferries provide daily roundtrip transportation to the island from June through October. Mountain bikes are welcome aboard the ferry (fee charged), and they provide ideal transportation once you reach the island. Self-reliant visitors are welcome to pitch a tent on Grand Island, but be advised there are currently no facilities. Sea kayakers were among the most ardent supporters of public ownership of Grand Island, and kayaks remain the best self-propelled means of reaching this preserve.

The Alger Underwater Preserve surrounds Grand Island, overlapping the adjacent Pictured Rocks National Lakeshore. The preserve was established to protect the many shipwrecks scattered across the harbor's floor. These wrecks are open to exploration by divers equipped to handle the cold waters of Lake Superior, but removing artifacts is strictly prohibited.

Against the backdrop of picturesque, 70-foot Munising Falls, you'll find the headquarters of 67,000-acre Pictured Rocks National Lakeshore. The visitor center here is open year-round, and rangers are happy to help you plan your day trip or arrange the necessary permits for a backcountry adventure.

The best means of viewing the awesome Pictured Rocks is by boat. From June through the colors of October, Pictured Rocks Boat Cruises (906-387-2379) regularly depart the Munising docks, offering two- to three-hour narrated tours of the inspiring cliffs. The pigment of the colorful cliffs is the result of water seeping through minerals locked within the 200-foot towers. These minerals stain the rock, and light dancing off the cliffs brings out the various hues.

TAHQUAMENON FALLS STATE PARK
P.O. Box 225
Star Rt. 48
Paradise, MI 49768
906/492-3415

Beloved Tahquamenon Falls is the golden centerpiece of upper Michigan's most popular state park. Each year, nearly half a million visitors watch as the Tahquamenon River drops its 200-foot-wide veil of gold over a fifty-foot sandstone cliff and into a foreboding pool of darkness below at Upper Falls. Four miles downstream, the Tahquamenon dances past an island, which braids the cascading river into two channels heading for a Lake Superior outlet 12 miles downstream.

The spring water of the Tahquamenon River originates near McMillan. It makes the final 16-mile leg of its 94-mile journey through the state park bearing its name. Prior to finding an outlet at Whitefish Bay on Lake Superior, the clean water flows through tamarack swamps, taking on an amber gold hue from the naturally occurring tannic acid that leaches from the swamps.

In "The Song of the Hiawatha," Longfellow's epic poem, the poet paid tribute to the mighty Tahquamenon and the self-reliant Ojibwa who once inhabited the river's shores. Along the "marsh of blueberries," according to Longfellow, Hiawatha built a canoe on the banks of the "rushing Tahquamenaw."

Tahquamenon Falls State Park is massive, both in terms of size and character. You'll find plenty of room to roam within the 35,733 acres under state park protection, and the park's backcountry is laced with 25 miles of hiking trails that meander past a dozen lakes and ponds.

Campers can choose from 319 sites, ranging from modern to rustic, within four campgrounds that are separated into two units.

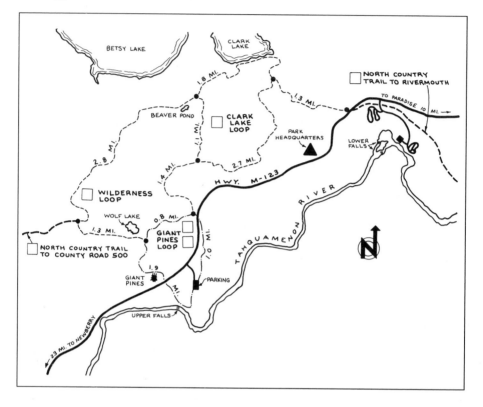

Fishing is popular along the Tahquamenon River, and anglers can often be found below the Lower Falls, casting spoons for northern pike, walleye, and muskies. In early spring and late October, steelhead (rainbow trout) make their way up the Tahquamenon from Lake Superior, and surfcasting opportunities await anglers at Whitefish Bay. Motorboats are outlawed on Betsy, Sheephead, and Clark lakes in the park's interior, but canoe access is allowed. The park maintains a boat launch at the Rivermouth Unit at Whitefish Bay, and a concessionaire rents motorboats and canoes at the Lower Falls.

The Upper and Lower Falls of the Tahquamenon River remain the park's chief attraction. The well-trodden access to these falls invites exploration by both young and old, as all discover the power and magic of the rushing Tahquamenon.

EXPLORING THE FALLS

The Upper Falls is a day use area accessible from a paved parking lot 21 miles east of Newberry on Highway 123. To allow wheelchair access, the pavement continues through a wooded grove to an overview of the cascades, where the sound of the flowing water is amplified by the surrounding forest. From the overview, the trail divides. The right fork leads to a staircase near the crest of the falls, and the left fork leads to a staircase that penetrates the river gorge.

The Lower Falls is located four miles downstream from the Upper Falls, and it's also accessible off Highway 123. Here the Tahquamenon wraps itself around an island in a series of shallow cascades. Although it lacks the awesome power of the Upper Falls, the Lower Falls is a pleasant attraction worthy of a visit. Access to the Lower Falls from the parking area is via the 1/2-mile Mainland Trail. Wide and well-traveled, the Mainland Trail leads to an observation platform before proceeding along the river to a group of picnic tables. The best view of the Lower Falls, though, is offered from the island. A park concessionaire rents both canoes and rowboats to make the brief river crossing, where a dock and short hiking trail await your arrival.

CAMPING

Tahquamenon Falls State Park offers four campgrounds within two separate units. At the Lower Falls, there are 183 modern campsites, complete with showers. These sites are divided between the Riverbend Campground and the Overlook Campground. Competition for the few sites located along the river is fierce, so consider yourself lucky if you secure one.

The second area offering campsites is the Rivermouth Unit, located near the shores of Whitefish Bay on Lake Superior. The modern campground offers 76 sites, while the less popular rustic campground offers 60 sites.

Although many campers take a chance on finding an open campsite, reservations are suggested if you require a site in the three modern campgrounds. Campsites are generally available in the rustic campground.

HIKING TRAILS

THE NORTH COUNTRY TRAIL

A 12-mile section of the planned 3,000-mile North Country Trail passes through Tahquamenon Falls State Park. The North Country Trail was dedicated in 1980 by the National Park Service. It is envisioned as a link between the Appalachian Trail in New York and the Lewis and Clark Trail in North Dakota. Michigan's Upper Peninsula will play an important role in this connection, and links to the North Country trail are already found in the Hiawatha National Forest and Mukallonge Lake State Park.

GIANT PINES LOOP

Aptly named, the 3.7-mile Giant Pines Loop Trail begins at the Upper Falls parking area, where it passes through a stand of massive pine trees. After skirting the falls, the trail crosses Highway 123 twice before returning to the Upper Falls parking lot.

WILDERNESS LOOP

The 7.4-mile Wilderness Loop begins north of M-123, where the Giant Pines Trail crosses the road east of the Upper Falls. The trail traverses the wilderness north of M-123.

CLARK LAKE LOOP

The trailhead to the 5.6-mile Clark Lake Loop is located at the end of a rough dirt road off M-123 west of the Lower Falls parking lot. Paddlers driving high-clearance vehicles use the Clark Lake access road to reach the put-in for Clark Lake, but it may be wise to hike the 1.3-mile track to the trailhead if you don't have a truck. The trail skirts the southern border of Clark Lake before looping through the wilderness north of M-123.

MUSKALLONGE LAKE STATE PARK
P.O. Box 245, Rt 1
Newberry, MI 49868
906/658-3338

Adventurous travelers who make the trek down the rough road to Muskallonge Lake State Park reap the rewards of a warm-water inland lake just a stone's throw away from Lake Superior.

Only a narrow, quarter-mile isthmus of land separates Muskallonge Lake from the agate-strewn shores of Lake Superior, but it can mean the difference between night and day for swimmers on those rare, hot days of summer.

Muskallonge Lake State Park was once the site of the village of Deer Park, a bustling lumber town of the 1800s. Dock pilings on Lake Superior and a large sawdust pile near Muskallonge Lake are all that remains of this chapter in the area's history.

The park offers 179 campsites in its modern campground along the shores of Muskallonge Lake. Mid-July through mid-August is the park's busy season, and making a reservation may help you avoid disappointment.

If the "no vacancy" sign is up, the park staff can help you find a campsite in one of the area's many rustic state forest campgrounds.

Muskallonge is noted for its northern pike fishing, and the park maintains an improved boat launch for those wishing to try their luck. There are no boat launching facilities on Lake Superior, but sea kayaks can be put in from the sand and pebble beach.

PICTURED ROCKS NATIONAL LAKESHORE
P.O. Box 40
Munising, MI 49862
906/387-4697
906/387-3700 (winter)

Colorful sandstone cliffs, known as "Pictured Rocks," meet the emerald waters of Lake Superior just outside of Munising, Michigan, in a setting as grand as any in mid-America. Sculpted by waves and wind into towers, arches, and caves, the sandstone escarpment reaches heights of up to 200 feet before giving way to a spectacular stretch of sand known as Twelve Mile Beach. Twelve Mile Beach, in turn, surrenders to mountains of sand at the Grand Sable Dunes, just outside the village of Grand Marais.

Pictured Rocks National Lakeshore protects this spectacular 42-mile stretch of coast, where the forces of Lake Superior battle the rugged shore of the inland sea. Forests of red, white, and jack pine mingle with aspen and birch, blanketing much of the park. White cedar, tamarack, and black spruce surround interior wetlands, while ferns and orchids find a home in the deep, dark interior woods. Wildflowers begin making their appearance in mid-May, and lichens, mosses, and mushrooms are found throughout the snow-free months.

In 1966 Congress took note of the striking topography of the region, and Pictured Rocks became America's first national lakeshore. Today the National Park Service protects and manages 33,550 acres bordering Lake Superior's shore, including vital inland watersheds such as the Beaver Basin. Adjacent to the lakeshore, an inland buffer zone encompasses an additional 37,850 acres. This buffer zone was established to stabilize and protect the Lake Superior shore and its nearby watersheds.

The national lakeshore area offers a wide variety of recreational possibilities, as well as the aesthetic pleasure of viewing the dunes and the Pictured Rocks. The opportunities range from long hikes down the coast to breaking trail on a backcountry winter ski trip. Backpackers will enjoy hitting the trail for an unforgettable hike along Grand Portal Point and pitching their tents in the spiritual confines of the Chapel Basin. Fishermen will have fun plying the park's inland lakes, hoping to net a trophy catch. Divers can explore the clear waters of the Alger Underwater Preserve, investigating the shipwrecks of days gone by, while those with less ambition enjoy easy access to numerous waterfalls and the inland escarpment that forms the lakeshore's rugged backbone.

Nature continues to mold the striking topography that characterizes Pictured Rocks National Lakeshore. When the last glacier retreated from the region 10,000 years ago, it left an exposed escarpment along the lakeshore. Slowly, as the level of Lake Superior dropped some forty feet, the shoreline expanded, leaving in its wake Miners Basin, Beaver Basin, and Chapel Lake—all rimmed by the inland escarpment

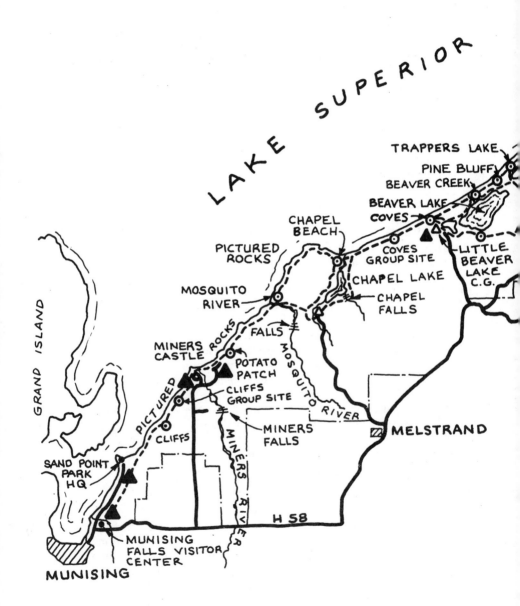

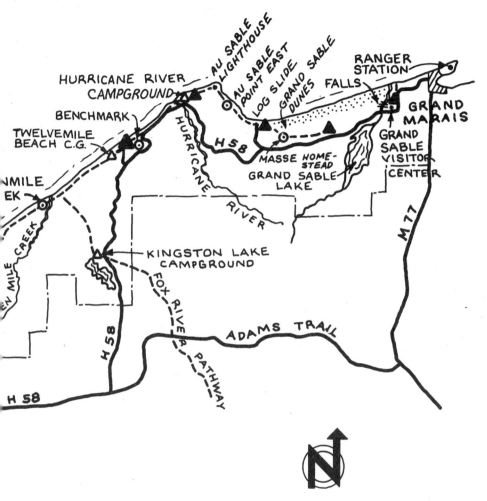

AU SABLE LIGHTHOUSE

AU SABLE POINT EAST

LOG SLIDE

GRAND SABLE DUNES

FALLS

RANGER STATION

HURRICANE RIVER CAMPGROUND

BENCHMARK

TWELVEMILE BEACH C.G.

HURRICANE RIVER

H 58

MASSE HOME-STEAD

GRAND SABLE LAKE

GRAND MARAIS

GRAND SABLE VISITOR CENTER

M 77

NMILE EK

EN MILE CREEK

KINGSTON LAKE CAMPGROUND

FOX RIVER PATHWAY

H 58

ADAMS TRAIL

H 58

N

ROADWAYS

--- HIKING TRAILS

.._._ LAKESHORE BOUNDARIES

△ DRIVE-IN CAMPGROUNDS

▲ TRAIL HEADS

⊙ BACKCOUNTRY CAMPGROUNDS

139

that once was battered by the pounding waves of Lake Superior. On the western boundary of the park, the exposed escarpment has been shaped by wind, frost, and waves into a fascinating array of towers, caves, arches, and cliffs. Collectively, we call these the Pictured Rocks, but individually each stack, arch, and cave maintains its unique character. Over the years, individual formations have been given names that reflect their grandeur, including Castle Rock, Grand Portal Point, Chapel Rock, and Battleship Row.

The best means of viewing the cliffs is from the water. Seated comfortably aboard a cruise ship or nestled within the cockpit of a sea kayak, you'll feel the magic of the escarpment and the power of the inland sea that surrounds it. From June 1 through October colors, tour boats depart several times daily from the docks of Munising. Late afternoon is the best time to capture the cliffs on film, since light dancing off the rocks will highlight the minerals that color the cliffs.

Most of the park's 300,000 annual visitors arrive during the short summer season, when July and August temperatures reach into the mid 70s. Even in the warm months, the chilling effect of Lake Superior remains an influence, so if you're boarding a cruise vessel to view the rocks from the lake, be sure to throw a sweater in your pack.

Winter blankets the lakeshore with abundant snowfall for nearly five months of the year. Snowmobilers, cross-country skiers, and winter campers typically find adequate snow from mid-December through March, and those venturing into the backcountry will discover a peaceful winter paradise.

Autumn colors begin in mid-September and peak within the next two weeks. This is a great time to hoist a pack, since you'll avoid the annoying black flies and mosquitoes that are present from May through July.

The park is headquartered in the city of Munising, and most visitors begin their exploration of the lakeshore from this gateway. A visitor center located at Munising Falls can be reached by following the signs from County Road H-58 in downtown Munising.

At the eastern end of the park, the village of Grand Marais is situated just outside of Grand Sable Dunes. County Road H-58 connects these communities, providing access to the entire length of the park. Beyond the Little Beaver Campground, however, H-58 turns into an unpaved washboard until you reach the visitor center at Grand Sable Dunes.

The cliffs we enjoy today held special meaning for the Ojibwa Indians, who fished the waters and hunted the forests of the region prior to the arrival of Europeans. The Ojibwa were year-round inhabitants of nearby Grand Island (listed separately), a national recreation area located just off the shores of Pictured Rocks National Lakeshore. French explorers reported that these first residents left offerings of tobacco along the cliffs of Pictured Rocks, to appease the spirits that control the unpredictable temperament of Lake Superior.

The arrival of the Europeans marked the beginning of the end for the lifestyle enjoyed by the Ojibwa. In 1836, a treaty with the natives ceded the region to the U.S. government, and the following year the Michigan Territory—including the Upper Peninsula—joined the Union.

Timber followed the fur trade as the area's chief economic draw. In 1867, hardwood from the forests of Pictured Rocks furnished charcoal for an iron furnace at Munising, and loggers soon brought their axes to bear on the white pine forests that covered the Kingston Plains south of what is now the park. Remnants of the park's timber era include a "log slide" once used to bring timber from the cliffs and dunes rimming the escarpment forest. The log slide allowed timber stacked along the escarpment to glide into Lake Superior, where waiting ships transported it to sawmills.

While lumberjacks toiled in the forest, commercial fishermen plied Lake Superior. When the forests were exhausted and the timber barons pulled up their stakes, some lumberjacks looked to the lake to provide a living. Fishing for lake trout and whitefish became an important part of the economy of Grand Marais, but fishing was soon eclipsed by tourism.

Since the first explorers spotted Pictured Rocks, visitors have been captivated by this land of rock, sea, and sand. A railroad spur that entered the region in 1882 opened the lakeshore to tourists, who relied on fishing boats to take them past the marvelous shoreside cliffs.

By the turn of the century, summer homes and fishing camps began to dot the inland lakes and the sandy Superior shores, but when Pictured Rocks National Lakeshore was established, these private holdings slowly disappeared from the landscape.

Today both timber and tourism play an important role in the area's development. Logging is still permitted on a sustained-yield basis within the park's inland buffer zone, and conservationists continue to battle a plan to pierce the lakeshore with a "scenic" Beaver Basin Rim road.

Despite the changes we have wrought upon the lakeshore region during our brief occupation, Lake Superior remains the dominant force. Its colorful cliffs and sweeping sand dunes have always been held in special reverence by visitors, and you may wish to leave your own offering to the cave-dwelling spirits of the Pictured Rocks—be it only a footprint in the sand or a vow to protect this lakeshore and its Superior beauty.

AUTO TOURS

A narrow ribbon of water drops some 50 feet over the inland escarpment of Pictured Rocks National Lakeshore, en route to Lake Superior at the Munising Falls visitor center, providing a wonderful beginning to your tour of the region.

To reach the seasonally staffed Munising Falls visitor center, follow the signs from the information center in Munising, a year-round facility located in the heart of town. You'll find park maps, backcountry permits, and advice regarding insects, weather, and camping options at either facility.

A well-developed trail begins at the Munising Falls visitor center, leading through a gorge carved by a rambling little stream fed by Munising Falls. The brief trail continues behind the waterfall, and you can witness the forces of nature at work from the dry protection of a hollow in the escarpment. Inside the visitor station, exhibits outline the history of Munising Bay, which, in the 1870s, hosted an iron smelting furnace and its workers.

Those anxious to get their feet in the sand will enjoy the two-mile, paved spur road leading to Sand Point, where you'll find a swimming beach and picnic tables. Sea kayakers often slide their boats in at Sand Point, and backpackers can begin their trek down the Lakeshore Trail from this location. The park's administrative headquarters is located in a former Coast Guard building at Sand Point, and relics of shipwrecks as well as an old Coast Guard boat are on display here. Across Munising Bay on the shores of Grand Island, the abandoned East Channel Lighthouse is visible. The wooden lighthouse, constructed in 1867, once guided ships past the dangerous reefs of Munising Bay.

Back on H-58, a five-mile drive down Miners Castle Road east of Munising Falls leads to the inspiring sandstone cliff known as Miners Castle. Named because erosion has carved its rocks into formations resembling castle turrets, this formation is one of the chief attractions on the lakeshore. You'll find easy access to the cliffs, thanks to wooden platforms that allow you to gaze over the edge of the rock precipice into the blue-green waters of Lake Superior. Steps and ramps then continue to a second viewing platform, which leads down to Miners Castle. In 1669, missionary Jacques Marquette is reported to have held religious services for the Ojibwa Indians, using Miners Castle as his altar.

From Miners Castle, a one-mile hike along the Lakeshore Trail leads through a pine forest to Miners Beach, where you'll find a picnic table and drinking water. Miners Beach is also accessible from a spur road just south of the Miners Castle parking area. From the beach parking lot, a trail passes the site of former cottages, then stairs descend the sand bluff to the beach.

Behind Miners Beach, the escarpment that forms Miners Castle arcs inland briefly to envelop Miners Basin, surfacing again on Lake Superior just east of the beach. The Lakeshore Trail follows this escarpment over the cliffs and ledges of the Pictured Rocks, and a short stroll down the path yields many rewards.

Backtracking on Miners Castle Road, a short spur leads to the trailhead of the Miners Falls. It's another one-mile hike to view the river tumbling over the inland escarpment, en route to marshy Miners Lake before it finds an outlet at Lake Superior.

A left turn on H-58 leads through the village of Melstrand, where another left turn leads six miles down an unpaved road to the Chapel Basin. This is a spectacular part of the park, but access is best for backpackers or for those wishing to enjoy a full day's hike.

Chapel Basin encloses a sand beach flanked by towering cliffs. It's a 2 1/2-mile one-way trek to the beach. Along the route you'll encounter both Chapel Falls, the longest waterfall in the park, and Chapel Lake, the deepest of the park's inland lakes. This is a favorite route of many weekend backpackers, who branch west off the trail to make the circular ten-mile route that leads past Grand Portal Point to the backcountry campground at Chapel Beach before returning to Chapel Lake and the parking lot.

Beyond Chapel Beach, Spray Falls tumbles over the Pictured Rocks in a remote section of shoreline traversed by the Lakeshore Trail. About one mile past Spray Falls, the lakeshore escarpment heads inland, revealing a seemingly endless ribbon of sand known as Twelve Mile Beach. Behind Twelve Mile beach, the inland escarpment encloses Beaver Lake and the remote Beaver Basin. Motorists who are willing to park and hike can gain access to this section of the park by taking Little Beaver Road, which leads to an eight-unit campground on Little Beaver Lake.

Little Beaver Lake provides a boat launch, but motorboats are restricted to ten horsepower or less. A small channel connects Little Beaver to Beaver Lake, which, at 800 acres, is the largest of the park's inland lakes.

Both day visitors and campers will enjoy the scenic 1 1/2-mile trail through planked wetlands to the sand and waves of Twelve Mile Beach. Those seeking a shorter hike should consider the .7-mile White Pine Trail, which leads along picturesque Beaver Creek before returning to the campground.

Returning to H-58, you'll find that the pavement ends beyond the three-mile spur road leading to the Beaver Basin Overlook. Situated on the inland escarpment surrounding the basin, this overlook provides a view above the treetops to the distant waters of Lake Superior. An old logging road built in the 1940s leads to Beaver Lake, two miles away. This trail provides access for trout anglers fishing the streams that drain Beaver Basin.

Motorists continuing on H-58 are warned that this unpaved section, though passable in summer, is rough and remote. Spur roads provide access to a number of rustic state forest campgrounds located on the inland lakes that dot the woods in an area known as Kingston Plains. An immense pine forest once covered these plains, and stumps still remain in testament to their former stately grandeur.

Kingston Lake, a state forest campground, is located within the park's inland buffer zone. This lake is noted for its fishing opportunities, and the campground often has vacancies when campsites within the national lakeshore are filled.

About four miles north of Kingston Lake, a spur road leads through a beautiful cathedral of white birch trees to a campground on Twelve Mile Beach. En route to the campground, parking is provided for day visitors and backpackers who wish to enjoy the delightful Lake Superior beach. Those wishing to take a hike will enjoy a jaunt down the Lakeshore Trail or a stroll on the self-guided, 1.6-mile White Birch Trail, which begins along the campground road.

The Hurricane River Campground is the next point of interest as you head east on H-58. The river was named by an expedition that camped here while on a mission to establish friendly relations with resident Indians. During the night, a powerful gale blew through the lakeshore, and the Cass expedition was forced to retreat to higher ground. Today, fishermen are often found surf casting at the river's mouth on Lake Superior.

Heading east down the lakeshore, Twelve Mile beach begins to give way to the rocks of Au Sable Point. Situated 1 1/2 miles down the Lakeshore Trail, you'll find the Au Sable Lighthouse. Along the trail, remnants of ships that fell victim to treacherous Au Sable Reef litter the beach, providing a vivid reminder of Lake Superior's hazards. Hidden under shallow water, Au Sable reef extends about one mile off shore, presenting imminent danger to unsuspecting mariners. To minimize this risk, the Au Sable Lighthouse was constructed by the Coast Guard in 1874. Today, restoration of the historic lighthouse is underway, but a modern beacon now warns ships of the impending danger.

Just east of the Hurricane River Campground on H-58, a former log slide reminds visitors that this was once the site of an immense logging operation. Viewing platforms atop the Grand Sable Banks allow you to look down the slope, where logs were shuttled from the crest of the bank down the wooden slide into Lake Superior.

The two viewing platforms rest on a formation known as the Grand Sable Banks. These glacial banks support the huge mountains of sand that characterize the Grand Sable Dunes. The east overlook provides a view of the Au Sable Point and the lighthouse, while the west overlook offers a striking glimpse of the awesome Grand Sable Dunes.

The dunes stretch for some five miles along the lakeshore, rising to heights of over 300 feet. Beyond the log slide overlook, H-58 provides access to the dunes just north of Grand Sable Lake, where a trail leads through the jack pines across the dunes to Lake Superior.

After H-58 winds through the park's forested sand dunes, you may wish to don your swimming suit for a dip in Grand Sable Lake. Be careful when driving this stretch, as the active Grand Sable Dunes frequently encroach on H-58, limiting travel to a single lane. The designated swimming beach at Grand Sable Lake will offer pleasant relief following the dusty drive down H-58. Changing stations and picnic tables are available at this day use area. Grand Sable Lake is also noted for its fishing opportunities. A boat launch can be reached from an access road located further east off H-58.

Beyond Grand Sable Lake, you'll be back on pavement for the drive to the Grand Sable visitor center. This station is open seasonally, occupying an old farmhouse that was once part of a dairy operation. From the visitor center, a one-mile trail leads along Sable Creek to Sable Falls. Those without the energy to take the hike can reach Sable Falls by continuing on H-58 to a parking area that provides easier access to the falls. The parking lot also provides access to Grand Sable Dunes, where you can wiggle your toes in the sand once more before bidding Pictured Rocks National Lakeshore farewell.

DRIVE-IN CAMPGROUNDS

The three drive-in campgrounds at Pictured Rocks National Lakeshore are rustic in character, but provide excellent access points to the park's many attractions.

The campgrounds are located at Little Beaver Lake, Twelve Mile Beach, and Hurricane River. Reservations are not accepted. If you hope to secure a campsite during peak summer season, plan to arrive mid-week. The sites offer a picnic table and a fire grate, and hand pumps and vault privies are centrally located.

Little Beaver Lake Campground contains eight campsites along inland Little Beaver Lake. Motorboats are restricted to ten horsepower or less. A self-guided nature trail starts at the campground, and a 1 1/2-mile trail leads to the beautiful cliffs and beaches of Lake Superior. H-58 is paved to Little Beaver Campground.

Twelve Mile Beach Campground is found 37 miles east of Munising via unpaved H-58. The campground's 37 campsites are located on a sandy bluff above the beach. The entrance road passes through a spectacular cathedral of lily-white birch trees. Twelve Mile Beach also features a self-guiding nature trail, which begins at the campground.

Hurricane River Campground is located three miles east of Twelve Mile Beach Campground, at the point where the Hurricane River empties into Lake Superior. A 1 1/2-mile stroll up the Lakeshore Trail leads past remnants of shipwrecks to the historic Au Sable Light Station.

These popular campgrounds fill almost every night in July and August. If you can't find a vacant site, the adjacent Hiawatha National Forest offers several camping options, including the 50-site Bay Furnace Campground located west of Munising on Lake Superior. Several rustic campgrounds are also located in the Lake Superior State Forest, adjacent to the national lakeshore. These campgrounds include 14-unit Kingston Lake, located in the lakeshore buffer zone.

At the eastern end of the lakeshore, adjacent to the village of Grand Marais, you'll find the 100-unit Woodland Park Campground, where electricity, showers, and tap water are available.

BACKCOUNTRY CAMPING

You can see Pictured Rocks National Lakeshore through the windshield, but you don't really experience it that way. To fully appreciate the power and grandeur of the lakeshore, you'll want to hoist a pack, pull a paddle, or take a stroll. Then the majesty of the cliffs and the sanctity of the sand dunes are likely to fill your heart with wonder.

Most interior visitors to Pictured Rocks National Lakeshore arrive with backpacks, but each summer an increasing number of sea kayakers are discovering the joy of paddling park waters.

Within the lakeshore there are 13 hike-in or paddle-in campgrounds, spaced at intervals of two to five miles. Each campground contains from three to 15 campsites, identified by numbered posts. Tents must be placed within 15 feet of these markers. The maximum party size per campsite is eight, but group campsites are available. Up to 30 percent of these backcountry campsites can be reserved in advance by calling 906/387-3700, with the rest available on a first-come, first-served basis. During July and August, backcountry campsites fill quickly, so it's wise to make reservations if your heart is set on exploring a specific part of the park.

During winter it's a different story. You'll still need a backcountry permit, available from the park's Munising office, but you may camp anywhere you wish, as long as there's six inches of snow on the ground. This is a great time to explore the peace of the lakeshore, but be prepared for deep snow and icy cold.

Except during winter, fires are permitted only in communal metal rings. It's best to bring a backpacking stove to minimize your impact and to ensure that you'll be able to fix a hot meal.

Water is available from lakes and streams throughout the backcountry, but it should be filtered or boiled. Water from park hand pumps is safe.

Dogs and pets are not permitted on backcountry trails or campgrounds, and the use of soap in lakes and streams is prohibited. You must keep all of your food out of your tent at all times, and it should be suspended at least ten feet from the ground and four feet from any branch or tree trunk.

HIKING TRAILS

The 43-mile Lakeshore Trail, an official segment of the North Country National Scenic Trail, stretches the entire length of the park. Only overnight visitors require permits to hike the trail, and access is available at trailheads spaced along the entire length.

The Chapel Basin is the most popular region to explore among weekend hikers. An easy two-day, nine-mile backpacking trip, which can also be a challenging one-day hike, begins at the Chapel parking area, 20 miles east of Munising. The trek takes hikers from the parking area past Chapel Lake to a backcountry campground (camping permit required). From here, you can proceed to Grand Portal Point, high atop the Pictured Rocks escarpment, before returning to the parking lot.

Beginning at the Chapel parking lot, it's best to follow the trail toward Chapel Falls, though you'll note that a parallel route west of Chapel Lake is also available.

A mile and a half from the parking area, you'll cross the creek on the footbridge and follow the sign out to the point on the left. A viewing platform here provides a spectacular look at 90-foot high

Chapel Falls, one of the highest cascades in the park. Below the falls in a narrow valley lies Chapel Lake. With depths reaching 128 feet, it's the deepest of the park's inland lakes.

Continuing on to Lake Superior, you'll find the trail leading to Chapel Rock. The "windows" in the rock, which today stand 40 feet above the lake level, were carved long ago by the wave and current action of an ancient lake.

Backcountry camping is available at Chapel Beach, but competition for these sites is often fierce during July and August, so it's best to reserve a site early.

Ascending the cliffs west of Chapel Beach, the trail continues for two miles to Grand Portal and Indianhead points. At 200 feet above Lake Superior, this is one of the highest sections of the Pictured Rocks escarpment, and it's certainly one of the most awesome. Do not venture too close to the cliff's edge, since the rock is weak and covered with loose gravel. The trail continues to the mouth of the Mosquito River before returning two miles to the parking lot. This trail can be hiked in either direction. Day hikers should be sure to pack water, lunch, and a swimsuit for a spiritually refreshing dip in the lake at Chapel Beach.

The Beaver Basin offers hikers access to the most remote sections of the park. Once you leave the drive-in campers behind at Beaver Lake, you'll see few others on Twelve Mile Beach until you near Twelve Mile Beach Campground.

Miners Basin, near the western edge of the lakeshore, and Grand Sable Dunes on the eastern border of the park provide excellent day hiking opportunities as well as access to overnight treks down the Lakeshore Trail.

PADDLING

Sea kayakers have access to the entire lakeshore, but permits are required of those planning an overnight visit. Before venturing along the Pictured Rocks, be sure to check the weather forecast, because options for retreat are limited along these steep cliffs.

Twelve Mile Beach is ideal for those attempting their first overnight on Lake Superior, as the sand beach provides a welcome escape if the lake vents its fury. Keep in mind, however, that many sections of the park are far from trailheads, and plan accordingly.

Little Beaver and Beaver lakes are well-suited to canoeing. Grand Sable Lake provides canoeing opportunities as well, but there is no restriction on motorcraft on this lake.

CROSS-COUNTRY SKIING

Groomed cross-country ski trails are located at each end of Pictured Rocks National Lakeshore, offering plenty of chances to enjoy the region's abundant winter snowfall.

The trails wind through a landscape that includes a variety of habitats and topography. Beech, maple, hemlock, pine, spruce and ancient plant communities grow on the sand uplands and rugged hills of the old glacial moraines and outwash plains.

Each trail offers a variety of loop lengths suitable for either a leisurely day ski or a quick workout. They're marked with a map at each intersection, and blue diamonds have been placed at intervals on the trail.

The Munising Ski Trails offer eleven miles of trails through the lakeshore, beginning one mile east of Munising off H-58. These trails vary in difficulty, winding through hills and forests along Lake Superior near Sand Point.

The Grand Marais Ski Trail offers a five-mile groomed route that begins near the Grand Sable visitor center one mile west of Grand Marais on H-58.

Those with the proper skill and equipment are welcome to break their own ski trails in the lakeshore backcountry. The snow is often deep, and snowshoes may prove a better mode of transportation, but it's unlikely that you'll encounter another soul—especially in the remote and scenic Beaver Basin.

WINTER CAMPING

Hearty winter campers have the lakeshore to themselves when snow blankets the backcountry. You'll need a backcountry permit, but you may camp anywhere as long as there's at least six inches of snow on the ground.

During winter, fires are permitted if you're more than one hundred feet from a trail, except in campgrounds where fires are restricted to designated fire grates.

SNOWMOBILING

Snowmobiling is permitted on unplowed sections of H-58 and on campground spur roads. Lake Superior is also open to snowmobiles, but operators should be sure of conditions before venturing out.

SENEY NATIONAL WILDLIFE REFUGE
HCR #2, Box 1
Seney, Michigan 49883
906/586-9851

Through the Windshield

Marshlands, fields, and forests provide a hiding place for wildlife, a nesting home for waterfowl, and even a sanctuary for people at the Seney National Wildlife Refuge.

Once exploited for its timber and scarred by fire, the 95,000-acre refuge area today resonates with the whir of wings and the yodels of loons. Eagles fish for meals within refuge pools, while geese nest on islands, hoping to elude hungry predators.

The Seney National Wildlife Refuge occupies the Kingston Plains, south of Pictured Rocks National Lakeshore. Over the years, the forces of nature and time and the hands of man have played a role in shaping Seney's unique landscape. When the last glacier retreated from the area, it left in its wake an intricate network of creeks and river channels, coupled with deposits of sand and gravel. Over the eons, wind and water have sculpted this landscape into the sandy knolls and ancient ridges you'll find on the refuge today.

Once left barren by axe and fire, the land has been mending for generations from the wounds that lumberjacks inflicted over a century ago. Lumberjacks first turned their attention to the huge red and white pine forests of upper Michigan, but when these woods were depleted, they took their axes to the less valuable northern hardwoods and swamp conifers of the Seney area. During this rough and tumble era, Seney was given the nickname "Hell Town in the Pine," based on the rowdy antics of lumberjacks in this logging boomtown.

When the trees came down, fires were set to clear the brush, and the plow would follow. These fires burned so deeply into the rich, organic soil that the seeds of the next generations were destroyed, setting back attempts to restore the huge forests that once covered the landscape.

As farmers moved to Seney, wetlands were drained and replaced with a developer's promise of rich farmland. These empty promises soon turned to dust in the poor soil of Seney, and one by one the farms were abandoned.

When the federal government established the Seney Wildlife Refuge in 1934, an intricate system of dikes, water control structures, ditches, and roads was built with the aid of the Civilian Conservation Corps. This system now impounds over 7,000 acres of open water in 21 major pools. The water for these pools is diverted from rivers that flow through the refuge. Wetlands management on the refuge is accomplished by raising and lowering water levels in the pools. By alternately raising and lowering them over several years, a natural wetland cycle is created.

Motorists may chance to see eagles, loons, sandhill cranes, and trumpeter swans heading for the Seney Wildlife Refuge pools, located between Seney and Germfask off M-77.

Just half a mile north of Seney's visitor center off M-77, you'll find the "Wigwams" rest area, where picnic tables and water are available for your convenience. A hiking trail leads to the refuge's visitor center but no camping is allowed.

Although the sanctuary's seventy miles of maintenance roads are open only to bicyclists and hikers, the refuge does maintain a seven-mile auto tour for motorists.

The one-way Marshland Wildlife Drive is open to motorists every day during daylight hours from May 15 to October 15. This one-hour tour of the refuge provides an excellent introduction to the unique landscape. Beginning across from the visitor center parking lot, the tour utilizes a printed leaflet with numbered stops to describe the refuge and its wild inhabitants. Recently, an active bald eagle nest has been clearly visible along the route.

The refuge offers both a wildlife observation deck and an eagle observation deck to increase your chances of viewing the 200 bird species and nearly 50 mammal species that have been recorded at Seney. Spring, late summer, and fall are the best seasons in which to schedule your stop. An early morning or late afternoon visit also increases your chances of spotting elusive mammals.

BICYCLING

Pedaling a bicycle is one of the best ways to experience Seney. The refuge offers nearly 70 miles of fine gravel roads, closed to vehicles but open to bicyclists. Mountain bikes are ideal, but just about any bike will do, since the roads do not require special wide tires.

One of the most popular bicycle routes is the seven-mile Marshland Wildlife Drive. This is a one-way route for both bicycles and autos. A pamphlet available at the beginning of the tour will help you better understand the wildland that surrounds you. The refuge closes at sunset, and managers ask that you plan your bike trip accordingly.

HIKING

Hikers will enjoy the 1.4-mile Pine Ridge Nature Trail, which begins just outside the visitor center. This trail offers an intimate look at refuge habitat, plants, and wildlife.

Other areas of the refuge are also open to exploration by foot. Hikers are encouraged to walk the gravel maintenance roads that cross the refuge, and those arriving during berry season are invited to enjoy wild blueberries found along the route.

PADDLING

Canoeing is popular on the Manistique River, which skirts the border of the refuge. Park managers will be happy to direct you to local outfitters who can rent you a canoe, offer advice, and provide shuttle service if you have your own boat.

Canoeing is permitted during daylight hours only on the Manistique, Driggs, and Creighton rivers, as well as on Walsh Creek. Boats are banned from refuge pools, in order to protect the waterfowl that find sanctuary here.

FISHING AND HUNTING

Northern pike fishing is popular on Seney's refuge pools, and those possessing a valid Michigan fishing license are welcome to cast from shore during daylight hours between May 15 and September 30. Boats are not permitted on refuge pools. Ice fishing is open from January 1 through February, and either live bait or artificial lures are permitted.

Only non-motorized watercraft are permitted on Walsh Creek and the Creighton and Driggs rivers. Boats with motors are permitted on the Manistique River.

Sections of the Seney Wildlife Refuge are open to big and small game hunting, including deer, bear, ruffed grouse, and woodcock. Special regulations apply, so check with the refuge manager for details.

CROSS-COUNTRY SKIING

A short cross-country ski trail through the Seney Wildlife Refuge begins next to the lookout tower near refuge headquarters off M-77.

An additional eight kilometers of groomed trails are located at the Northern Hardwoods Cross-Country Ski Area, including a two-kilometer advanced loop. To reach this set of trails, take M-77 into Germfask, and turn west on the road just south of Grace Lutheran Church. The parking lot is located 1/2 mile west of M-77.

GRAND ISLAND NATIONAL RECREATION AREA
Hiawatha National Forest
400 East Munising Ave.
Munising, MI 49862
906/387-3700
906/387-2512 (off season)

The reverence Ojibwa Indians felt for Grand Island is shared by today's self-reliant visitors, who embark on this island preserve to find black bears still roaming free along sand beaches, inland lakes, and sheer sandstone cliffs.

Situated just half a mile offshore from Munising, in the shadow of Pictured Rocks National Lakeshore, Grand Island is accessible by daily commercial ferry service during the summer season and across the frozen ice in winter.

The Ojibwa called it *Kitichi Minis*, the Great Island, and it was one of the few sites on Lake Superior that hosted a permanent population of native people.

In legend, the Ojibwa tell of the origin of their island home and the hills surrounding Munising. They explain that Kitchi Manito, the Great Spirit, fashioned several huge giants. When these giants were completed, he fretted that they might become even more powerful than he was if given life, so he abandoned the creatures. He cast one of the them into the waters of Lake Superior, and this "sleeping giant" became Grand Island, with nearby Wood and Williams islands representing the giant's hands rising from the depths of Superior. The other outcasts became the hills surrounding Munising—all of them giants sleeping under the watchful eye of Kitchi Manito.

French explorers were equally impressed by the size and character of the three-island chain, and they christened the archipelago "Les Grandes Isles," adopting the Indian's literal description.

Today, Grand Island remains true to its name. Protecting Munising Bay, it's the largest island on Lake Superior's south shore, and some would argue that it's the most beautiful. It stretches north for eight miles, from its southernmost point at Williams Landing in Munising Bay to its northern border at North Point. Only three miles across at its widest point, Grand Island offers 35 miles of shoreline, encompassing over 13,500 forested acres. Streams divide its rugged hills, and sandstone cliffs reach for the sky above the clear waters of Lake Superior. Sand beaches stretch along the exterior shoreline, and marsh grass sways along the shores of inland Echo and Duck lakes.

Archeological investigations indicate that Grand Island has probably been inhabited for the last 2,300 years. By the time Europeans arrived to establish fur trading posts in the late 1700s, Ojibwa culture was thriving.

In the summer of 1840, at the invitation of Grand Island Ojibwa chief Omonomonee, Abraham H. Williams of Decatur, Illinois, arrived on Grand Island with his family, becoming the first white settlers. Williams had met Omonomonee during the annual Ojibwa rendezvous at Sault Ste. Marie, and the powerful chief approved his plans of setting up a trading post on the island. Williams Landing takes its name from this steadfast pioneer, but an island cemetery offers a glimpse of the hardships these homesteaders must have endured. Williams' 16-year-old son, Isaiah, was the first laid to rest in the cemetery, followed two years later by Abraham's wife.

It's believed that shipwreck victims are also buried in the Williams cemetery, casualties of the treacherous reefs, persistent fog, and unpredictable weather of Lake Superior. Air currents rising from the sand dunes of the lakeshore, combined with the cold air of Superior, often create fog that blankets Grand Island and the surrounding

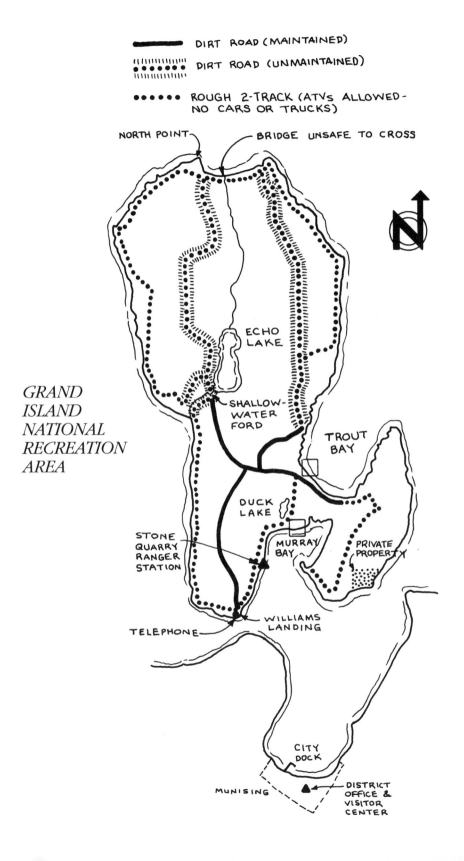

DIRT ROAD (MAINTAINED)

DIRT ROAD (UNMAINTAINED)

ROUGH 2-TRACK (ATVs ALLOWED — NO CARS OR TRUCKS)

NORTH POINT

BRIDGE UNSAFE TO CROSS

N

ECHO LAKE

SHALLOW-WATER FORD

TROUT BAY

GRAND ISLAND NATIONAL RECREATION AREA

DUCK LAKE

STONE QUARRY RANGER STATION

MURRAY BAY

PRIVATE PROPERTY

TELEPHONE

WILLIAMS LANDING

CITY DOCK

MUNISING

DISTRICT OFFICE & VISITOR CENTER

Pictured Rocks National Lakeshore. This fog, coupled with high winds and shallow reefs, combined to wreak havoc on early mariners. Today, ten shipwrecks lie strewn in a watery grave across the lake bottom near Munising. The Alger Underwater Preserve was established by the state of Michigan in 1981 to protect the integrity of these shipwrecks. The preserves encompasses all waters surrounding Grand Island, overlapping with the boundaries of the mainland Pictured Rocks National Lakeshore. Recreational diving is permitted within the preserve, but removal of artifacts in strictly prohibited. During summer months, buoys mark the locations of several famous wrecks. For information on charter boats specializing in shipwreck dives, contact the Alger Chamber of Commerce (906/387-2138).

In 1900 the Cleveland Cliffs Iron Company purchased Grand Island from The Munising Company and Williams' heirs for $93,071.61. Impressed with the virgin wilderness they had acquired, company officials opted against industrial development. Instead, they decided to turn the unspoiled island into a wild game preserve and tourist destination.

In 1902 the Cleveland Cliffs president, William Mather, purchased 11 elk and released them on Grand Island. Over the next few years he added moose, caribou, antelope, several species of deer, and even a mountain goat to his island menagerie. Imported trees and shrubs were planted on the island to accommodate the diets of these exotic species and the animals were allowed to roam free.

This abundance of game proved too tempting a target to a lone female wolf that crossed the winter ice in 1906 to pursue its prey. After the wolf devoured 19 animals, Mr. Mather reached the end of his patience and ordered the wolf killed at any cost. A total of 27 skilled hunters took to the island's forests and marshlands with a mission to kill the predator. The wily wolf avoided the hunters for ten days before finally falling to a bullet, in what many call the most expensive hunt ever to take place on Michigan's Upper Peninsula.

William Mather died in 1951, and the exotic game he transplanted to Grand Island eventually disappeared over the same winter ice the predator had crossed years before. Timber was selectively harvested by Cleveland Cliff over the years, but the company remained a fine steward of their Grand Island paradise.

In 1990, a new chapter in the history of Grand Island was written when the Cleveland Cliffs Iron Company relinquished its ownership of the island. When the company indicated its desire to sell its Grand Island holdings, the Minnesota-based Trust for Public Lands stepped in, acting as an interim owner until the U.S. Forest Service made its acquisition. Today the Forest Service manages the Grand Island National Recreation Area as a component of the Hiawatha National Forest.

A small parcel of private property remains on Grand Island, and all of the buildings with the exception of the Stone Quarry Ranger Station are privately owned. For many years, these property owners had Grand Island to themselves, and many still rely on all-terrain and four-wheel drive vehicles to negotiate the island's rustic roads. Please respect the privacy of these property owners, and they'll respect your right to visit.

GETTING THERE

GRAND ISLAND FERRY SERVICE
PICTURED ROCKS CRUISES, INC.
ELM AVE
MUNISING, MI 49862
906/387-2379

Most visitors to Grand Island arrive aboard the Grand Island Ferry. Adult fare is approximately $10.00 roundtrip, $5.00 for children under age 12. Bicycles are welcome for an additional $3.00. You must be self-sufficient once you reach the island, and headnets are recommended during the black fly season.

The Grand Island Ferry departs the Munising City Pier during June, September, and October at 9:00 a.m. and 4:45 p.m., with a return trip at 9:30 a.m. and 5:15 p.m. It's about a 20-minute trip to the island. During July and August, the ferry leaves Munising at 7:45 a.m., 11:45 a.m., and 5:45 p.m., and departs Grand Island at 8:15 a.m., 12:15 p.m. and 6:15 p.m.

Motorboats are welcome to visit Grand Island, but travel can be hazardous. Obtain a reliable weather forecast and be prepared to navigate in thick fog. There are no public docks on the island, but you may load and unload at Williams Landing. When the Forest Service tug or the passenger ferry arrive, you must vacate the dock. Private boats may be moored overnight in Murray and Trout Bay. A free permit is required from the Forest Service before leaving a boat unattended.

Experienced canoeists often make the trip to Grand Island without incident, but sea kayaks provide a much safer means of travel. Keep a close eye on the weather, and be sure to have a compass and chart along. A wetsuit is standard equipment for Lake Superior travel.

GETTING AROUND

Many of today's Grand Island visitors arrive on the island with only their legs as transportation. While hiking is a fine means of seeing Grand Island, especially for backpackers, mountain bikes provide the best transportation. The island's rough dirt roads are tailor-made for the wide tires of a mountain bike, and even the island's nasty black flies can't keep up with a mountain bike coasting along the trails.

Sea kayaks provide excellent coastal access for paddlers wishing to explore the remote north shore of Grand Island. It takes at least two days to circumnavigate the island by sea kayak, and paddlers should keep in mind that the only area off limits to camping is the remote but ecologically sensitive North Beach.

Snowmobiles are the vehicle of choice for many winter visitors who cross the frozen ice of Munising Bay to ride the well-developed trails of Grand Island.

CAMPING

Camping is permitted just about anywhere on Grand Island. Exceptions include North Beach, where camping is prohibited to protect the pristine setting. At Murray's Bay and Trout Bay beaches, camping is restricted to designated campsites.

Backcountry campsites should be located at least 50 feet from creeks and lakes, and the use of a portable stove is recommended. No beach fires are allowed and you must, of course, pack out whatever you pack in.

When choosing your backcountry campsite, it's imperative that you choose a site on the windward side of the island. A fresh breeze blowing through your campsite will keep the black flies from inflicting their nasty damage.

FISHING AND HUNTING

It's a long, tough canoe portage to inland Echo Lake, which offers opportunities to snare bass, northern pike, and panfish. Much of the shore of this one-mile-long inland waterway is surrounded by marshlands, and during early summer the mosquitoes and black flies can be a force to contend with. Trout Bay and the waters surrounding Grand Island are noted for their lake trout and coho salmon populations. Trolling is the most effective means of enticing a strike.

Grand Island is open to small and big game hunting. Resident species include black bear, white-tailed deer, ruffed grouse, rabbit, and waterfowl. A Michigan fishing and/or hunting license is required on Grand Island. Contact the Michigan Department of Natural Resources (517/373-1220) for details.

HAZARDS

The island's remote character and its robust insect population represent the greatest hazards to an enjoyable visit. The black flies are present from May through July, and many visitors time their travels to avoid peak fly populations. In the event of an emergency, you can use a telephone near the island dock to alert the Ferry Service of difficulties.

HIAWATHA NATIONAL FOREST
2727 North Lincoln Rd.
Escanaba, MI 49829
906/786-4062

The two units of upper Michigan's Hiawatha National Forest stretch from the shores of three Great Lakes to encompass over 860,000 acres of woods and water. Taking its name from Longfellow's celebrated poem, "Song of Hiawatha," the forest and its landscape often remain as wild as the waves pounding its shores.

Over 775 miles of rivers and streams flow through the Hiawatha before finding an outlet at Lake Michigan, Lake Huron, or Lake Superior. Along these three Great Lakes, 77 miles of shoreline are managed as national forest, providing important public access to the greatest freshwater basin in the world.

Fishermen delight in the diversity of the forest's 413 inland lakes, where loons can often be found adding to the song of Hiawatha. Canoeists will relish the forest's 163 miles of designated canoe routes, and sea kayakers will find much variety between the sand dunes of Lake Michigan and the islands of Lake Huron. The northern section of the forest is noted for its abundant snowfall, providing opportunities for both cross-country skiing and snowmobiling.

The Great Lakes that surround the Hiawatha influence both climate and recreation in the forest. Snowfall on the southern shores of the forest averages just 54 inches per year, while on the north shore the average is over 240 inches per year.

Sunbathers can be found all summer long enjoying the beach life on lakes Huron and Michigan, while on Lake Superior, visitors are donning sweaters and wearing long pants.

Due to the forest's remote character, trophy whitetail deer often elude hunters during Michigan's big game season. In more accessible areas, up to 90 percent of all antlered bucks are harvested; here, over half of the antlered deer in remote sections escape each season. Black bear also frequent the Hiawatha, and a few native or reintroduced moose are occasionally spotted.

September marks not only the fall hunting season on the Hiawatha, but also autumn colors. During late September, the forested acres begin radiating the colors of crimson, yellow, gold, and green. Maple, oak, birch, beech, and aspen trees provide the reds, golds, and yellows; the pine, spruce, hemlock, and cedar trees provide the greens.

Biting and stinging insects, such as mosquitoes and black flies, are an unpleasant part of the Hiawatha scene. You can best deal with them by using long sleeves, headnets, and insect repellent. Don't let the presence of bugs deter you from a trip to the forest—just be prepared.

Finally, the Hiawatha is a place to find peace. There are six designated wilderness areas within the forest. These pristine tracts protect virgin white pine forests, sweeping sand dunes, and crystal-clear lakes, offering a home for wildlife and a retreat for visitors who attune their ears to the song of Hiawatha.

MAPS

An excellent large-scale map featuring campgrounds, roads, and recreational areas is available for a nominal fee from the Hiawatha National Forest headquarters in Escanaba. Write to the address at the beginning of this section, or give the headquarters a call.

CAMPING

Drive-in campgrounds dot both units of the Hiawatha National Forest, and most are located on a scenic lake in a northwoods setting. The campsites are generously spaced, and are serviced by hand pumps and vault privies. Electrical hookups and showers are not available, but most of the campsites will accommodate trailers.

Due to budget constraints, several of the campgrounds in the forest, particularly in the Munising area, are operated by private concessionaires. Reservations may be required during July and August at these campgrounds, and it's often best to phone the ranger district office for information.

Dispersed camping—which means pitching a tent or parking an RV outside the boundaries of established recreational areas—is free, and is permitted throughout the Hiawatha National Forest. Some dispersed campsites offer a cleared tent pad and fire ring, but most simply provide space beneath the stars.

Primitive campsites are usually located along inland lakes, and offer a private, secluded setting away from the more popular developed campgrounds. Primitive sites can be reserved, and camping permits (fee charged) are required. You may obtain a primitive campsite permit by writing or visiting the district ranger station for the area you wish to visit.

HIAWATHA NATIONAL FOREST— WEST UNIT CAMPGROUND

MANISTIQUE RANGER DISTRICT
DEVELOPED CAMPGROUNDS
499 E. Lake Shore Dr..
Manistique, MI 49854
906/341-5666

CAMP 7 LAKE CAMPGROUND
41 sites

Camp 7 Lake Campground is 60 acres in size. Swimming, boating, and fishing for rainbow trout are popular here, and a nature trail is nearby. Seven sites are available for the handicapped. Camp 7 Lake is located 37 miles south of Munising. Take Highway 13 to paved County Road 442, and head east eight miles to Camp 7 Lake.

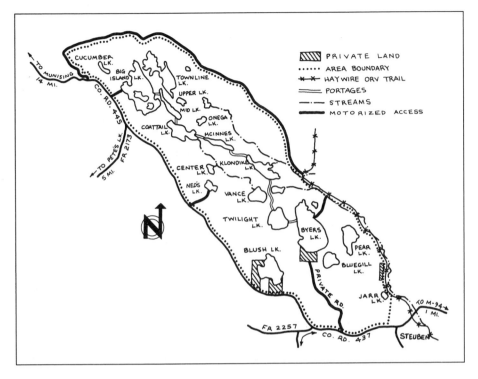

COLWELL LAKE CAMPGROUND
34 sites

A sand beach and excellent northern pike and largemouth bass fishing combine to make the 145-acre Colwell Lake a popular destination for both swimmers and anglers. Colwell Lake Campground is located 20 miles south of Munising. Exit M-94 at Forest Road 2246 to Colwell Lake.

CORNER LAKE CAMPGROUND
9 sites

The 156-acre Corner Lake is home to walleye, northern pike, bass, and panfish. Its back-in boat launch, however, does not easily accommodate large boats. The campground is located 15 miles south of Munising, off H-13 via Forest Road 2259.

INDIAN RIVER CAMPGROUND
11 sites

The Indian River Campground is situated on a bluff overlooking the river itself. The campground is near the halfway point on the Indian River Canoe Trail, and is a convenient overnight for canoeists. You'll find it on the west side of M-94, 20 miles north of Manistique.

LITTLE BASS LAKE CAMPGROUND
12 sites

Little Bass is an 84-acre lake offering carry-in boat access to anglers pursuing resident largemouth bass, northern pike, and panfish. The campground is located 25 miles southeast of Munising. Take M-94 to County Road 437 west, then take the first road south (left) to Little Bass Lake.

RAPID RIVER RANGER DISTRICT DEVELOPED CAMPGROUNDS
8181 Highway 2
Rapid River, MI 49878
906/474-6442

LITTLE BAY DE NOC
38 sites

Boat access to Lake Michigan's Little Bay de Noc is offered from this 38-unit campground. Fishing for walleye and northern pike can be quite good. Handicap accessible. Located 15 miles from Rapid River, south on U.S. 2, then onto County 513.

FLOWING WELL
10 sites

The Flowing Well Campground is situated along the banks of the Sturgeon River, among large trees and wildflowers. The "flowing well" itself is 1,160 feet deep, and was originally drilled for oil in 1929, but only water resulted. Flowing Well Campground is located 14 miles east of Rapid River. Exit Highway 13 off U.S. 2 and head north three miles to the campground.

MUNISING RANGER DISTRICT
400 E. Munising
Munising, MI 49862
906/387-2512

AU TRAIN LAKE CAMPGROUND
37 sites

At 830 acres, Au Train Lake is the largest inland lake in the area, and it provides many boating options. Canoeing is popular on both Au Train Lake and the Au Train River. The campground is located 10 miles west of Munising. Travel south on H-03 four miles, then head east one mile on Forest Road 2276. Go two miles north on Forest Road 2596 to Au Train Lake Campground.

BAY FURNACE CAMPGROUND
50 sites

Located on the shores of Lake Superior, Bay Furnace Campground is within easy reach of Pictured Rocks National Lakeshore, Grand Island, the Alger Underwater Preserve, and many nearby waterfalls. Only the iron kiln ruins remain from the once-prosperous iron smelting town of Onota, which was founded here in 1869. Bay Furnace Campground is located five miles west of Munising on M-28.

ISLAND LAKE CAMPGROUND
45 sites
Concessionaire-operated

Tiny, 32-acre Island Lake is less popular than other campgrounds in the Munising District, which means you're more likely to find an open campsite on a busy summer weekend. Carry-in boat access provides canoeing opportunities. To reach Island Lake, proceed south from Munising on Forest Highway 13 for 10 miles, then west on Forest Road 2268 to the campground.

PETE'S LAKE CAMPGROUND
41 sites
Concessionaire-operated

Pete's Lake is a popular campground with a great swimming beach and improved boat launch. The 900-acre lake is clean and clear. Paved roads in the area offer great bike-riding potential. Reservations are suggested during the peak summer season. Pete's Lake Campground is located 12 miles south of Munising off Forest Highway 13.

WIDEWATERS CAMPGROUND
34 sites
Concessionaire-operated.

Widewaters Campground occupies a "wide" spot along the Indian River. The Indian River offers excellent quietwater canoeing from the campground, which is located 13 miles south of Munising. Take Forest Highway 13 south to Forest Road 2262, then head 1/2 mile northwest to the Indian River.

HIAWATHA NATIONAL FOREST— EAST UNIT CAMPGROUNDS

SAULT STE. MARIE RANGER DISTRICT CAMPGROUNDS
4000 I-75 Business Spur
Sault Ste. Marie, MI 49783
906/635-5311

BAY VIEW CAMPGROUND
24 sites

Bay View Campground is located along the shores of Lake Superior's Whitefish Bay, and provides an excellent stop for Circle Tour drivers. The sand beach of the bay continues for miles, and beautiful sunsets can be enjoyed "by the shore of Gitchi Gummi, by the Shining Big-Sea-Waters." The campground is located on the lakeshore, about 35 miles west of Sault Ste. Marie on Forest Road 3150 (Lake Shore Drive).

MONOCLE LAKE CAMPGROUND
44 sites

A sandy beach, a boat launch, and many nearby attractions make 172-acre Monocle Lake an attractive vacation spot. The campground is located near the historic Point Iroquois Lighthouse. Monocle Lake Campground is seven miles west of Brimley off Forest Road 3150 (Lake Shore Drive).

SOLDIER LAKE CAMPGROUND
44 sites

Trout and perch are found in 15-acre Soldier Lake, but no motors are permitted, so you'll have to use a canoe to fish these waters. A sand beach makes for pleasant swimming. Soldier Lake Campground is located 30 miles from Sault Ste. Marie, off M-28 at Forest Road 3138.

THREE LAKES CAMPGROUND
28 sites

Three Lakes Campground is a peaceful hideaway located on Walker Lake, one of the "three lakes" that surround the area. Rainbow trout are found in this 19-acre lake, but no motors are allowed. There is no marked swimming beach, but sandy areas along the water invite a dip on a hot day. Three Lakes Campground is located 38 miles west of Sault Ste. Marie, two miles south of M-28 at Strongs Corner on Forest Road 3142.

ST. IGNACE RANGER DISTRICT CAMPGROUNDS
1498 West U.S. 2
ST. Ignace, MI 49781
906/643-7900

BREVOORT LAKE CAMPGROUND
70 sites

Brevoort Lake is one of the popular campgrounds in the St. Ignace Ranger district, and many families return year after year to the 4,233-acre lake. Camping is available on a first-come, first-served basis. Boat access is offered, and fishing for walleye remains a popular pastime. Brevoort Lake Campground is 20 miles west of St. Ignace. From U.S. 2, turn north on the Brevoort Camp Road (FR 3108) then right on FR 3473 to the campground entrance.

CARP RIVER CAMPGROUND
44 sites

Trout fishermen will find brook, brown, and rainbow trout in the Camp River, easily accessible from the campground. Nearby, at the mouth of the river at St. Martin Bay on Lake Huron, both steelhead and salmon make seasonal runs. The Carp River Campground is eight miles north of St. Ignace city limits off H-63, commonly called the Old Mackinac Trail.

FOLEY CREEK CAMPGROUND
54 sites

The Foley Creek Campground is located just six miles from St. Ignace, the gateway to popular Mackinac Island. You'll find a sandy beach on Lake Huron one mile from the campground at the end of the Horseshoe Bay Hiking Trail, so be sure to pack a swimsuit. The Foley Creek Campground is located six miles north of St. Ignace off H-63, the Old Mackinac Trail.

LAKE MICHIGAN CAMPGROUND
35 sites

When the wind is whipping, bodysurfing waves rush the sandy shores of the Lake Michigan Campground. Swimmers cautious of the undertow will have a great time. Most of the tent campsites are spacious and comfortable, located between sand dunes up to 30 feet high. The campground is very popular in the summer, so it's best to arrive early in the day, mid-week. The Lake Michigan Campground is 18 miles west of St. Ignace between U.S. 2 and the Lake Michigan shoreline.

CANOEING

A canoe will allow you to experience the Hiawatha National Forest in peace and harmony. Paddlers anxious to dip a blade in clean quietwater will be pleased to note that the national forest contains over 160 miles of designated canoe routes. These routes vary in length from an hour to several days, and most offer plenty of options to suit individual interests.

For safety's sake, a personal flotation device (PFD) should be worn when canoeing, especially in the spring, when rivers run cold and weather changes abruptly. It's wise to leave an itinerary with friends who can report to authorities if you're overdue in returning from your planned outing.

AU TRAIN RIVER CANOE ROUTE

The slow-moving, meandering Au Train River offers an excellent four- to six-hour canoe trip. While this doesn't seem like a very long trip, it can be quite lengthy for inexperienced paddlers. If this is your first outing, consider shortening the distance by taking your canoe out at one of the access points along the route.

The trail begins at the Forest Service boat launch in the Au Train Lake Campground, and proceeds north approximately ten miles to Lake Superior.

Today, the absence of rapids and portages makes for a quiet, relaxing trip. Numerous sloughs along the route harbor a wide variety of wildlife, including ducks, songbirds, great blue herons, kingfishers, muskrats, and turtles. Walleye, perch, sucks, and bullheads inhabit the river all year, while steelhead (rainbow trout) make a spring run and salmon run in fall.

The first access point is located on Au Train Lake at the Forest Service boat launch, approximately 5.5 miles south of the village of Au Train. It's best to avoid this access point when strong north winds are blowing. The second put-in or take-out is located at the southern bridge, where H-03 crosses the Au Train River, approximately 1.5 miles south of the village of Au Train. The third access point is located at the northern bridge, where H-03 crosses the Au Train River. The take-out is located off M-28 at the mouth of the Au Train River on Lake Superior.

Canoes are available for rent from resorts along Au Train Lake. For information on rental or current river conditions, call the Au Train Tourist Association at 906/892-8144 or 906/892-8350.

CARP RIVER CANOE TRAIL

The Carp River Canoe Trail offers a pleasant two or three day float down a winding quietwater river, well-suited for beginners.

The Carp flows east 25 miles from the first recommended put-in off Forest Road 3458 to its outlet in Lake Huron's St. Martin Bay. Along the route it passes through pine, aspen, maple, and paper birch forests.

The Carp has been designated a second-quality trout mainstream by the Michigan Department of Natural Resources. Anglers may catch brook, rainbow, or brown trout in pools along the route, and steelhead and salmon may be caught seasonally near the river's mouth.

A developed campground with pit toilets and water pumps is located about two miles from Lake Huron. There are no other developed sites along the river, but camping is permitted. Make sure you're at least 100 feet from the river or other water sources.

The first access point is located on Forest Road 3458. To reach this put-in, take M-123 north of St. Ignace to Forest Road 3124. Head west to Forest Road 3458, then east one mile to the Carp River.

It's six miles from FR 3458 to Michigan State Highway 123, the second put-in or the first take-out. From Highway 123, the river continues eight miles through a proposed wilderness area to East Lake Road, passing the North Branch at the six-mile mark. There is a small section of fast water on the route, but nothing to worry about. This is also a very peaceful stretch of water, since no motorized equipment or motor vehicles are permitted in the area.

From East Lake Road (FR 3119) the Carp passes through two small, easy rapids en route to Carp River Campground six miles downstream. From the campground, the river continues past Flat Creek a mile downstream to Red Creek, three miles from the campground. It's another 1.5 miles from Red Creek to the boat landing at St. Martin Bay.

INDIAN RIVER CANOE ROUTE

The gentle flow of the Indian River, combined with its scenic beauty, will impress any canoeist. A trip of one to several days is possible along the 36-mile route from Fish Lake to Indian Lake.

You'll travel deep into the Hiawatha National Forest, where you'll drift past northern hardwoods, mixed conifers, rolling hills, and marshland swamps.

The average width of the Indian River is 30 to 50 feet, and its average depth is just one to three feet. Don't let this depth lull you into a false sense of security. The Indian River is deadly cold in spring, and paddlers should dress accordingly.

The trail begins at Fish Lake, where paddlers travel the widest stretch of river for 1/2 mile to the second access point, Widewaters Campground. This area offers toilets, tables, fireplaces, and drinking water.

From Widewaters you travel to 10-Mile Bridge. There is a bit of fast water above Forest Highway 13 to add to your canoeing excitement, but nothing to worry about. West of the bridge you can paddle into Straits Lake, Deep Lake, and Corner Lake, but remain in your boat, since both the shore and islands of these lakes are private.

From 10-Mile Bridge, the third access point, to Thunder Lake Road, the Indian River flows through the northern boundary of the Iron Jaw semi-primitive, non-motorized area. This is a remote, scenic stretch where there are steep banks. Erosion is evident on these banks, and the Forest Service asks that you avoid the slopes.

The fourth access point is at Thunder Lake Road, and continues to the Indian River Campground. This is not the best stretch for beginners, since skill is often required to avoid logs in the river and portaging may be necessary. Just south of Steuben you will drift past 30-foot river banks, and you are again advised to avoid the slopes. At the Indian River Campground, you can use the footbridge area for put-ins and take-outs. The campground (fee charged) has tables, toilets, and drinking water.

From Indian River Campground, the fifth access point, to 8-Mile Bridge, the river meanders through marshlands, much to the delight of nature photographers.

The sixth access point is located at 8-Mile Bridge. Be advised that from here there are no roads or access points until you reach Michigan's Palms Brook State Park, ten miles downstream. Below 8-Mile Bridge, the river enters "the Spreads," a series of shallow, maze-like braids. An alternative route is suggested in this area in order to avoid portaging and dragging your canoe.

Indian Lake is 8 miles downstream from 8-Mile Bridge, but the state park boat launch is another two miles down the lakeshore. You're advised to use caution on Indian Lake, since waves can often whip up during strong winds. For safety, it's best to paddle close to shore.

STURGEON RIVER CANOE ROUTE

Only experienced paddlers should canoe the Sturgeon River, since the best time to paddle the river is during high water—typically between April 30 and the end of June, or after mid-September. In early spring, the Sturgeon runs deep, swift, and cold. Experienced paddlers equipped with wet suits and waterproof bags will find the trip enjoyable.

The Sturgeon River Trail is 44 miles long. The river is relatively slow-moving, meandering frequently, but fallen trees and heavy brush occasionally block the route, making portages necessary. There are two sections of rapids, adding excitement to the outing.

The first access point is located on County Road 440, accessible off Forest Highway 13 south of Munising. From this put-in, it's usually a two-day trip to the second access point at County Road 442. There are no intermediate access points, and this is the most remote section of the river. When camping, check the Forest Service map to be sure you are not pitching a tent on the private property that lines the river. Log jams, heavy brush, and rocky riffles on the last two miles of this stretch may require portaging.

From County Road 442, the second access point, to Forest Highway 13, the Sturgeon River runs entirely through national forest lands. A few log jams require liftovers, but in general this section is easy going. There is no intermediate access.

The stretch between Forest Highway 13, the third access point, and Flow Well Campground is also entirely within national forest lands. Along this stretch, ten-mile rapids challenge experienced paddlers. Beginners should avoid it altogether.

From Flowing Well Campground, the fourth access point, the next access is Country Road 497. This is a good day trip for those camping at the national forest campground. There is one mile of private property above U.S. 2.

From County Road 497, the fifth access point, to the river's end at Big Bay de Noc, the meandering river is often blocked by log jams or is too shallow to run. This stretch is best avoided.

CANOEING THE BIG ISLAND LAKE WILDERNESS

The Big Island Lake Wilderness includes more than 20 inland lakes nestled within rolling woodlands. It's a landscape of solitude.

Located 15 miles southeast of Munising, the wilderness offers secluded paddling, fishing, hiking, and backcountry/winter camping.

The area includes over 6600 acres, and it's roadless except for limited access to three of the lakes by motorized vehicles.

White birch, maple, and aspen cover the wooded hills that surround the lakes, and berries, mushrooms, and wildflowers grow throughout the area.

There are no developed campsites, but low-impact, backcountry camping is permitted in the entire area. Permits are not required, but campers must limit their stay at any site to 14 days, and must remain at least 100 feet from any lake to protect the area's water quality.

Daytime temperatures range from 55 to 90 degrees between late spring and early fall. Average annual rainfall is about 30 inches, and winter snowfall averages about 160 inches, thanks to the influence of Lake Superior.

The lakes and small streams within the designated wilderness offer a secluded opportunity for anglers. Special fishing regulations by the Michigan Department of Natural Resources apply, however, including special size and creel limits for muskie, northern pike, bass, trout, and panfish. Consult the Michigan DNR for details.

Paddles offer the best means of travel through the Big Island Lake area. The chain is linked by eight portage trails ranging in length from 102 to 1800 feet.

To reach the Big Island Lake Wilderness from the east, take Highway M-94 to Country Road 437. From the west, take Forest Highway 13 to County Road 445 or Forest Road 2173. From the south, access is via County Road 437 off U.S. 2. From these roads, access spurs lead to Big Island Lake, Neds Lake, and Byers Lake.

HIKING

The Hiawatha National Forest includes two segments of the North Country Trail, a national scenic trail that, when completed, will extend from New York to North Dakota.

Approximately 35 miles of the trail lies within the St. Ignace District, and 42 miles within the Sault Ste. Marie District. The former segment begins at Castle Rock Road (FR 3104) and ends at FR 3323 near Maple Hill, one of the highest points within the district. Along the way, the trail passes through stands of northern white cedar, aspen, pine, and northern hardwoods. This section of trail is relatively flat. The trail is fully marked with blue diamonds painted on trees to mark the way, but not all sections of the trail been brought up to scenic trail standards, and wet areas may be encountered.

A section of the trail passes through the developed campground at Brevoort Lake (fee charged). Elsewhere, free primitive campsites are scattered along the route.

The Sault Ste. Marie section of trail joins the St. Ignace section at Forest Road 3323, passing through pine plantations, hardwoods, wetlands, and dunal ridges until it meets the shore of Lake Superior. Again, backcountry camping is permitted, but horses and motorized vehicles are not allowed. This section of trail ends near Lake Superior, at the Forest Highway 42 parking area on Tahquamenon Bay.

Bruno's Run is another popular hiking trail in the Hiawatha National Forest. Access to the 7.25-mile loop is available at both Widewaters and Pete's Lake campgrounds, from Forest Highway 13 at Moccasin Lake, and from Forest Road 2173 at Grassy Lake.

Winding its way through valleys, across hills, and along overlooks, the trail takes hikers past a host of small lakes. Permits are not required for camping along the trail, making this a pleasant overnight backpacking trip.

CROSS-COUNTRY SKIING

The Munising District offers nordic skiers plenty of opportunities to take advantage of Lake Superior's abundant snowfalls. The five ski trails found within the district offer groomed loops ranging from easy to highly difficult.

The Valley Spur ski trailhead (fee charged) is just off State Highway M-94, six miles southwest of Munising. Here you'll find eleven miles of groomed ski trails, ranging from easy to most difficult.

McKeever Hills Ski Trail (fee charged) is located on Forest Highway 13. Most skiers park at the Forest Glen Store. The seven miles of groomed trails vary from easy to most difficult.

The 12.6 miles of groomed trails within the Buckhorn Ski Trail system (fee charged) include a 3.5-mile skating loop. Parking is available at the Buckhorn Lodge on FR 2254, off M-94 south of Munising.

An illuminated two-mile groomed trail can be found at the Christmas Ski Trail (fee charged). Parking is available at Jerry and Pat's store.

In the Rapid River District, you'll find challenging hills at the Rapid River Ski Trail, which offers over 9 miles of groomed trail. The trailhead is seven miles north of Rapid River, off U.S. 41.

In the Sault Ste. Marie District, the McNearney Ski Trail offers eight miles of trail, traversing ancient sand dunes covered by a second-growth hardwood forest. The trailhead is located five miles north of Strongs Corners at the junction of M-28 and Salt Point Road.

The St. Ignace District features ten miles of groomed trails at the Sand Dunes Cross Country Ski Trail. The trail takes you through old Lake Michigan sand dunes, formed by blowing sand. The trailhead is on the west side of Brevoort Lake Road (H-57) about 1/2 mile north of U.S. 2.

COPPER COUNTRY
The Keweenaw and Isle Royale

Through the Windshield

The fifty-mile-long, 15-mile-wide Keweenaw Peninsula juts into Lake Superior like a crooked finger, enclosed by the clear, shimmering waters of the surrounding inland sea. From its shores, visitors embark on explorations of Isle Royale National Park, a roadless island preserve where wolves prey on moose and visitors seek quiet renewal.

At the turn of the 20th century "King Copper," the red metal, ruled this region of Michigan's Upper Peninsula, bringing wealth and prosperity.

Today, a narrow spine of pure copper still exists, but its importance is overshadowed by the region's other natural resources—clean water, fresh air, and forested hills.

Isle Royale is the next destination on your Lake Superior Circle Tour, but this leg of the adventure should not be rushed. There are lakes to be paddled, streams to be fished, and trails to be hiked as you make your way across Copper Country.

Departing the Munising city limits and heading west on M-28, you'll pass two campgrounds, both offering campsites on the shores of Lake Superior. The 50-unit Bay Furnace Campground is located where the iron-smelting town of Onota stood in 1869. Eight years later, a fire destroyed the town, leaving only the iron kiln ruins seen today. The Munising Tourist Campground, just two miles east of Christmas, also offers camping opportunities.

The Christmas post office has become quite famous, since holiday cards arrive there from throughout the nation to be hand-stamped with the Christmas, Michigan postmark.

West of Christmas you'll pass Scott Falls, a small drop visible from the highway, before reaching the AuTrain River where both fidgeting children and the flowing river find an outlet at Lake Superior. The Au Train River is noted for its excellent quietwater canoeing, and nearby outfitters offer boat rentals and advice. Children and the young at heart will enjoy taking a summer swim where the warmer waters of the AuTrain River cushion the icy chill of Lake Superior.

The Circle Tour skirts the lakeshore, providing plenty of chances to get your feet wet. Highway M-28 heads inland briefly before reaching Lake Superior once again at the Sand River. It leads onward to Marquette, a bustling commercial and cultural center.

With a population of over 23,000, Marquette is the largest community in Michigan's Upper Peninsula. It takes its name from Father Jacques Marquette, a Jesuit missionary who arrived on the southern shores of Lake Superior by canoe, spreading the white man's religion to the Ojibwa.

Along the shores of Lake Superior, historic brownstone buildings rise above the city's red brick sidewalks, and sailboats dot the waters surrounding Marquette.

Presque Isle Park is the city's most popular natural attraction. Not actually an island, Presque Isle occupies a 328-acre peninsula surrounded by the blue waters of Lake Superior. Boaters find refuge in the 95-slip marina adjacent to Presque Isle since, depending on its mood, Lake Superior either gently caresses or violently pounds the park shores. There are opportunities to play tennis, picnic, or hike within park boundaries. Kids enjoy romping in the park's swimming pools or visiting the small zoo, where whitetail deer roam among the pines. A short cross-country ski trail traverses the park, but winter storms can leave the trail icy and dangerous.

Marquette is one of the educational centers of the Upper Peninsula, serving the 8,000 students of North Michigan University. The university is also home to the U.S. Olympic Education Center and the NMU Sports Training Complex, where world-class athletes train in 29 of the 37 Olympic events.

Beach-lovers will enjoy a visit to the Marquette Maritime Museum Lakeshore (fee charged). Located east of the U.S. Coast Guard station, the museum offers lessons in Great Lakes maritime history. It's open seven days a week from Memorial Day to December.

The city's abundant snowfall attracts cross-country and downhill skiers, as well as snowmobilers who explore hundreds of groomed trails through the surrounding forest. Marquette Mountain, just three miles from downtown Marquette, offers downhill skiers a 600-foot vertical drop. Cross-country skiers enjoy the groomed trails of Blueberry Ridge, a Michigan DNR pathway near Marquette at the junction of county roads 480 and 553. Don't be surprised, however, if an Olympic athlete flies past you like a rocket while you're taking a breather.

Heading west out of Marquette on M-28 and U.S. 41, you're rolling toward the Upper Peninsula communities of Negaunee and Ishpeming. Some six miles west of Marquette, you'll find the Jackson Mine Museum, open during the summer, which displays mining equipment dating back to the mid-1800s.

Iron Ore Monument, located on Highway 41, pays tribute to the iron mines of the Marquette Range. Teal Lake, near Negaunee, produced the area's first hint of iron when ore was discovered in the roots of a fallen tree along its shores.

Just south of Negaunee on old M-35, you'll find Lucy Hill, home of the first natural luge course in the United States. The course meets new International Luge Federation standards. This "toboggan run" drops near 300 feet over its 2500-foot length. There are 29 curves on the winding track, each representing one of the 29 iron ore mines that were once active in the city of Negaunee. Visitors are welcome to stop by on winter weekends and watch as speedy sleds tear down the icy track at harrowing speeds.

The drive between Negaunee and Ishpeming takes you from a luge course to a ski jump at Suicide Hill. Each February, competitors from Canada, Europe, and Japan converge on Ishpeming to take part in the annual International Ski Jumping competition.

Located in the heart of Marquette's Iron Range, Ishpeming is the home of the National Ski Hall of Fame. Ishpeming is proud of its claim that American skiing began here when Scandinavian miners strapped skis on their feet, then shuffled across the snow to work the iron mines.

Rolling west on M-28 out of Ishpeming, the route traces the northern shores of Lake Michigamme. Resorts dot sections of this massive, island-studded lake, but much of the shoreline remains wild and undisturbed. The Michigamme River drains the lake, winding through the Michigamme State Forest before emptying into Michigamme Reservoir. Paddling and fishing opportunities are numerous along this stretch of river, but check the water level and insect population before launching.

Michigan's Van Riper State Park (listed separately), located on the shores of Lake Michigamme, offers modern campsites, a sand swimming beach, and a boat launch. Van Riper also serves as headquarters for a rustic campground situated along the Peshekee River just west of the park. If you're seeking a wilderness cabin or a backcountry canoe trip, the park staff can help you arrange a trip to nearby Craig Lake (listed separately), where rustic state park cabins are available for rent. Craig Lake is linked by canoe portage to a series of wilderness lakes, and backcountry camping is permitted if you acquire the necessary permits from rangers at Van Riper State Park.

Approximately 12 miles north of Champion off County Road 607, the McCormick Wilderness (listed separately) occupies 27 square miles of forested land and scattered lakes. This wilderness is named after former owner Cyrus H. McCormick, the inventor of the reaping machine. It's now managed as a unit of the Ottawa National Forest, and its springs serve as headwaters of the Yellow Dog, Dead, and Peshekee rivers. No-trace camping is permitted in this wilderness, and those who carry a backpack are sure to find solitude in this land of rocky cliffs and soggy swamps.

Fifteen miles west of Lake Michigamme, Highway 41 forks toward the Keweenaw Peninsula. You're now en route to Copper Country, traveling through a heavily forested area where moose again roam following a long absence. In 1985, Michigan exchanged wild turkeys for Ontario moose, in the hope of restoring this stately creature to its traditional habitat. The herd is still roaming the central U.P., but consider yourself lucky if you spot one of these huge animals rambling into the forest.

En route to L'anse, you'll pass over the Sturgeon River, where a roadside park provides a great place to stretch your legs and take a ten-minute stroll. An interpretive hiking trail leads to a wonderful gorge and a series of waterfalls.

Situated on the southern shores of Keweenaw Harbor, the community of L'anse takes its name from a French word meaning "bay." The Keweenaw band of Ojibwa (or Chippewa as they're known today) has a reservation in this region, and nearby you'll find a historic Indian burial ground. The Ojibwa believed that when life ended, provisions were needed to sustain the soul on its journey to the afterlife. For this reason, food was often left with those buried. A shelter with a small opening was erected over the grave, to protect its occupant and to allow the soul to reach the hereafter.

Overlooking the shores of Keweenaw Bay, high atop Red Rock Bluff between Baraga and L'Anse, a memorial commemorates Bishop Frederic Baraga. The Catholic missionary gained fame as "The Snowshoe Priest" because he traveled on foot great distances in the winters between 1831 and 1868 to minister to his Indian converts. Appropriately, the 35-foot statue of the priest depicts the missionary clasping a huge pair of copper snowshoes.

Across from L'anse, on the shores of Keweenaw Bay, Baraga State Park (listed separately) offers hot showers and welcome campsites for travelers who are preparing for their trek to Isle Royale National Park. You may need reservations at Baraga during the busiest weekends of the year, since the park offers swimming, boating, and picnicking opportunities. To make a reservation, call 906/353-6558.

From Baraga, the Circle Tour continues up the Keweenaw Bay through a series of small villages to Chassel, home of the Sturgeon River Wilderness Area. Migrating waterfowl rest on the sloughs of this sanctuary during their flights to nesting sites. From an observation platform east of the village, you can watch these waterfowl take to the sky.

Highway 41 pierces Houghton and the campus of the city's 7,000-student Michigan Technological University. Houghton is a town built in the boom days of the copper bonanza. Its stately downtown has survived a mining economy turned sour. The city is named after Douglass Houghton, the state's first geologist, who is credited with documenting the rich copper deposits of the Keweenaw. Today, the large student population keeps the city lively and vivacious.

Houghton serves as the headquarters of Isle Royale National Park (listed separately), and it's one of two Keweenaw Peninsula locations from which to launch your exploration of Isle Royale. The National Park Service operates the 165-foot *Ranger III*, which departs twice weekly from Houghton, ferrying passengers to the lodges, campgrounds, and trails of this island park. Accommodations, campgrounds, and backcountry camping are available on Isle Royale, but you'll need reservations for the ferry and for lodging once you're on the island.

Houghton is separated from Hancock, its neighbor to the north, by the narrow Keweenaw Waterway, which divides the 50-mile-long peninsula. The Portage Lift Bridge spans the waterway at Portage Lake, forming the connection for travelers en route to Copper Harbor at the tip of the Keweenaw Peninsula.

Overlooking Houghton and the Keweenaw Waterway, Quincy Hill offers winter visitors a chance to enjoy the area's 180-inch annual snowfall on downhill skis.

From Houghton, Circle Tour travelers can head directly north on Highway 41 to Copper Harbor or skirt Portage Lake on M-26 and pay a visit to the Arcadian Copper Mine at Ripley. From June through mid-October, underground tours (fee charged) of this mine offer a glimpse of the area's rich mining past.

Michigan Highway 26 joins Highway 41 near Calumet, named after an Ojibwa term meaning "pipe of peace." When granted final federal approval, this historic copper mining town will be designated headquarters of the Keweenaw Mining District National Historic Park. A self-guided walking tour of Calumet's historic downtown allows you to trace the history of a city built with "red metal dollars."

The Circle Tour continues through the deserted mining towns that dot the spine of the Keweenaw Peninsula to Delaware, eleven miles south of Copper Harbor. Guided, 45-minute tours begin at this ghost town from late May through mid-October, taking visitors 1400 feet into the sloping shaft of a copper mine.

A canopy of trees, alive with color in the fall, encloses Highway 41 as the road makes its final approach to Copper Harbor. The peninsula receives an incredible amount of snowfall each winter. A record 394 inches of "white gold" was measured during the winter of 1978-79, making the Keweenaw a preferred destination for snowmobilers, cross-country skiers, and winter campers who treasure a white playground.

The 100 year-round residents of Copper Harbor are a hardy crew who welcome visitors with lodging, restaurants, gift shops, and a marina. At the entrance to the harbor a lighthouse and museum faces the village, but access to the site is difficult without a boat.

From Copper Harbor, daily departures to Isle Royale National Park are offered aboard the *Isle Royale Queen III.* The *Queen* shaves two hours off the trip to Isle Royale, but in rough seas a ride on this vessel can be a stomach-turning experience.

Many campers spend the night at Fort Wilkins State Park just northeast of Copper Harbor, where a morning shower awaits them prior to their Isle Royale departure. Situated along the shores of inland Lake Fanny Hoe, the 199-acre site was established as an army post in 1844 to keep the peace between copper miners and resident Indians. The anticipated trouble never arose, and the post's stockade became something of a home for the rough-and-tumble miners the army was sent to protect.

Scuba divers often explore the Coast Guard cutter *Mesquite*, which lies in about 80 feet of water within Keystone Bay, off the Keweenaw Peninsula. The 180-foot vessel ran aground on the reefs of Keweenaw

Point, less than one mile offshore, in December of 1989. Rather than attempting to salvage the old vessel, the Coast Guard towed the ship two miles south of the dangerous reef, then sent it to a watery grave on the floor of Keystone Bay.

If you're interested in hiking through a land of giant trees, follow the signs from Copper Harbor to Estivant Pines. The Estivant Pines represent the last stand of privately owned virgin white pines in Michigan. The stand's famous 500-year-old "leaning giant," once Michigan's champion white pine, has fallen, but its majestic counterparts remain standing. Although privately owned, the Estivant Pines are open for public enjoyment.

To minimize backtracking on your trip down the Keweenaw, take Michigan Highway 26 along the peninsula's western lakeshore. You'll delight in the scenic views along nine-mile Brockway Mountain Drive. Touted as the highest above-sea level drive between the Rockies and the Alleghenies, Brockway Mountain peaks at 700 feet. On a clear day, you may see Isle Royale in the distance or spot hawks and eagles during their annual migration.

Highway 26 passes Eagle Harbor, home of the Eagle Harbor Lighthouse and the Keweenaw Country Historical Museum, before rejoining Highway 41 two miles southeast of Eagle River.

Backtracking on Highway 41 to Calumet, you'll find State Road 203 skirting the Keweenaw Waterway en route to F.J. McLain State Park. Situated at the mouth of the Portage Lake Ship Canal, the park offers fiery sunsets visible along its nearly two miles of Lake Superior shoreline. McLain is often busy during summer weekends, and reservations may be necessary to secure one of the park's 100 modern campsites. For reservations, call 906/482-0278.

Continuing south down State Route 26 through once-booming mining towns, you're heading for your final destination in Copper Country—Twin Lakes State Park. Swimmers will be pleased to note that Lake Roland, the centerpiece of the park, is often touted as the warmest lake in the Upper Peninsula. The park's 62 modern campsites are rarely full, and campers arriving early in the day during mid-week may secure a site right on the shores of the 292-acre Roland Lake.

VAN RIPER STATE PARK
P.O. Box 66
Champion, MI 49814
906/339-4461

A fine sand swimming beach and prime walleye fishing on Lake Michigamme keep campers coming back year after year to Van Riper State Park.

The campground is divided into two units, separated by Highway M-28. The southern unit features a modern, 151-unit campground at the eastern end of Lake Michigamme. None of the campsites are located directly on the lake, but access to the water is never far away. The northern campground offers campers a more rustic experience along the shores of the Peshekee River, and much of the park's 1,100 acres surround this rustic campground.

Brook trout can be found in the Peshekee River north of the campground, and a developed boat launch serves anglers pursuing Lake Michigamme's excellent population of walleye and northern pike.

The park's sand beach draws a fair number of day visitors who arrive to take advantage of upper Michigan's short summer.

Like all Michigan state parks, Van Riper is open to exploration in winter. There are no groomed ski or snowmobile trails, however, so winter activity is limited.

CRAIG LAKE STATE PARK
c/o Van Riper State Park
P.O. Box 66
Champion, MI 49814
906/339-4461

You'll need a canoe or a pair of sturdy hiking boots to explore the wilderness lakes and rugged environs of Craig Lake State Park.

Getting to the put-in for this wilderness is a challenge in itself. A high-clearance vehicle or four-by-four may be the only means of reaching this remote park. Van Riper State Park serves as headquarters for Craig Lake as well, so it's prudent to stop at Van Riper for a map and advice on road conditions prior to taking on the old logging roads that access the park. Poorly marked logging roads lead seven miles off Highway M-28 to a small parking lot that serves as trailhead to the wilderness.

Those who ignore the hassle of getting there are rewarded with a series of six wilderness lakes, cradled within the wild forest of Michigan's Upper Peninsula. Motorboats and ATVs are banned from this park, making it a favored destination for silent-sport enthusiasts.

The striking, 374-acre Craig Lake, studded with six islands, serves as the centerpiece of the park. Most visitors begin their exploration of the area by portaging a canoe the short distance to the Craig Lake put-in, then head off to explore Crooked or Clair lakes, both accessible by portage trail.

Cabins along the shores of Craig Lake offer tentless visitors a chance to escape the black flies of June and the thunderstorms of August. The cabins are accessible by paddle and portage or by hiking a 1.5-mile trail. The largest of the two cabins sleeps 14, while the smaller sleeps six. The cabins are very popular among fishermen, and it's best to reserve them well in advance to avoid disappointment.

Before pitching a tent, you must obtain a camping permit from Van Riper State Park. There are only two designated camping areas within the wilderness, but backcountry camping is permitted if you set up camp at least 150 feet from shore. The Sandy Beach Camping Area is situated on the east shore of Craig Lake, and it offers room to pitch three tents. The Eagle Nest Camping Area is located on Crooked Lake near the portage from Craig Lake.

Fishing for muskie, walleye, bass, and northern pike can be very good, but anglers are restricted to artificial lures, and northern pike and muskies must be released immediately. Other fishing restrictions apply, so check with rangers at Van Riper prior to making the long trip down the rugged road to Craig Lake.

THE McCORMICK WILDERNESS
Ottawa National Forest
Kenton Ranger District
Kenton, MI 49943
906/852-3501

The McCormick Wilderness straddles the divide between the Lake Superior and Lake Michigan watersheds, protecting 18 small lakes that sparkle on the landscape. Situated in the north central part of Michigan's Upper Peninsula, the McCormick Wilderness is located 12 miles north of Champion, and fifty miles west of Marquette. Access to the southwest corner of this little-visited, 27-square-mile preserve is via County Road 607, an old Huron Bay railroad grade.

The lay of the land within the McCormick Wilderness varies from nearly level to rocky and rugged. Its boundaries encompass the headwaters of the Huron, Yellow Dog, Dead, and Peshekee rivers.

Numerous swamps and muskegs rim the area's waterways, more reminiscent of waters found further north on the Canadian Shield than the more fertile lakes of the Upper Peninsula. Game and fish populations are low as a result, but the insect life remains robust. Those who visit the wilderness during May, June, or July should plan accordingly.

Northern hardwood and lowland conifer forests have reclaimed the glacier-scoured hills of the McCormick Wilderness following the logging era of the early 1900s. Small tracts of towering white pines that escaped the logger's axe remind us how the woods looked prior to the arrival of Europeans.

Thanks to reintroduction programs, the moose has returned to the McCormick landscape, joining the white-tailed deer, black bear, otter, mink, beaver, and fox, which have always been a part of this wilderness.

Fishing is limited to the small population of largemouth bass, northern pike, and trout that swim the area's network of lakes and streams.

For many years, this wilderness served as the private vacation retreat of Cyrus H. McCormick, son of Cyrus Hall McCormick, inventor of the reaping machine. The inventor's son first visited the Upper Peninsula around 1885, planning to hunt, fish, and camp. He was impressed with the area and, with Chicago attorney Cyrus Bentley, McCormick acquired land around White Deer Lake from logging companies.

Between 1902 and 1906, the pair built a lodge on an island in White Deer Lake. Known as the Chimney Cabin, the lodge was built on the island to protect it from forest fires. Other cabins were built on the island for guests. Surprisingly, the dining room of the house was located on the mainland. The McCormicks and Bentleys lived on the island and ate on the mainland, using a hand-operated raft for transportation to and from the house to the dining room.

Both McCormick and Bentley loved the outdoors, and both were members of the Huron Mountain Club, an exclusive summer colony on the shores of Lake Superior in northern Marquette County. Bentley loved hiking so much that he had a 26-mile trail brushed out from White Deer Lake Camp to the Huron Mountain Club.

The last owner, Gordon McCormick, donated the family estate to the U.S. Forest Service upon his death in 1967. Because of its unique characteristics, it became part of the National Wilderness Preservation System in December of 1987.

Access to the backcountry is limited, but a three-mile foot trail beyond a gated road connects County Road 607 to White Deer Lake, where the McCormick estate building once stood. Cyrus McCormick was an avid hiker, and over 100 miles of hiking trails once crossed the area. Today vegetation has overtaken these trails, making them difficult to locate.

The rugged landscape of the McCormick tract appeals to those preferring to hike, backpack, fish, hunt, and camp free of permits and designated campsites. Paddlers are limited by long portages between lakes, and cross-country skiing is limited by deep snow and poor winter access from County Road 607.

Nevertheless, those making the effort to visit the McCormick Wilderness will not be disappointed when they discover the waterfalls of the Yellow Dog River and the solitude of a peaceful northern forest.

BARAGA STATE PARK
P.O. Box566
Rt. 1
Baraga, MI 49908
906/353-6558

Because of its location at a crossroad along the way to many upper Michigan attractions, Baraga State Park is an excellent overnight stop for weary travelers.

The 56-acre park offers a fine view of Keweenaw Bay from its day use area, which serves as a great picnicking site. Traffic from Highway 41, which dissects the park, can be annoying to light sleepers, but the park's modern facilities are sure to refresh even the most exhausted visitors.

You'll appreciate the park's 109 modern campsites if you've just returned from the backcountry of Isle Royale, and the park serves as a stepping stone to the Copper Country of the Keweenaw Peninsula.

ISLE ROYALE NATIONAL PARK
87 N. Ripley Street
Houghton, MI 49931
906/482-0984

Isle Royale National Park rises above the wind-swept waves of Lake Superior to reveal a castle of wilderness, where wildlife reigns and man is merely a visitor. Isolated for eons by miles of open water, this island preserve harbors unspoiled forests, pristine inland lakes, and rugged, rocky shores.

Isle Royale National Park was authorized by Congress in 1931, in order to "conserve a prime example of Northwoods Wilderness." The park has remained true to its mission and, in 1981, the United Nations designated this wilderness oasis an International Biosphere Reserve, affording it worldwide protection.

Today, 15,000 annual visitors embark on Isle Royale from mid-May through October. They arrive by commercial ferry, sea plane, private vessel, and even sea kayak. During winter, true wilderness returns and the island is left to wildlife, together with a handful of scientists who study the island's true inhabitants.

Most summer visitors arrive at Rock Harbor on the island's southeastern shore, aboard boats departing the mainland from Houghton or Copper Harbor, Michigan. Arrival from Grand Portage, Minnesota, is also an option aboard the *Wenonah*, which stops at Windigo on the island's western shore before continuing to Rock Harbor. You're welcome to bring your own vessel to the Isle Royale, as long as you feel comfortable crossing the open waters of Lake Superior. Gas and oil are available at both Rock Island and Windigo from mid-May through mid-October.

Most visitors to Rock Island plan on camping, but lodging and housekeeping facilities are available at Rock Harbor (reservations required). Small stores at Rock Harbor and Windigo accommodate visitors by offering food, insect repellent, and hot showers. Camping is available at Windigo, located on Washington Harbor, but there are no lodging facilities.

Isle Royale is a special place. For many it provides the challenge of hoisting a pack over a rocky trail, of pitching a tent in the forest, or of finding a bull moose and watching as it feeds in a beaver pond. To others it offers a stroll through the woods before spending the night in a comfortable lodge. To still others, it presents a quiet cove during stormy seas, a haven of tranquility in the protected waters of Duncan Bay.

Isle Royale is more than a single island. The park acually encompasses a 200-island archipelago. Although water is everywhere in this wilderness, swimming is not popular at Isle Royale, due to the temperature of Lake Superior and the leeches found in the park's inland lakes.

At least ten shipwrecks litter the waters surrounding Isle Royale, permitting exploration by scuba divers. Divers must register at a ranger station prior to making a dive.

You won't need a license to fish the park's inland lakes, where lucky anglers may tangle with a feisty northern pike. If you plan to fish the productive waters of Lake Superior, however, you'll need a Michigan fishing license.

Isle Royale is a long way from civilization. There are no telephones, and medical services are not available within the park. Seriously ill or injured folks are transported to the mainland for asisstance at their own expense. All travelers should pack a first-aid kit and know how to use it. Pets are not permitted on Rock Island, even those kept aboard a boat that is docked offshore. There are no poisonous snakes or spiders on the island, but mosquitoes, black flies, and gnats can prove bothersome to the unprepared. Veteran backcountry travelers pack a headnet, long sleeves, long pants, and repellent. It's also wise to bring along an extra sweater, rain gear, and even a wool cap and gloves. Due to the influence of Lake Superior, Isle Royale can be a cold place, even in July.

Backpacking is the most popular means of experiencing the park's interior, and even beginners will find trails to match their enthusiasm. There are over 165 miles of trail traversing this roadless park, offering enough variety to challenge even the hardened backpacker. Hikers accustomed to putting 12 miles behind them by day's end are often dead tired and ready to call it quits after just eight miles or so on Isle Royale.

Isle Royale's unique geology accounts for the challenge of its rugged trails. Hiking across the island, one is struck by its long and narrow topography. Stretching some 45 miles from tip to tip but only 8.5 miles wide at its broadest point, the island dips and rises between ridges and troughs that parallel the park's interior backbone, the

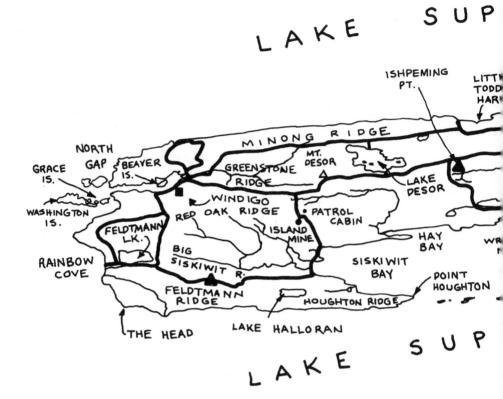

Greenstone Ridge. Traversed by a hiking trail connecting both ends of the island, the Greenstone Ridge rises three times to heights of over 1300 feet, reaching its 1394-foot summit at Mount Desor, the highest point on the island. North and south of the Greenstone Ridge, inland lakes gouged out by glacial activity and filled by meltwater beckon exploration by paddlers anxious to make a meal of the island's northern pike.

The Isle Royale story is inseparable from the water that surrounds it. Some 80 percent of the national park is underwater, lying beneath shallow ponds, small streams, inland lakes, and the cold blue waters of Lake Superior.

Indians were the earliest known visitors to the island, arriving some 4,000 years ago. To these early peoples, Isle Royale was a mysterious object floating on the blue horizon, tempting the brave explorers to reach it by challenging the open waters of Lake Superior. It's believed

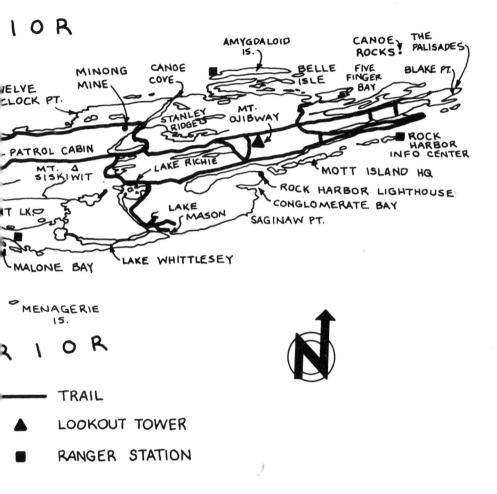

I O R

AMYGDALOID IS.

CANOE ROCKS! THE PALISADES

MINONG MINE   CANOE COVE

BELLE ISLE   FIVE FINGER BAY   BLAKE PT.

VELVE CLOCK PT.

STANLEY RIDGE   MT. OJIBWAY

PATROL CABIN

ROCK HARBOR INFO CENTER

MT. SISKIWIT   LAKE RICHIE

MOTT ISLAND HQ

ROCK HARBOR LIGHTHOUSE

T LK   LAKE MASON

CONGLOMERATE BAY

SAGINAW PT.

MALONE BAY   LAKE WHITTLESEY

MENAGERIE IS.

R I O R

N

——— TRAIL

▲ LOOKOUT TOWER

■ RANGER STATION

that these Indians paddled their canoes the fifteen miles from what are now Canadian shores to reach the island's pure copper, which served as valuable trading stock. They, too, were only summer visitors, retreating to their homes on the mainland before the approach of winter storms.

White explorers learned of the island's copper in the 17th century, prompting exploration by the French, who gave the island its name. Whether through negotiation or a mapmaker's error, somehow Isle Royale became part of the U.S. when boundaries were drawn separating Canada, then controlled by England, from the newly formed United States in 1783.

Fishermen began discovering the rich fishing grounds of Isle Royale in the 18th century, and by 1837 seven fishing camps and 33 fishermen inhabited the Isle Royale and its surrounding archipelago. Sport fishermen still ply the waters of Isle Royale hoping to land a trophy lake trout, but commercial fishing has largely disappeared, remembered only by park naturalists who conduct tours of the once-thriving commercial fisheries.

In 1837 Isle Royale became part of the Michigan Territory, despite the fact that it was closer to the shores of Minnesota.

Soon after, in 1844, Ojibwa Indians relinquished their claim to the island by signing a treaty with the United States that opened the island to miners who were anxious to stake a claim on the island's copper. Despite many endeavors, a mother lode of copper never materialized on Isle Royale, and these enterprises collapsed by the early 1900s. They were soon replaced by tourism and summer resorts.

Congress took note of this island wilderness in the 1920s, passing a bill in 1931 that created Isle Royale National Park. Today it's one of the nation's smallest national parks, but also one of the most beloved. Due to the relative difficulty of access, Isle Royale is a destination park. Visitors don't pass through Isle Royale en route elsewhere—they arrive to enjoy its splendor for several days or a week at a time. This allows time to hike the trails, paddle the lakes, and touch the heart of this primeval land, which in turn touches the souls of all who visit.

WOLVES AND WILDLIFE

In February of 1990, stunned scientists who were conducting winter wolf research watched in awe as the ancient cycle of predator and prey unfolded before them. While surveying the island's 450-wolf pack, consisting of a dominant alpha male, his mate, and their three pups, the scientists watched as the wolves entered a thicket of trees near the island's southeastern shore. The wolves emerged in pursuit of a moose, following inches behind it until, in a desperate lunge, the Alpha male locked onto the back leg of the fleeing animal.

The alpha female arrived to assist her mate, and soon the hapless moose was dragging the pair through the snow. Now tearing at the animal's rump, the wolves inflicted mortal damage despite attempts by the moose to shake free by dragging its tormentors over logs and whirling them into trees. Such is the balance of nature on Isle Royale.

The modern history of wolves on Isle Royale began during the winter of 1948, when a handful of wolves crossed the 15-mile ice bridge separating the wilds of the Canadian mainland from the isolation of Isle Royale. They discovered a rich hunting ground where prey was plentiful and hunting was undisturbed. By 1967, over 30 wolves roamed the island, as others are thought to have followed the same ice bridge to the island's prey.

In 1980, the island's wolf population peaked at over 50 animals in five territorial packs. Moose, the wolves' major prey, plummeted to an all-time low of 550 animals on the island by 1983. Researchers believed this predator/prey fluctuation reflected the cycle of nature until 1983, when the wolf population suddenly plunged to just fourteen animals. The population rebounded to more than 20 wolves in 1984, but that year marked the beginning of a five-year decline.

During the late 1980s, wildlife biologists reversed the "hands off" policy they had adopted regarding the wolves, and began trapping and radio-collaring the animals in an attempt to understand the population decrease.

Researchers have concluded that the problem appears to be a lack of genetic diversity within the Isle Royale wolf population. Those wolves examined are as closely related to each other as family members.

In 1990 there were 15 wolves patrolling the forests of Isle Royale, offering some hope for the local survival of this species. Few visitors actually see a wolf on the island, but a fresh footprint on a portage trail indicates that the call of the wild is nearby.

Moose have thrived on Isle Royale since the first animals swam over from the mainland in the early 1900s. During the 1930s an estimated 3,000 moose lived on Isle Royale, but the population subsequently crashed. Despite an infestation of winter ticks, which has reduced the population by 25 percent from the island's most recent peak of over 1600 animals, the herd now appears to be thriving. You may encounter moose anywhere on the island, even near busy Rock Harbor. Those with their hearts set on seeing a moose should shoulder a backpack and head for Lake Ritchie, where the animals enjoy feeding on the lake's vegetation. Keep in mind that moose are powerful, strong-willed animals, best viewed from a safe distance.

Whitetail deer and black bears never made the journey to Isle Royale. Don't be lulled into a false sense of security, however, thinking your food pack is safe. Hungry red foxes are very common on the island, and they'll quickly snatch any food left unguarded. It's best to avoid the temptation of feeding the occasional camp fox that arrives at your site looking for a handout. You won't be here in winter, but your friendly fox will, and it must learn to fend for itself.

Eagles and osprey are continuing to make a recovery on Isle Royale, and both species are actively nesting on the island.

During the past several years, over ten peregrine falcons have been released on the island. In 1989, a jet-setting female peregrine that hatched on Isle Royale in 1988 found a mate from Chicago, and the pair nested successfully on a building in downtown Milwaukee!

GETTING THERE

Because Isle Royale is an island, you'll need a boat or a sea plane to reach the preserve. From June through mid-September, the double-decked, 165-foot National Park Service *Ranger III* sails from Houghton to Rock Harbor on Tuesdays and Fridays, returning to Houghton the following day. Trip length is 6 1/2 hours. A ranger on board can help you plot your trip and issue your backcountry permit. For a fee, canoes, hand-loaded boats, and motorboats up to 20 feet long can be transported aboard. Reservations are required. Contact Isle Royale National Park, 87 N. Ripley Street, Houghton MI 49931 or call 906/482-0984.

Departing Copper Harbor, Michigan, the 81-foot, 100-passenger *Isle Royale Queen III* makes its 4 1/2-hour trip to the island from mid-May through September. This can be a rock-and-rolling ride during heavy seas. Canoes, hand-loaded boats, and motors can be carried for a fee. From mid-June through early-September, the *Queen III* makes roundtrip voyages every day except Wednesday and Sunday, adding Sunday departures to its schedule during July and August. Reservations are required. Contact Isle Royale Ferry Service, Copper Harbor, MI 49918 or call 906/482-4950 (winter) or 906/289-4437 (summer).

From Grand Portage, Minnesota, the 65-foot, 49-passenger *Wenonah* departs on Mondays, Wednesdays, and Fridays for the 2 1/2-hour one-way trip to Windigo. The *Wenonah* then proceeds to Rock Harbor, where it overnights before returning to Grand Portage on Tuesdays, Thursdays, and Sundays.

Sea plane service is available for up to five passengers from Houghton to Rock Harbor or Windigo. The flight takes only 45 minutes, but you may be delayed by fog on the island. Contact Isle Royale Seaplane Service, Box 371, Houghton, MI or call 906/482-8850.

GETTING AROUND

Backpackers can begin their Isle Royale hike at a location other than Rock Harbor or Windigo by boarding the 63-foot *Voyageur*, which circumnavigates Isle Royale in a clockwise direction. This is a great way to arrange a one-way hike or to access remote trailheads of the island. Contact Grand Portage-Isle Royale Transportation Lines, 1332 London Road, Box 754, Duluth, MN 55805 or call 218/728-1237.

LODGING

Housekeeping cottages and rooms in the Rock Harbor Lodge are available from mid-May through September at Rock Harbor. The Rock Harbor Lodge also offers a dining room, snack bar, gift shop, marina, sightseeing tours, and guided fishing excursions. Reservations are required. From mid-May through September write: National Park Concessions, Inc., Rock Harbor Lodge, Isle Royale National Park, P.O. Box 405, Houghton, MI 49931 or call 906/482-0984. During the off season, write National Park Concessions, Inc., Mammoth Cave, Kentucky, 42259.

CAMPING

Isle Royale is a great place to pitch a tent, but it's not suited for base camping. For example, campground stays are limited to only one night at Rock Harbor and to a maximum of five nights at Belle Isle. The Park Service expects visitors to the island to move from campground to campground, enjoying the wonderful variety the park offers.

Many of the park's interior campgrounds offer both tent pads and screened, three-sided shelters, each accommodating up to six people. During periods of rain, competition for the island's limited number of shelters is fierce, so it's best to begin hiking early in the day and secure a campsite early in the afternoon. A limited number of group camping sites can accommodate up to ten people. You must camp in the sites designated on your backcountry permit. If you arrive at a full campground, be prepared to move on.

Campfires are permitted on Isle Royale only where a metal fire grate is provided. Backpacking stoves are mandatory. All water, with the exception of water obtained from spigots at Rock Harbor or Windigo, should be filtered or boiled for two minutes prior to consumption.

PERMITS

All campers and boaters must secure a free permit upon arrival at Isle Royale. You must plan your itinerary in advance, but rangers can help you if you give them an idea of your interests and limitations.

HIKING AND BACKPACKING

Most visitors to Isle Royale National Park wisely arrive with a fully loaded backpack, because the park offers the best hiking opportunities in mid-America. Trips can be tailored to any skill level, but remember that the terrain of Isle Royale is rugged and demanding. The wilderness takes no pity on visitors with twisted ankles, insect welts, or throbbing sunburn. Those arriving with headnets, insect repellent, quality rain gear, waterproof tent, backpacking stove, and water filter will have a wonderful adventure on Isle Royale. Seasoned visitors often toss a wool cap, pile sweater, and winter gloves in their backpacks, because the island can get chilly even during July.

Day hikers staying at the Rock Harbor Lodge should bring a comfortable day pack, water bottle, and sturdy shoes. Those who rise with the songbirds will have plenty of chances to see wildlife right outside the lodge.

To avoid the busy campgrounds located within a day's hike of Rock Harbor, backpackers should consider boarding the *Voyageur* or the *Wenonah* to access remote trailheads. You'll see more wildlife, encounter fewer people, and find more open campsites by arranging for a backcountry drop off.

PADDLING

A sea kayak or canoe is as valuable to Isle Royale visitors as a pair of sturdy hiking boots. The island offers many choices to both canoeists and sea kayakers who are willing to bear the expense of bringing a boat to the island. It's worth the trouble. Portages, brutal as they may be, link nine lakes within the park's interior. Fishing for northern pike is productive on these remote lakes, and you'll have many opportunities to spot wildlife. A limited number of rental canoes are available from the Rock Harbor Lodge. All boaters should invest in nautical chart #14976, entitled "Isle Royale," which is available at park headquarters.

The Five Fingers Bay region in the park's northeastern corner provides stunning beauty and welcome protection to sea kayakers who brave the often-rough passage around Blake Point. This passage can be avoided by making a long, dreadful portage into Duncan Bay. Park rangers discourage paddlers from challenging the island's unprotected south shore, as campsites are spaced rather far apart, and protection from the fury of Lake Superior is minimal.

BOATING

Isle Royale offers 600 square miles of waterways for boating enthusiasts, allowing you to motor into a secluded harbor or troll for lake trout on Lake Superior. All boaters must, however, secure a permit upon arrival at the park.

The marina at Rock Harbor Lodge is open from mid-May through mid-September, and can accommodate boats up to 65 feet long. Boat gasoline and oil are available at Rock Harbor and Windigo. Channel 16 FM is monitored by the U.S. Coast Guard, and by Mott Island and Windigo ranger stations. Small motorboats are available for rent through the Rock Harbor Lodge, which maintains the marina. All boaters are advised to carry nautical chart #14976, "Isle Royale."

FORT WILKINS STATE PARK
U.S. 41 East
Copper Harbor, MI 49918
906/289-4315

Resting on a narrow strip of land near the tip of the Keweenaw Peninsula, Fort Wilkins State Park separates the waters of Lake Superior's Copper Harbor from inland Lake Fanny Hoe.

The old wooden fort still stands, surviving as a monument to the days when copper was king and force ruled the Keweenaw. The fort was built in 1844 to protect copper miners from the threat of Ojibwa Indians who were expected to make an attempt to reclaim the land that was taken from them.

This uprising never materialized, and the soldiers more often ended up protecting the raucous miners and prospectors from each other. Over 100 soldiers were stationed at the fort in 1845, but they soon discovered the hardship of winter in the Keweenaw frontier. By 1846, less than two years after it was built, Fort Wilkins was abandoned.

Although it was reoccupied briefly by soldiers returning from the Civil War, its true value lay in its wonderful location on an isthmus separating two bodies of water.

Today, visitors arrive at the park to tour the historic fort and ponder the rugged life of a soldier on the upper Michigan frontier. From mid-June through Labor Day, park staff members dressed in period costumes offer tours of the fort and recall its brief history and the life of its soldiers.

Camping is available within the park's two modern campgrounds, which offer a total of 165 campsites. The campground is a great place to stay before departing for Isle Royale National Park, as it offers a hot shower and easy access to the early morning ferry. It's best to reserve a campsite during July and August, because many visitors to the Keweenaw launch their exploration from this campground.

Besides encompassing two miles of shoreline along Lake Superior and Lake Fanny Hoe, Fort Wilkins State Park encompasses a number of islands and the Copper Harbor Lighthouse. Access to the restored lighthouse is difficult, since a boat is required. Check with park staff for details.

F.J. McLAIN STATE PARK
M-203
Hancock, MI 49930
906/482-0278

Sunset is the most popular time of the day at F.J. McLain State Park. Located on the western shore of the Keweenaw Peninsula, the park's shoreline bluff provides an excellent grandstand from which to enjoy a crimson sun over the endless waters of Lake Superior.

McLain's 100-site, modern campground is a popular destination for summer and fall visitors to the Keweenaw. Many arrive to enjoy the park's two miles of Lake Superior shoreline while camping on the bluff overlooking the lake. The park also offers 26 rustic campsites, but during July and August campers without reservations risk being turned away.

A sand beach, located on the Portage Lake Ship Canal and protected by a breakwater, appeals to sunbathers anxious to shake off a long midwestern winter. The breakwater also serves fishermen who try their luck casting spoons off the pier, hoping to coax a strike from a trout or salmon.

A three-mile hiking trail that begins at park headquarters skirts the shores of inland Bear Lake, while a two-mile fitness trail caters to those who wish to burn a little energy. Be sure you return in time to catch the sunset. It's the best show in the park.

In winter, novice skiers will enjoy the four-mile Bear Lake cross-country ski trail, as it's groomed and level.

PORCUPINE MOUNTAINS
Up the Porkies to a Lake in the Clouds

Through the Windshield

Departing Michigan's Keweenaw Peninsula, you're rolling into the Porcupine Mountains, where old-growth forests blanket the highest range of mountains between the Alleghenies and the Black Hills.

U.S. Highway 45 and M-38 converge in Ontonagon, gateway to "the Porkies," as this mountain range is affectionately dubbed by those who cherish its scenic views and rugged trails. Ontonagon serves as the western anchor of the Copper Range, and mining continues to play an important role in the local economy. A marina, located at the mouth of the Ontonagon River, serves boaters cruising the waters of Lake Superior in search of trophy lake trout or scenic shores. Upstream, the Ontonagon tumbles over a wide rock outcropping at Bond Falls, producing an awesome spectacle especially during winter.

Ontonagon serves travelers as a crossroads to adventure. Backpackers may wish to head west down M-64 toward Michigan's Porcupine Wilderness State Park (listed separately), while paddlers often can't resist heading south down U.S.45 to dip a blade in the pristine lakes of the Sylvania Wilderness (listed separately).

The route down U.S. 45 dissects the heart of the massive, 953,000-acre Ottawa National Forest (listed separately). The forest's 27 campgrounds provide overnight visitors access to lakes and streams where swimming, fishing, and boating are popular pastimes. At Bruce Crossing, Michigan highway M-28 intersects with U.S. 45, providing an east-west route through the Ottawa. East of Bruce Crossing at Sidnaw, scenic Forest Road 2200 provides both hikers and photographers access to the rapids and waterfalls of the Sturgeon River Gorge Wilderness (listed separately). A section of the North Country National Scenic Trail skirts the border of this wilderness, offering hikers a ribbon of trail through the remote and peaceful land of the Ottawa.

Highway 45 intersects U.S. 2 near the Sylvania visitor center. Open during the summer season, the center and its staff offer history, advice, and information about the Ottawa National Forest and its impressive resources. This is a great place to plan your canoe trip to the nearby lakes of the Sylvania Wilderness. Accessible by canoe, the 35 spring-fed lakes of the Sylvania Wilderness are linked by portage trails and surrounded by majestic stands of old-growth forest. A drive-in campground at Clark Lake features a beautiful sand beach that whets the appetite for a backcountry visit.

From Ontonagon, Highway M-64 parallels the Lake Superior shore before intersecting with M-107 at Silver City. Between 1872 and 1877, silver fever struck this area when a small find was uncovered. Mills were built to process the silver, but the dividends were few. Today, the only silver found at the village is the coinage left by travelers during their visit to the Porkies.

From Silver City, M-64 heads south to White, while scenic M-107 continues following the lakeshore to Porcupine Mountains State Park (listed separately). You'll need a Michigan state park vehicle permit to park your car at the end of M-107, but the view is well worth the price of admission. During the summer, visitors can purchase vehicle permits at the visitor center just off M-107 on South Boundary Road. The center provides a great introduction to the Porkies, featuring a slide show, maps, and camping information. At the end of M-107, a short stroll leads to a spectacular overlook of the famous Lake of the Clouds. The beautiful blue water of this lake is rimmed by an expansive green forest and drained by a pair of trout streams.

In winter, M-107 dead-ends at the Porkies ski area, ranked by many as the finest ski hill in mid-America. The hill caters to a wide variety of skill levels, offering runs of up to 6,000 feet. Over 20 miles of groomed cross-country ski trails surround the ski area, and a heated chalet delivers a cozy fire on a chilly winter day.

Travelers taking the southern route down M-64 will pass through White Pine, site of the world's largest underground copper mine. The mine doesn't offer tours, but the town of White Pine caters to visitors, offering lodging, restaurants, and a variety of shops.

Continuing through the village of Bergland, M-64 skirts the shores of Lake Gogebic, noted for its walleye fishing. Michigan's Gogebic State Park is situated along the shores, offering modern campsites, boating, swimming, and fishing opportunities.

You'll consider the small village of Merriweather aptly named if you've arrived to ski. Highway M-28 intersects M-64 at this small community, and M-64 in turn leads to Wakefield and the heart of upper Michigan's "Big Snow Country." Plenty of natural snowfall occurs here, and there are four major ski resorts within a short drive of Wakefield: Indianhead, Big Powderhorn, Blackjack, and Whitecap. For current snow conditions, call the Gogebic visitor's bureau snow line, 800/BSC-7000.

From Wakefield, a 16-mile spin up County Road 519 leads to the picturesque Presque Isle River, at the western boundary of Porcupine Mountains Wilderness Park. Hiking trails provide access to views of the river's beautiful cascades, and a modern campground is situated along the shores of Lake Superior.

U.S. 2 heads west from Wakefield, taking Circle Tour drivers into Bessemer and Ironwood. En route, an excellent sidetrack down County Route 513 leads to Black River Harbor, part of the Ottawa National Forest. You'll benefit from an overnight visit to the Black River Harbor, as there's a great deal to do and see. Trails along the river offer views of its seven magnificent waterfalls, and a well-developed national forest campground offers camping opportunities. Fishing charters are available at the mouth of the river, and a boat launch and marina can accommodate virtually any boat. The Black River Campground is an excellent location from which to plan the next leg of your adventure, as we'll soon be entering Wisconsin, home of the Apostle Islands.

OTTAWA NATIONAL FOREST
2100 E. Cloverland Drive
Ironwood, MI 49938
906/932-1330
800/562-1201 (Upper Michigan)

The Ottawa National Forest is a robust land of tall trees, wild rivers, and clear lakes situated in the heart of Lake Superior's "Big Snow Country."

Annual snowfall in the forest averages 200 inches, attracting snowmobilers, cross-country skiers, snowshoers, and winter campers. Within its 954,000 acres, the Ottawa also harbors more than 500 lakes and 1500 miles of rivers and streams. These waters are home to trout, salmon, walleye, northern pike, and bass.

A 106-mile section of the North Country Trail traverses the Ottawa, allowing hikers to step back in time and enjoy the natural world. The trail runs the width of the northern tier of the forest, between the towns of Kenton on the east and Bessemer on the west. Camping is permitted anywhere along the trail, but those who tackle it should be completely self-sufficient.

The Black River Harbor recreation area, located 15 miles north of Bessemer, is one of the most scenic parts of the Ottawa National Forest. The Black River flows through a forest of huge pine, hemlock, and hardwood trees. It cascades in a series of waterfalls as it drops to meet Lake Superior. Stairways and observation platforms overlook the Black River and the scenic Gorge and Potawatomi waterfalls. The harbor offers one of the area's few access points to Lake Superior, providing a boat ramp. A forty-unit campground accessible by paved road allows visitors to linger in the area and enjoy its wonderful scenery.

The history of the Ottawa is steeped in ice, axe, pick, and shovel. Some 10,000 years ago, glacial sheets from the Wisconsin Ice Age covered the land of the Ottawa. As the glaciers retreated, they left in their wake the rolling hills, bedrock outcrops, deep river valleys, lakes, and wetlands that we enjoy today.

When the first Europeans arrived here, they found mature pine, hemlock, sugar maple, and yellow birch forests. Logging during the late 1800s and early 1900s, followed by wildfires, drastically altered the complexion of the forest. Today aspen, paper birch, and balsam fir trees dominate much of the forest. Logging and forest industry products continue to be an important source of income to those who depend on the Ottawa for a livelihood.

Native Americans mined and traded copper long before the arrival of Europeans. Copper artifacts that originated in the Upper Peninsula have been discovered elsewhere in North America, indicating their value as trade items. Remnants of the first European mining enterprises can be found in protected depressions and foundations scattered throughout the Ottawa. These hardy miners depended on black powder, picks, and shovels to carve a living from the often-hostile wilderness that surrounded them.

Today, the Ottawa National Forest offers 27 campgrounds to visitors. Whether you plan to spend a day or a month in the western Upper Peninsula, you're sure to find a road to follow, a trail to ski, or a lake to paddle in the land of the Ottawa.

MAPS

An excellent map of the Ottawa National Forest is available for a small fee from the park headquarters. This map identifies public land within the forest and features campgrounds, suggested canoe routes, and scenic drives.

DRIVE-IN CAMPGROUNDS

The 27 drive-in campgrounds of the Ottawa National Forest offer visitors a wide spectrum of camping opportunities. All are accessible by road, serving both tent and trailer campers. Most are located on lakes or streams that offer fishing and swimming. Several, such as the campground at Bobcat Lake, contain beaches with changing facilities.

All campgrounds within the Ottawa offer picnic tables, tent pads, fire grates, and toilet facilities. Most have drinking water and can accommodate trailers up to 22 feet in length. Campers planning to stay at Blockhouse, Burned Dam, and Paint River Forks should plan to bring their own water, as there is no safe water supply available at these campgrounds. Most of the campgrounds within the forest open in mid-May. Bob and Courtney Lake campgrounds, along with the Clark Lake Campground located at the edge of the Sylvania Wilderness, open the last week in May. Most campgrounds close after Labor Day, though a few remain open into the fall.

The three campgrounds with the most highly developed facilities are Lake Ottawa, Sylvania (Clark Lake), and Black River. Each has a paved access road, pressurized water system, and flush toilets. Black River and Lake Ottawa also have trailer dump stations. No showers or electricity are available. Other campgrounds within the forest range in size from 3 to 41 sites, offering more rustic facilities and, often, greater solitude. A nightly fee is charged at all campgrounds except those at Burned Dam, Robbins Pond, Matchwood Tower, Paint River Forks, and Blockhouse.

RESERVATIONS

Campground reservations are accepted through the Mistix Reservation System by calling 800/283-CAMP for campsites at Norway Lake, Perch Lake, and Lake Ste. Kathryn. Reservations for campsites within the Sylvania Wilderness must be made directly with the Sylvania visitor center (listed separately). All other campgrounds within the Ottawa National Forest are open on a first-come, first-served basis.

Information concerning campgrounds can be obtained at any time of the year by calling or writing the forest supervisor's office.

HIKING

There's something for everyone who wishes to take a hike in the Ottawa National Forest. Nearly 200 miles of hiking and backpacking trails cross the forest, the trails ranging from short, easy walks to waterfalls and historic sites to multi-day backpacking trips.

Some of the forest's most popular trails are located in the Black River Harbor area, north of Bessemer and Ironwood in Gogebic County. These trails vary in length from 1/4 to 1 1/2 miles, providing access to Great Conglomerate, Gorge Potawatomi, Sandstone, and Rainbow Falls. All trails descend rather steeply from the rim of the Black River gorge to overlook points beyond.

Over 100 miles of the North Country National Scenic Trail cross the Ottawa National Forest in an east-west direction. When completed, the North Country Trail will extend for 3,000 miles, linking the Appalachian Trail in Vermont to the Lewis and Clark Trail in North Dakota. The North Country Trail is challenging, as most stream crossings must be made without bridges. It's best to contact the forest supervisor's office in Ironwood and secure a detailed trail guide before tackling this route.

In addition to its outstanding canoeing opportunities, the Sylvania Wilderness near Watersmeet also offers nearly 30 miles of foot trails. These trails traverse old-growth forests along the shores of several lakes. They're well-suited for both day hiking and overnight trips. Overnight campers must stay at one of the area's 81 designated campsites.

PADDLING AND FISHING

With over 500 lakes and 1800 miles of streams, the Ottawa National Forest offers plenty of paddling and fishing adventures.

Michigan Highway 28 separates two types of canoeing within the forest. South of M-28 the forest is relatively flat, and hundreds of small lakes dot the landscape as you approach the Wisconsin border. Rivers in this section of the Ottawa generally offer quietwater with only moderate currents or small rapids. In contrast, the area lying north of M-28 is rugged, with many high hills and ridges. Rivers in this section are beginning their descent to Lake Superior. Here, fast water, rock ledges, and waterfalls that demand portages are common.

During spring run-off, the rivers of the Ottawa flow fast and furious. Quietwater rivers can become dangerous torrents, demanding your respect. However, these same rivers may be so low during summer that canoeing is impossible.

The Presque Isle River usually has ample water all summer long. Beginners who have some paddling experience should have no trouble on the section below M-28. Paddling above M-28 is not recommended. The put-ins for the most popular trips are located off Forest Road 8100 on the west branch north of the Henry Lake Campground, or on the east branch south of Hawk Lake one mile west of Michigan Highway 64. The branches join south of Marenisco. The trip from there has a long portage at Yondata Falls. Fishing for trout and northern pike can be very productive.

Other rivers suitable for paddling include the Ontonagon and its east and west branches, as well as the Paint and Brule rivers. The forest supervisor's office in Ironwood offers a rather detailed guide to paddling these rivers, and it's best to secure both the guide and current water level information prior to making your visit.

STURGEON RIVER GORGE WILDERNESS
Ottawa National Forest
Kenton Ranger District
Kenton, MI 49943
906/852-3501

Steep-sided rock walls up to 300 feet high and one mile wide enclose the Sturgeon River and its tributaries. Volcanic rock outcrops above the 20-foot Sturgeon Falls and overlooks on the gorges's eastern rim provide panoramas of the gorge, the river, its whitewater rapids, and the falls.

Access to this 14,139-acre wilderness is primarily via Highway M-28 and Forest Road 2200 from Sidnaw, Michigan. A nine-unit national forest drive-in campground is located just outside the wilderness boundary along F.R. 2200. This rustic campground serves as a great base from which to explore the gorge and its wilderness interior. No-trace hiking and backcountry camping are permitted throughout the wilderness, but there are no established trails. Hikers wishing to access the interior should be equipped with a topographical map and compass, as the overgrown logging roads that cross the wilderness are difficult to find and harder to follow. A segment of the North Country National Scenic Trail parallels the northern and eastern boundaries of the wilderness.

Those exploring the rugged interior of the gorge will relish the waterfalls, rapids, oxbow, and terraces of the Sturgeon River. With the exception of a few bare slopes created by natural erosion, most of the area is forested with a mixture of pine, hemlock, aspen, sugar maple, birch, and basswood trees. The variety of trees provides an array of color during autumn that peaks in the latter half of September. The rim of the gorge provides the best viewing opportunities. A parking area north of the gorge provides a vista from Silver Mountain, and a spur trail has been proposed that would allow hikers to crest its peak.

The Sturgeon River and its tributaries are primarily trout streams, although they're not highly productive. However, anglers who value the sight of an osprey or eagle fishing beside them will enjoy dipping a line in the Sturgeon.

Skilled whitewater paddlers can canoe and kayak the 13 miles of river through the gorge during spring run-off or in fall when the river is running high. It's best to call the Kenton Ranger District of the Ottawa National Forest before leaving home. You should also be sure of your skills before pushing off the river's banks.

SYLVANIA WILDERNESS
Ottawa National Forest
Watersmeet Ranger District
Watersmeet, MI 49969
906-358-4551

Like stars fallen from the sky, the clear, blue-green lakes of the Sylvania Wilderness sparkle among the hills of the ancient forest surrounding them. Dipping a paddle in these deep, pristine waters is truly a wilderness delight.

Nearly all of Sylvania's 36 named lakes are landlocked, fed by springs, bogs, rain, and snow. Rimmed by magnificent old-growth trees and speckled with white sand beaches, the Sylvania bears comparison to its larger and better-known Lake Superior neighbor, the Boundary Waters Canoe Area Wilderness.

The interior lakes of the Sylvania are linked by canoe portage trails, allowing paddlers to base camp, then explore with empty boats. Hiking trails traverse the interior, following rugged roads that once provided access to private cabins that dotted the lakes.

Scattered patches of ancient white pine, Michigan's state tree, tower above the landscape, but most of the area is cloaked in virgin northern hardwood forest. These hemlock, yellow birch, basswood, and sugar maple trees twinkle with color each fall, creating a wonderful spectacle for mid-September visitors.

A stroll through the Sylvania forest allows visitors to step back and enjoy a glimpse of mid-America prior to European settlement. Many of Sylvania's trees are over 200 years old, and a few date back to the 1500s, offering a portrait of our natural history.

Of Sylvania's 36 lakes, six cover more than 250 acres. Numerous smaller lakes, ponds, and bogs are scattered throughout the region. The Sylvania lies on the divide between the Lake Superior and

Mississippi drainage basins, yet most of these wilderness lakes have no outlet. Due to this closed environment, the large, older fish of these lakes require special protection to ensure their survival. Bass fishing is excellent on the lakes of the Sylvania, but fishermen are required to release their catch unharmed.

Wildlife is abundant, and quiet paddlers may encounter white-tailed deer, black bears, otters, fishers, and coyotes. Waterfowl and woodland birds including bald eagles, loons, and osprey are frequently sighted by patient visitors.

From the last glacier's retreat until the late 1800s, little is known about Sylvania's history. Artifacts from prehistoric peoples have been found, but a comprehensive cultural survey has not been completed.

We do know that A.D. Johnston, a Wisconsin timber speculator, purchased 80 acres near the south end of Clark Lake in 1895, planning to cut pine. After visiting the property, however, Johnston decided it was too beautiful to cut. Instead, he built his home there. Shortly thereafter, Johnston invited a few friends to visit and fish lakes that have since become quite famous for smallmouth bass. These friends, executives of Pennsylvania's U.S. Steel, then purchased adjacent lands and formed the Sylvania Club, naming it in honor of their home state.

Under private ownership, the Sylvania tract was spared the logger's axe and escaped the fires that swept across the surrounding land, perhaps because it was green and growing. The Sylvania Club also hired caretakers to put out fires and guard the lakes from trespassers. Many stories have been told about people sneaking in to fish, only to have a warning shot fired in their direction by hired guards. The Sylvania Club built lodges, cabins, and bathhouses on the larger lakes, together with a road system to connect them.

Ownership changed hands through the years, but by 1960 Larry Fisher owned three-quarters interest, with C.M. Christiansen controlling the remaining quarter. After the death of these men, the Fisher heirs indicated that they wished to dispose of their interest in the property.

In 1966, the federal government purchased the Sylvania tract at a cost of $5,740,000, opening the area to the public in the following year. Today, few wilderness areas east of the Mississippi compare to Sylvania. Paddlers can skip from lake to lake via portage trails, swimming and fishing along their route. Backpackers can hike the old Sylvania Club roads, walking beneath majestic trees and startling ruffed grouse along the trail. Car campers can pull into a campground on the edge of the wilderness and enjoy a picnic while the children swim nearby.

ACCESS

The entrance to Sylvania is located four miles west of Wastersmeet, Michigan, on U.S. Highway 2. Access is by County Road #535, which skirts the north portion of the wilderness. Signs along the road will direct you to your destination. From Memorial Day through Labor Day, an attendant is stationed at the Sylvania information station from 7:30 a.m. to 4 p.m. Boat landings are located on Crooked, Clark, and Long lakes. You must use the parking areas provided.

The Sylvania visitor center is located at the intersection of U.S. Highways 2 and 45. The staff there is prepared to answer your questions and offer advice on the Sylvania Wilderness and other attractions of the Ottawa National Forest.

For lodging accommodations or information on canoe rentals and outfitting, write the Watersmeet Chamber of Commerce, Watersmeet, MI 49969.

DRIVE-IN CAMPGROUNDS

Adjacent to the Sylvania Wilderness, the Sylvania Recreation Area provides a 48-unit drive-in campground on Clark Lake (fee charged). Running water, flush toilets, sand beach, picnic area, and access to the wilderness makes this a very appealing campground. Open from Memorial Day through Labor Day.

BACKCOUNTRY CAMPING AND PERMITS

Unfortunately, our love of the Sylvania is having an impact. The area was once one of Michigan's best-kept wilderness secrets, but the increasing number of visitors discovering the Sylvania each year are taking a toll on this fragile land. Permits are required of overnight visitors, and travelers must do their best to lessen their impact. Those who travel quietly, step lightly, and visit off season will discover the Sylvania of yesterday, and will find themselves surrounded by an ancient forest on a moonlit night.

In 1987, 18,327 acres of the 21,000-acre Sylvania Recreation Area were designated by Congress as wilderness, an area where nature comes first and man is only a visitor. To better protect the values of the Sylvania, new rules went into effect in 1992, and visitors must be aware of these.

From May 15 to September 15, all visitors to the Sylvania must register, and those planning to camp are required to secure a permit prior to pitching a tent. Camp reservations should be secured in advance to avoid disappointment upon arrival. Campers must use only designated campsites, and cooking is restricted to these campsites. Backpacking stoves are recommended, since fire grates at some campsites will be removed. Cans, bottles, styrofoam containers, and pets are banned from the backcountry. Mountain biking and mechanical portaging are also disallowed.

To protect nesting loons, landing on islands will be prohibited from ice-off to July 15. Motor size on Crooked Lake is limited to 25 horsepower, and no-wake zones have been established.

RESERVATIONS

In 1992, the Sylvania visitor center began accepting reservations for its 81 wilderness campsites. Subject to change, reservations ($5 fee) are currently accepted by mail only from January 15 to February 1, for camping dates between May 15 and September 15. After February 1, reservations are accepted by visiting, writing, or calling the Sylvania Visitor Center, Ottawa National Forest, Watersmeet, MI 49969. The phone number is 906/358-4742.

FISHING

Fishing is a popular sport in the Sylvania Wilderness, and bass fishing can be excellent. Because the clear waters of the Sylvania do not contain much food, special regulations exist to protect the slow-growing fish of these unique lakes. Only artificial lures are allowed, and bass must be released unharmed. The use of barbless hooks is encouraged. Other species can be taken if certain size restrictions are met. Check with rangers for details.

CROSS-COUNTRY SKIING

Deep snow and few visitors add to the winter appeal of cross-country skiing in the Sylvania Wilderness. Ski trails through the Sylvania are not groomed, but skiers frequently break trail. Winter camping is wonderful for those with the equipment and attitude to enjoy a campfire in the snow.

PORCUPINE MOUNTAINS WILDERNESS STATE PARK
599 M-107
Ontonagon, MI 49953
906/885-5275

Upper Michigan's Porcupine Mountains rise from the shores of Lake Superior to cradle clear lakes and virgin timber in a wilderness setting that's laced by hiking trails and sprinkled with rustic cabins.

Those seeking adventure need only shoulder a backpack to disappear beneath the old growth and step back into Michigan's past. Harboring over 65,000 acres of woods and water, the Porkies encompass four inland lakes, numerous trout streams, and an impressive 26-mile section of Lake Superior shoreline.

Access to the eastern section of the park is via M-107, seventeen miles west of Ontonagon. In winter this road dead-ends at the park's famous ski area, but summer visitors will find the highway continues to within strolling distance of the Lake of the Clouds Overlook, one of

Michigan's most beloved scenic attractions. Perched on a 300-foot rock escarpment, visitors contemplate shimmering Lake of the Clouds, which unfolds beneath them as turkey vultures soar overhead.

The South Boundary Road provides a 26-mile long link between the visitor center, located on the eastern end of the park, and the popular Presque Isle Campground, situated near the park's western border. The visitor center is an excellent first stop for travelers. A multi-image slide show takes you on an "arm chair adventure" through the Porkies while you're planning your visit. Maps, permits, and camping and cabin information is also available. During winter, sections of the South Boundary Road often remain unplowed, so visitors should plan accordingly.

At Presque Isle Campground, the Summit Peak Road exits South Boundary Road 13 miles from M-107. This spur road leads travelers to a pair of observation towers that overlook the heart of the Porkies. After an easy 1/2-mile hike down a well-trodden path, you'll reach the Summit Observation Towers, which straddle Summit Peak. Panoramic views of Lake Superior and Wisconsin's Apostle Islands are here for your viewing pleasure. At 1,958 feet, Summit Peak is the highest point in the park, serving as the forested crown of the highest range of mountains between the Alleghenies and the Black Hills.

South Boundary Road continues to bypass backcountry trailheads that afford hiking access to backpackers and interior cabin users. It joins County Road 519 about one mile south of the Presque Isle Campground at the western fringe of the park. From Wakefield and U.S. 2, it's a 16-mile trip up Country 519 to the mouth of the Presque Isle River, another famous attraction. The developed, drive-in campground near Presque Isle Falls is popular with overnight visitors, and reservations may be necessary during the busy months of July and August.

The Presque Isle Campground is one of many points backpackers use to access the park's 87 miles of hiking trails. Those without the equipment, skill, or desire to pitch a tent in the park's rugged interior can enjoy backcountry beauty from the comfort of the park's 16 rustic "Trailside Cabins." These cabins, accessible by foot trail, offer bunks, a woodstove, and a dry roof on a rainy day. The park is also served by five drive-in campgrounds with sites that range from modern units complete with showers to more rustic offerings.

The abundant snowfall that blankets the Porkies between December and March makes the park a favorite winter destination for downhill, telemark, and cross-country skiers. Downhill slopes carved from the mountain's forests cater to both experts and beginners, offering some of the longest runs and highest vertical drops in mid-America. The Porkies also offer high-capacity chairlifts and views of the surrounding wilderness, making it (according to many skiers) the best alpine terrain in mid-America. The park's reasonable lift ticket rates and spectacular views have kept generations of skiers returning year after year.

Cross-country and backcountry skiers will also find challenging groomed trails and ample room within the park's interior. A special discounted one-lift ticket allows cross-country skiers to avoid the climb up the mountain and begin at the park's alpine peak.

The Porcupine Mountains were so named because the range is thought to resemble a porcupine hunched over the shores of Lake Superior. The appearance of the area today is much as it was over a century ago, when treasure-seeking miners took to these hills in search of copper. Miners first tunneled into the mountains during the 1850s. After failing to discover large deposits of rich copper ore, the enterprises were eventually abandoned. Silver also attracted the interest of mining entrepreneurs, but a mine opened at what is now called "Silver City" also failed to produce a profit.

Today, visitors to the Porkies seek riches not in the park's mineral wealth, but in its natural beauty. The mountains themselves, roughly paralleling Lake Superior, consist of a spectacular series of irregular ranges rising to heights of nearly 2,000 feet. For the most part, these slopes are covered with an impressive stand of hardwood—hemlock coupled with scattered patches of pine, maple, birch, and basswood. From the escarpment trail, Lake of the Clouds mirrors the sky brilliantly as hikers feel the weight of their packs lighten thanks to the beauty below. Draining the lakes, the Carp and Little Carp rivers have carved deep valleys between high hills reaching to the shores of Lake Superior.

Meanwhile, at the southwestern boundary of the park, the Presque Isle River impresses all who visit, as it plunges through narrow gorges in a torrent of swirling foam, cascading over shelves of sandstone to find an outlet at Lake Superior.

Due to its demanding topography, the Porkies managed to elude the axes of 19th-century lumberjacks, who were unable to pay the demanding price of harvesting its forested slopes. As the 1940s rolled around however, wartime demand for wood reached its peak. Loggers again began eyeing the virgin timber of the Porcupine Mountains. Aware of this mounting pressure, Michigan's Conservation Commission intervened, declaring that the purchase of the Porkies should not be delayed, since "logging companies are nibbling at the fringes and promise to invade the interior at an early date." Acquisition of the Porkies began a year after the commission issued its report.

Today, Porcupine Mountains Wilderness State Park preserves Michigan's last stand of mixed hardwoods and hemlock within a living museum of woods, water, and wildlife.

INSECTS

The Porcupine Mountains have a robust insect population. Visitors arriving in May, June, and early July should be equipped with headnets, long sleeves, and insect repellent.

MAPS

Park maps are available at the visitor center, or from park headquarters. These maps show the trails and cabin locations, but they do not indicate the topography. Backpackers should consider purchasing topographic maps, or should study the 3-D relief model at the visitor center prior to hitting the trail.

INFORMATION CENTERS

To reach the park's visitor center on South Boundary Road, watch for the sign just off M-107. This should be the first stop for visitors to the park. An excellent slide presentation reveals the park's attractions and history. You'll also find maps, backcountry permits, advice, and even a scale model of the park available at the center, along with information regarding the area's rich natural history.

CAMPING

Porcupine Mountains Wilderness State Park maintains two modern campgrounds and three rustic, drive-in units. Showers are available at both the 95-unit Union Bay Campground, located on M-107 near the visitor center, and the 88-unit Presque Isle Campground, on the park's western edge at the end of County Road 519. The Union Bay Campground is the only campground in the park that offers electricity.

It's best to secure reservations during July and August by calling park headquarters prior to your visit.

The small, rustic campgrounds that the park considers "outposts" are also available for those seeking a bit more privacy, or for use as overflow when the popular modern campgrounds are filled.

Winter campers planning a trip to the Porkies will find massive snow and ice sculptures, a sparkling landscape, and often deep, fresh powder. They'll also find temperatures that can dip to 40 degrees below zero, coupled with frigid wind chills.

Prior to departure, winter campers must register at the ski chalet, file an itinerary, and pay the required camping fee. Depending on your destination, both snowshoes and backcountry skis may be recommended. Camping and winter campfires are permitted anywhere in the wilderness.

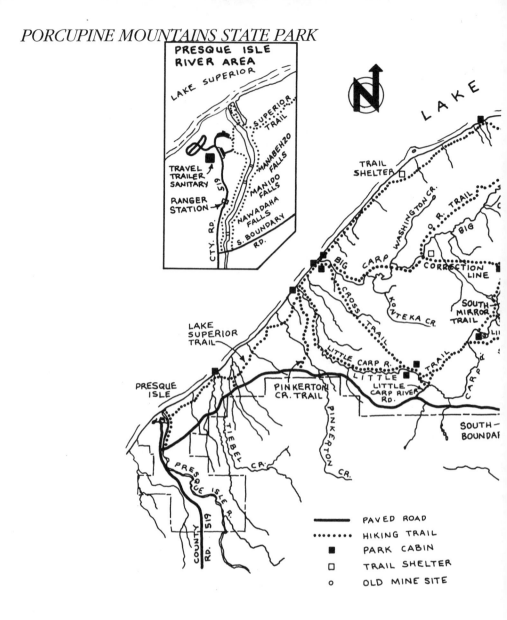

TRAILSIDE CABINS

The park's 16 trailside cabins, located deep within the interior of the Porcupine Mountains, provide backcountry access to visitors seeking the comfort of a rustic shelter.

The cabins are available for rental between April 1 and November 30. Three have now been opened for winter rental as well. Access is gained by foot trail only. The closest cabins are located one mile from the nearest trailhead, with the most remote located four miles in. There's one eight-bunk cabin at Mirror Lake, but most accommodate four guests.

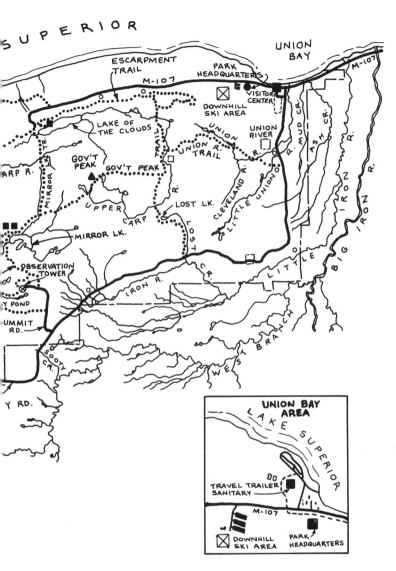

Bunks and mattresses are provided, but pillows and linens are not. It's best to pack in a sleeping bag. Woodstoves provide heat, but should be augmented by a portable cookstove because the stoves are not particularly well-suited for cooking. Due to the distance from modern utilities, conveniences such as electricity and running water are not supplied. Only water taken from the park's modern campgrounds is considered safe to drink. Water from other sources—from creeks, lakes, and springs, for example—should be boiled or filtered.

The trailside cabins are extremely popular during the summer months and fall colors. Cabin reservations can be made up to 366 days in advance, and it's always best to make reservations at least two months in advance. Telephone reservations are accepted, but are not confirmed until payment is received.

BACKPACKING

The Porcupine Mountains are ideal for backpacking. Be advised, however, that the trails are demanding. You'll encounter ankle-deep mud, unbridged stream crossings, and hungry black flies. The rewards include pristine streams, towering trees, and grand vistas.

Prior to hitting the trail, be sure to pick up a backcountry permit (fee charged) available at either the visitor center or park headquarters. With your permit in your possession, you may travel and camp anywhere in the interior of the park, except within a quarter of a mile of roads, cabins, or shelters.

There are three free trailside shelters available to backpackers on a first-come, first-served basis: one on the Lake Superior Trail, one on the Correction Line Trail, and one on the Govern Peak Trail. These shelters are popular and hikers must carry a waterproof tent with them, as there's no guarantee that the shelters will be open when you arrive.

The Porkies are noted for a large population of black bears. Campers who fail to adequately protect their food invite an unwanted visit from these animals.

The Lake Superior Trail is the longest, most challenging trail in the park. It follows the rocky shore of Lake Superior for 16 miles, offering many outstanding views.

The four-mile Escarpment Trail is considered by many to be the park's most spectacular trail, because it offers outstanding views of Lake of the Clouds. If time permits, backpackers hiking the Porkies for the first time should consider planning a circle hike that includes sections of both the Lake Superior Trail and the Escarpment Trail.

Brook trout fishermen will enjoy both the 11-mile Little Carp River Trail and the 9-mile Big Carp River Trail. Don't let the names fool you. Both of these rivers are noted for their excellent brook trout fishing.

These trails represent just a few of the many that traverse the rugged hills of the Porkies. Hikers often combine trail sections to create circular loops. An ideal route might begin on the park's escarpment, touch the Lake Superior shore, and follow one of the park's many trout streams to an interior lake before leading back to civilization.

WINTER SPORTS

Located in the Lake Superior "snowbelt," the Porcupine Mountains offer some of the finest downhill skiing in mid-America. With a 600-foot vertical drop and nearly 200 inches of annual snowfall, the Porkies region is a winter-lover's paradise. A pair of chair lifts, a cozy chalet, and reasonable lift ticket prices keep skiers coming back.

Cross-country skiers will find 23 miles of groomed ski trails, while backcountry skiers encounter plenty of virgin powder deep within the park's interior. A specially priced, one-ride lift ticket gives skiers quick access to the center of the Porkies without a heart-pounding uphill climb.

Overnight lodging is available in three of the trailside cabins, and in the nearby communities of Silver City, White Pine, and Ontonagon. For information, contact the Porcupine Mountain Promotional Chamber, P.O. Box 493, White Pine, MI 49971 or call them at 906/885-5885.

THE APOSTLES
Superior's South Shore

Through the Windshield

Sand beaches and pillars of stone. Historic lighthouses and crashing waves. Sea caves and sailboats, silhouetted against a setting sun. These are the among the sights that await you on Lake Superior's south shore, home of Wisconsin's Apostle Islands.

The story of Lake Superior's south shore is inseparable from the story of the Great Lakes. Inhabited by native Americans for nearly 12,000 years, the Wisconsin shores of Lake Superior were first seen by Europeans in their search for a water route to the Orient. French explorers plied the waters of almost every navigable stream along Wisconsin's coasts, little realizing that these same streams would soon become waterways of commerce for a growing nation.

The area's abundant natural resources have always attracted the attention of speculative pioneers. At first, it was the lure of the valuable beaver pelt. Then the magnificent white pine became valuable—even necessary—for an expanding nation, before industrial growth led to the need for iron and copper ore. All of these resources provided boom periods for the south shore of the lake and were the major impetus for the area's settlement and development. Unfortunately, they were over-utilized, because exploitation—not conservation—was the rule of the era.

Later in Wisconsin's story, lumbering, mining, manufacturing, and many other pursuits all relied on the easy transportation provided by the Great Lakes. River mouths and natural harbors, long the favorite locations for Indian camps, were chosen as ideal sites for white settlements. Soon these coastal hamlets became thriving cities. The days in which Goodrich steamships brought daily mail and supplies to every village on the Lake Superior coast are gone, but today as we tour the south shore we'll see windows into the past, and a glimpse of the future.

Rambling out of Michigan, U.S. 2 crosses the Wisconsin border separating the city of Ironwood, Michigan from Hurley, Wisconsin. Situated along the banks of the Montreal River, Hurley is known as the "queen of the north woods." Notorious for its bawdy "red light district" during the lumber era, Hurley today enjoys a more wholesome reputation based on its cordial hospitality to winter visitors who relish the area's abundant snowfall. Just south of Hurley at Whitecap Mountain, downhill skiers will find a wide variety of runs catering to both beginners and experts. Whitecap is located off Highway 77 at Montreal.

Historic Ashland, cradled along the shores of Lake Superior's Chequamegon Bay, is the next stop on your Circle Tour. U.S. 2 leads directly through this thriving city of over 9,000, a community that serves as home to Ashland College and the Sigurd Olson Institute of Environmental Studies.

In 1854, Asaph Whittlesey built the first home here and became Ashland's first permanent white settler. Later, during the heyday of lumbering and mining in the 1890s, Ashland was the third-largest port on the entire Great Lakes, and had shipped a total of ten million tons of Gogebic iron ore. Today, Ashland's waterfront is important not as a Great Lakes port, but as a recreational center for pleasure boaters, windsurfers, and fishermen enjoying the protected waters of Chequamegon Bay. Residents celebrate this wonderful resource during the annual "Bay Days" festival in mid-July. An exciting sailboat race from Bayfield to Ashland tops the agenda, and bicyclists may wish to enter the 40-mile race from Ashland to Benoit. Runners compete in a 15K race, and everyone enjoys the ethnic foods served during the event. Before leaving Ashland, those longing for a swim will find an inviting beach, picnicking spot, and RV camp at Jean Kreher Park.

Just west of the city, Highway 13 arcs up Chequamegon Bay to climb the Bayfield Peninsula, gateway to Apostle Islands National Lakeshore (listed separately). The Apostles are a land of sea caves and stone cliffs, sand beaches and black bears. Each summer the National Park Service welcomes thousands of visitors to the Apostle Islands, and most begin their exploration of the archipelago from the village of Bayfield.

En route to Bayfield, Highway 13 crosses Fish Creek Slough. This 1,000-acre natural area is an important wetland, as it provides outstanding habitat for waterfowl and fur-bearing animals.

Midway to Bayfield, the community of Washburn rests along the shores of Chequamegon Bay. Known to its residents as "just a little town on the Big Lake," Washburn has the kind of small-town charm for which northern Wisconsin is noted. Sailing and fishing charters for excursions on Lake Superior are available from Washburn's city-owned marina. A pair of city-operated campgrounds are located at Memorial and West End parks, providing showers and electrical hookups. Call 715/373-5645 for reservations.

Washburn also serves as one of the gateways to the nearby Chequamegon National Forest. This 854,000-acre forest takes its name from an Ojibwa (Chippewa) term meaning "place of shallow water," which refers to the Superior's Chequamegon Bay. Campsites within the national forest are available at the Birch Grove Campground, located about 15 miles west of Washburn via Highway C and forest roads 252 and 435.

When the snow is falling, you'll find groomed cross-country ski trails traversing the forest ten miles west of Washburn on County C at the Valhalla Winter Sports Area.

Before putting your skis away, check out Mt. Ashwabay, north of Washburn off Highway 13 (fee charged). Located just two miles south of Bayfield, Mt. Ashwabay offers both cross-county and downhill skiing, rewarding all who visit with winter views of the nearby Apostle Islands. Mt. Ashwabay's 40 kilometers of cross-country trails cater to both beginners and experts, with trails groomed for classic and skate skiing. A t-bar and 4 rope tows serve downhill skiers on the hill's 11 Alpine runs. For information, call 715/779-3227.

During the summer, Mt. Ashwabay brings culture under canvas by hosting Lake Superior's Big Top Chautauqua (fee charged). From mid-June through early September, programs combine music, legend, history, and lore to entertain visitors beneath an all-weather canvas tent, to the delight of sell-out crowds.

Rolling into the vacation village of Bayfield, you'll find the beauty of New England combined with the charm of Wisconsin. Bayfield serves as headquarters of the Apostle Islands National Lakeshore (listed separately), and most visitors depart on their island adventures from this scenic port.

Bayfield is Wisconsin's sailing capital. Many charter operations offer both sailing lessons and captained vessels for those wishing to join the white-masted fleet patrolling the protected waters offshore.

Steeped in history and rich in culture, Bayfield contains impressive architecture that allows visitors to reflect on the days when nearby brownstone quarries provided the building blocks for a growing nation. "Brownstone and Bargeboard," a historic guide published by the chamber of commerce, takes visitors on a walking tour past 25 of Bayfield's well-known architectural treasures.

Many visitors plan their tour of Bayfield so that it coincides with the village's annual Apple Festival in early October. The festival occurs during autumn colors, and allows visitors to sample apple treats from the orchards that dot the peninsula.

Accommodations in Bayfield range from historic bed and breakfast mansions to tent sites overlooking the national lakeshore. Located just three miles north of Bayfield on the shores of Lake Superior, the rustic 30-site, city-run Dalrymple Campground is a popular overnight spot for tent campers who are preparing for a trip to the Apostle Islands.

The best place to begin your visit to Apostle Islands National Lakeshore is at the park's visitor center, located in Bayfield's historic old brownstone courthouse. Here you can arrange transportation to the islands, plan a mainland trip, or just enjoy the interesting interpretive displays.

Bayfield is also the launching point for excursions to nearby Madeline Island (listed separately). Madeline is the largest of the 22 Apostle Islands, and is the only island within the chain that's not preserved as national lakeshore. A 15-minute car ferry ride from Bayfield takes visitors to Madeline Island's year-round village of La Pointe. Many of the island's attractions, including a beach, restaurant, and historical museum, are within walking distance of the ferry dock. If you plan to explore Big Bay State Park or Big Bay Island Town Park, both located on Madeline's eastern shore, you'll have to bring your car or bicycle, because it's a seven-mile trek to the park. Big Bay State

Park offers a 55-unit campground and a wonderful 1.5-mile sand beach. This park is very popular during July and August, so it's best to check campsite availability or secure reservations before leaving the mainland. Mail reservations are suggested. For further information, call 715/779-3346.

Adjacent to the state park, the town of LaPoint operates Big Bay Island Park. You won't need a state park vehicle permit to camp at Big Bay Island Park, but its 44 rustic campsites, available on a first-come, first-served basis, also fill quickly during July and August.

If raindrops put a damper on your island excursion, the Bayfield swimming pool can rescue your vacation. The 25-meter pool is open to the public for a small fee, and offers two racquetball courts and a whirlpool as well.

Just north of Bayfield, Highway 13 pierces the Red Cliff Indian Reservation before providing access to the 12-mile-long mainland unit of Apostle Islands National Lakeshore. The Red Cliff Reservation preserves the heritage of the Ojibwa (Chippewa) Indians, who migrated to Lake Superior 500 years ago. Campers will find a place to overnight at the 40-unit tribal campground, and a 45-slip marina caters to boaters visiting the Apostle Islands. The Buffalo Art Center exhibits Indian art work, and pow wows are held on the reservation each summer. The tribe also operates a bowling alley and bingo center for those who seek indoor activities on a rainy day.

Exiting Highway 13, County K leads to the Little Sand Bay visitor center off Little Sand Bay Road. This is a great place to launch your mainland exploration of Apostle Islands National Lakeshore. Park rangers offer guided tours of the Hokenson Brother Fishery, and Sand Island is visible offshore, tempting sea kayakers to slide in their boats for an open-water crossing.

Returning to Highway 13, Meyers Road provides access to Squaw Bay just north of the village of Cornucopia. The sea caves of Squaw Bay are a favorite paddling destination for skilled sea kayakers who maneuver their vessels into the sandstone fissures. Paddlers should only depart for the caves under favorable weather conditions, because once you reach the caves there are few opportunities to retreat.

Long-range plans call for the park to develop a 10- to 12-mile hiking and skiing trail along the shoreline bluffs between Squaw Bay and Little Sand Bay. Once completed, this is will be a spectacular route, offering island vistas from shoreside cliffs.

The Circle Tour continues to Cornucopia, Wisconsin's northernmost village on Lake Superior's south shore. Cornucopia boasts of having the region's largest sand beach. Hidden waterfalls and spectacular sunsets also await those interested in exploration. A trip to the village wharf is not complete without purchasing the "catch of the day" from a local fisherman, and boat launching facilities are available if you'd like to try your luck.

West of Cornucopia you'll find Herbster, where the scenic beach road provides a great view of the lake and campers can roll out their tents at the town campground. Sun lovers will enjoy the sandy beach, and fishermen can frequently be spotted surf casting right from shore.

Seven miles west of Herbster you'll reach Port Wing, one of the last important commercial fishing villages on Lake Superior's south shore. Port Wing was the first community in the country to provide free bus transportation for school children. Today the village provides easy access for fishermen hoping to land a Lake Superior trout, or for hunters wishing to bag a Chequamegon National Forest white-tailed deer.

Continuing west on Highway 13, your journey will take you across the famous Brule River into the Brule River State Forest that surrounds it. The Brule has always attracted the attention of travelers. French explorers followed the lead of native Americans by using the Brule as a link between Lake Superior and the Mississippi River. Today the Brule remains a popular stream with trout fishermen, but these anglers share the river and its surrounding forest with canoeists, hikers, and sightseers.

Highway 13 joins U.S. 2 just south of Superior. Located ten miles east of Superior on Highway 2, Amnicon Falls State Park (listed separately) is a popular camping and picnicking stop for Circle Tour motorists. Within the park, the Amnicon River divides into two streams, while cascading over a series of rock outcroppings before reaching its outlet some thirty miles downstream at Lake Superior. Campers can roll out a sleeping bag at one of the park's 36 rustic campsites (no showers or electrical hookups), and swimmers can be found frolicking below the falls in the warm water of the Amnicon, although there is no designated swimming beach or lifeguard on duty. The Amnicon takes its root-beer color from naturally occurring tannic acid that leaches from the headwater swamps and bogs.

West of Amnicon Falls State Park, Circle Tour drivers who began their trek in Duluth reach the end of their journey at the port city of Superior (pop. 29,606). Superior was founded in 1854 by speculator Henry M. Rice. Plans to build a railroad and make the community the western terminus of Lake Superior were dashed in 1857 due to an economic downturn. The population of the region plummeted from nearly 3,000 to about 1,000 residents.

Insult was then added to injury. In 1870, the railroad terminus Superior had sought was located in nearby Duluth. Showing its resilience, Superior became a city in 1889, and by 1890 it had become the second-largest city in Wisconsin, housing grain elevators that were among the world's largest.

Today the Duluth-Superior harbor remains one of the most important ports on the Great Lakes, and although residents will assert claims to the contrary, in many ways Duluth and Superior remain "twin" cities.

Barker's Island, a manmade island, is the recreational center of Superior. Here visitors can enjoy a tour of the *S.S. Meteor*, the world's only surviving "whaleback ship" (fee charged). Built in 1896, the *Meteor* is listed on the National Register of Historic Sites, and is the last surviving ship of the whaleback fleet built in Duluth/Superior in the late 1800s. Swimming, fishing, and a 360-slip marina add to the appeal of Barker's Island. The best way to view the Duluth/Superior harbor is from a boat, and those without their own watercraft can board excursion boats on Barker's Island. The *Vista King* and *Vista Queen* excursion boats offer daily service. Reservations are recommended, and can be obtained by calling 218/722-6218. To reach Barker's Island, follow U.S. 2-53 and Highway 13, two miles from I-53 via I-535.

If you're interested in a less "commercial" Superior experience, you'll want to visit Wisconsin Point. This barrier island offers a sandy shore perfect for picnicking, with an outstanding view of Lake Superior. The Superior entry to the harbor at the tip of Wisconsin Point is the best spot from which to enjoy the ship traffic and admire the lighthouse. You may also want to stroll down the breakwater and enjoy the expansive lake surrounding you, while reflecting on your exploration of the world's greatest inland sea. To reach Wisconsin Point, exit U.S. 2-53 at Moccasin Mike Road east of Superior.

APOSTLE ISLANDS NATIONAL LAKESHORE
Route 1
Box 4
Bayfield, WI 54814
715/779-3397

Aptly named, the Apostle Islands are indeed a spiritual place. Over eons, the relentless power of Lady Superior has sculpted fascinating rock and cave formations in the Apostles' reddish-brown sandstone, while sprinkling island shores with beaches of fine white sand.

The Apostles are anchored off the tip of Wisconsin's Bayfield Peninsula, and folklore holds that early European explorers counted only 12 islands in the chain and christened them accordingly. In reality, there are 22 islands in the archipelago, each harboring natural treasures.

Public access to this 720-square-mile land of sand, sea, and forest was ensured in 1970, when 2500 acres on the northern tip of the Bayfield Peninsula and 20 of the islands were designated national parkland by the U.S. Government. Today, the Apostle Islands National Lakeshore encompasses 21 islands and a 12-mile stretch of wild and wonderful mainland.

The islands within the park vary both in size and character. Stockton Island, for example, is a 10,000-acre preserve laced with hiking trails and hosting beaver, bear, and deer. Three-acre Gull Island, on the other hand, serves as a bird rookery, providing sanctuary to thousands of shore birds. Devil's Island supports a mixed coniferous forest, while Long Island is breeding ground for the rare, endangered piping plover. Madeline (listed separately), the only island in the chain with a year-round population, is not part of the national lakeshore. Thanks to its accessibility by car ferry, many visitors include Madeline Island on their agenda as they enjoy the magic and mystery of adventuring on the Apostle Islands.

Legend, history, facts, and fables abound in this land of blue water and green plateaus. Hermit Island is said to harbor buried treasure, and Objibwa legends tell of life beginning on Madeline Island. French fur trappers established trading posts on the islands, and later settlers built seasonal hunting and fishing camps, summer cabins, and homesteads.

The Apostle Island archipelago was formed nearly 12,000 years ago, during the last great Ice Age. Today's islands are the visible peaks of tall, rounded hills formed by the sea of ice that crept southward, sculpting the earth in its path. As the glacier retreated, mighty Lake Superior surrounded these green plateaus, creating sea caves and sand beaches.

Before Columbus set sail for America, nomadic woodland Indians pitched camp on Madeline Island. Like the modern vacationers who arrive today, bands of Iroquois, Fox, Huron and Sioux Indians were drawn to the Apostles by the area's rich natural bounty of fish and game. By 1700 the Ojibwa Indians had made Madeline Island their tribal home.

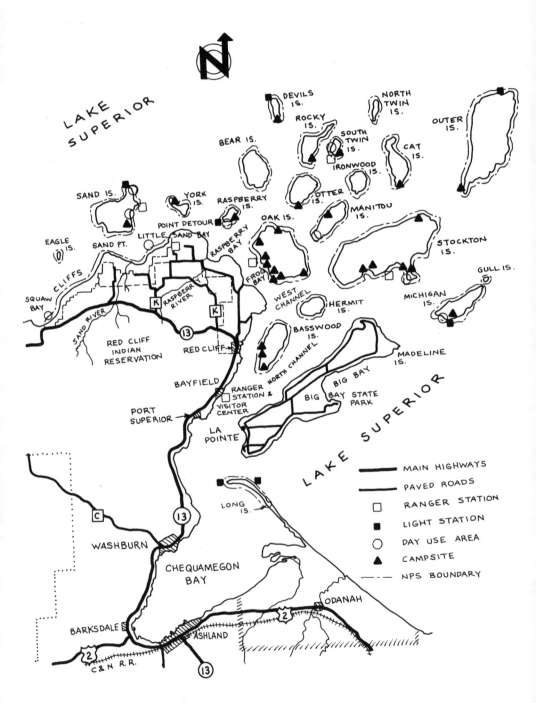

French explorers and missionaries traveling the waterways of the Great Lakes arrived in the mid-1600s. They dubbed this region the "Chequamegon" after an Ojibwa word meaning "place of shallow waters." These explorers found the Apostles rich in fur-bearing animals and sheltered from Lake Superior's storms. Trading with the Indians was brisk, and early explorers exchanged knives, needles, and pots for the beaver pelts prized by Europeans for use in making robes and hats. As the fur trade grew, fur companies hired trappers and voyageurs who hauled the goods down the 2,500-mile Voyageurs Highway in birch bark canoes. During the peak of the fur trade era, just two of the major fur trade operators took 106,000 beaver pelts in a single year.

Shortly after the turn of the 18th century, demand for fur began to diminish. That's when the American Fur Company turned to the commercial fishing trade as a means of economic survival. From the 1830s to 1841, this company began to catch and sell lake trout, whitefish, and lake herring to folks living around Lake Michigan and Lake Erie. In 1839, over 5,000 barrels of salted fish were shipped from La Pointe on Madeline Island to company warehouses in Detroit. Without the means of transporting the fish inland, however, demand was limited, and American Fur closed its doors in 1841.

The 1880s saw the rebirth of the fishing trade when an influx of Scandinavian immigrants arrived in the area. Experienced fishermen, these newcomers were eager to put their commercial fishing skills to work in their new surroundings. When railroads reached Bayfield in 1883, the fishermen had a way to get their products to new markets. Meanwhile, as steam engines replaced traditional sailing vessels, fishermen were able to tend a greater number of nets, thus increasing their catch. The increase is reflected in state statistics indicating that, between the years 1888 and 1896, the total catch in the Bayfield district increased from 1.7 million to 7.8 million pounds.

Commercial fishing was still an important industry when Leo, Eskel, and Roy Hokenson began their commercial fishing operations along the shores of Little Sand Bay in the 1920s. The three brothers were sons of Swedish immigrants who turned to the inland sea to supplement their farming income. The Hokensons retired in the mid-1960s, and the Park Service subsequently purchased their property, docks, and sheds. Today park historians offer a firsthand look at the Hokenson Brothers Fishery on guided tours that recount the days of pound nets and herring sheds.

The city of Bayfield was founded on the mainland in 1856, opposite Madeline Island. Fed by vast forests of hemlock and pine, Bayfield grew with the lumbering industry. Only Raspberry, Devils North Twin, Eagle, and Gull islands were spared the logger's axe. At about this time, a shipping canal pierced the treacherous rapids of Sault Ste. Marie. The "Soo" canals opened Lake Superior to inter-lake shipping, and the Apostle Islands became the western terminus of a 1,000-mile liquid highway. Its ships often carried brown sandstone chiseled from both mainland and island quarries, for use in constructing the fashionable brownstone buildings that were popular in the east and midwest during the period.

Soon lighthouses were needed to safely illuminate shipping lanes, due to dangerous reefs and shoals that surround the archipelago. In 1857, the first of seven light stations built on the Apostle Islands was erected on Michigan Island. By 1891, lights had also been built on Madeline, Long, Raspberry, Sand, Outer, and Devils islands. Each light station was illuminated by a beehive-shaped piece of glass known as the Fresnel Lens. This beautifully ground lens magnified a small flame into a highly visible beam of light. It was the task of the lightkeeper to keep the flame burning. Since one of the lightkeepers' chores involved trimming the wick of the burner, they earned the nickname "wickies."

Today modern navigational beacons have replaced the Fresnel lens in leading vessels through shipping lanes. The history of the light stations remains accessible, though, as the Park Service restores the stations and guides visitors through the shipping world of yesterday.

During the 1890s, wealthy folks from the city began discovering the beauty of this region. They built summer homes in the mainland communities of Bayfield and Cornucopia, and at La Pointe on Madeline Island. By the time of the Great Depression, the Apostle Islands—ravaged by loggers' axes and laid bare by fire—no longer held appeal to vacationers.

Fortunately, the Apostles are once again nearly as wild as those visited by Indians in birch bark canoes. Sugar maple, yellow birch, hemlock, and pine trees are reclaiming the islands, hiding much of man's earlier carnage. Wildflowers, including violets, trillium, starflowers, and Canada dogwood, greet visitors along with black bears, white-tailed deer, and the clean waters of the inland sea.

TOURING

Nearly 90 percent of the visitors to the Apostle Islands National Lakeshore arrive between June and September. August is the most popular month to visit, since it's also the month when the island's insects are the least bothersome.

About two-thirds of all island visitors arrive by sailboat, setting off from Bayfield, Washburn, Port Superior, or Madeline Island.

Sea kayaks also provide access to the islands for those with the skill and equipment required to enjoy paddling Lake Superior.

A private concessionaire authorized by the Park Service provides visitors who don't have private access to boats the opportunity to visit the islands via scheduled boat tour or water taxi service.

Whether you're planning a visit by land or lake, it's best to begin your tour of the Apostle Islands with a stop at the lakeshore's visitor center, located in the Old Bayfield County Courthouse. Be sure to watch the ten-minute introductory film about the lakeshore. You'll also enjoy exhibits on display that illustrate the cultural and natural history of the area, and a ranger will be on hand to answer your questions and help you plan your visit. The visitor center is open daily from Memorial

Day through Labor Day, and restricted hours during the off season.

If time is tight and you have only a few hours to enjoy the Apostle Islands, you may find yourself limited to a mainland visit. Alternately, it's possible to take a quick ferry trip to Madeline Island, or a one-hour water taxi cruise around Basswood and Hermit islands but, considering the time restraints, you're likely to find a mainland trip more enjoyable.

On the mainland, visit the Little Sand Bay, 13 miles north of Bayfield via Highways 13 and K. Here you can explore the Hokenson Brothers Fishery, take in the exhibits at the information station, walk along a sandy beach, and view several offshore islands from the mainland. If you time your visit properly, you'll enjoy the ranger-led tour of the fishery.

Apostle Islands National Lakeshore is a water-oriented park. If you wish to truly experience the islands within the national lakeshore, you'll need at least four hours, as the shortest cruise offered by the Apostle Island Cruise Service is three hours long.

If you have a full day, you'll also have time to get out on the lake for a trip to the islands. The Apostle Islands Cruise Service is the only public transportation to the islands that's authorized by the National Park Service. Write to them at Box 691, Bayfield, WI 54814, or call 715/779-3925.

The cruise service offers a variety of excursion boat tours, as well as a water taxi service that allows you to view the islands from aboard the vessel or land on an island for a few hours or a few days.

The Apostle Islands Cruise Service offers regularly scheduled excursion tours to Stockton, Raspberry, and Manitou islands, and camping is available. Sand, Oak, and Basswood islands are also accessible by boat, but you may have to arrange water taxi service.

At over 10,000 acres, Stockton is the largest island within the national lakeshore. A visitor center at Presque Isle offers exhibits and information on the natural and cultural history of the island. Rangers lead hikes and present campfire programs frequently during the summer season. Hiking trails traverse the island, and sand beaches are found at Julian, Presque Isle, and Quarry bays.

On Raspberry Island, you can tour a restored 1863 light station and take a short one-half mile stroll to a sand spit, where an inviting sand beach awaits you.

On Manitou Island, you'll discover what life was like for a commercial fishermen during the 1930s at a fish camp. Park rangers lead tours through restored historic buildings, demonstrating the resourcefulness of those who lived and worked at this remote fishing camp. Trails lead hikers to either the northwest beach or a prehistoric fishing site.

Sailboats provide an excellent means of enjoying the Apostle Islands. It's estimated that over half of the sailboats plying the Apostles are charters. In fact, the Bayfield area hosts the largest sail charter fleet in the country. If you'd like to learn to sail or hire a captained charter, the Apostle Islands are your kind of place. Contact the Bayfield Chamber of Commerce, Box 138, Bayfield, WI 54814, or call 800/447-4094 to make the necessary connections.

CAMPING

If you plan to camp on the islands within the national lakeshore, you must obtain a free permit prior to your departure. Permits are available from the Apostle Islands visitor center and from the visitor center at Little Sand Bay. The permits cannot be reserved, and you can obtain them no earlier than the day prior to your departure for the islands.

Campsites are limited to parties of six or less. Group campsites are available on Stockton, Sand, Oak, and Basswood islands, but must be reserved in advance.

The Apostle Islands offer both designated campsites and backcountry camping. Backcountry sites cannot be established within 500 feet of any designated campsite, or within view of any lighthouse grounds or historic structure. Campfires are not permitted in the backcountry. The following areas are closed to camping:

- Private land
- Eagle, Gull, and North Twin islands
- Raspberry and Devils islands, except at designated sites
- Certain additional areas may be closed to protect wildlife.

Well water, safe for drinking, is available on some islands. Lake water should be boiled or filtered. Black bears are found on several of the Apostle Islands, so campers must protect their food.

Biting insects and ticks are prevalent from June to September. Headnets, long sleeves, long pants, and insect repellent are mandatory items if you're to be comfortable.

HIKING

Hiking trails traverse many of the Apostle Islands. Stockton Island is the favored destination of most backpackers, since it offers over 14 miles of trail and backpack camping opportunities.

Shoreline hiking is very rugged, and often impossible. Park rangers recommend that you avoid attempting to hike "around" an island. Off-trail hiking is difficult and, if you attempt it, be sure to bring a topographic map and compass.

PADDLING

Due to cold temperatures, rough seas, fog, and sudden squalls, paddling open canoes on Lake Superior is not recommended.

Average daytime temperatures range from a high of 60 degrees in May to the upper 70s in mid-summer, dropping to the mid-60s in September. Lows vary from 40 degrees in May to the upper 50s in mid-summer and about 50 in September. Average water temperatures in

May and June are only about 40 degrees. Even in late summer, surface temperature rarely exceed 60 degrees, except in protected bays.

If you have the skill, equipment, and necessary respect for Lake Superior, sea kayaking is an excellent means of enjoying the Apostle Islands.

Sea kayakers should wear a wet suit at all times while paddling in the Apostle Islands. A dry suit is standard equipment for those challenging Lake Superior during April, May, and September. Signalling equipment, self and group rescue skills, and sound judgment are also mandatory.

Sand, Raspberry, and Oak islands are the most popular targets for sea kayakers. Sand Island, with its sea caves and beaches, makes an excellent destination for experienced paddlers on their first excursion into the Apostles.

Several outfitters offer guided sea kayak tours of the Apostles, including day trips to the spectacular sea caves of Squaw Bay. Paddling guides are familiar with Lake Superior and its many moods. If this is your first outing on Superior, they can provide you with the guidance required to make your trip memorable.

Each summer the Inland Sea Society, a non-profit environmental group, hosts a Sea Kayak Symposium in Bayfield. This is an excellent opportunity for beginners to immerse themselves in the sport while under the watchful eye of skilled instructors. For information, contact the Inland Sea Society, P.O. Box 1202, Bayfield, WI 54814.

THE ISLANDS

SAND ISLAND
2,949 acres

Sand Island, is a favorite destination for sea kayakers, thanks to the sea caves located on the island's northwest corner. Several private cabins and an old hunting lodge remain on the south shore. Two of these, the Shaw farm and the Sevona cabin, are listed on the National Register of Historic Places.

At East Bay you'll find a dock, three campsites, a well, and a vault toilet. A seasonal ranger's residence is stationed on the island about half a mile from the campsites and dock. Backcountry camping is permitted.

A light station built in 1881 sits on the northern tip of the island. A natural rock ledge directly in front provides a fair-weather boat landing, but the lake is often too rough for docking here.

RASPBERRY ISLAND
296 acres

A sand spit provides a good landing site on the southeast end of one-mile-long, 1/2-mile-wide Raspberry Island. The bay on the east side of the island is a favored overnight mooring spot for sailboats.

Raspberry is one of the few islands in the chain that escaped logging, and there is a thick understory of yew.

A 3/4-mile hiking trail connects the island's historic 1862 light station with two campsites on the sand spit. These campsites are subject to relocation because of the delicate environment on which they stand.

OAK ISLAND
5,078 acres

Oak Island, 3.5 miles by 2.5 miles, is the highest of the Apostle Islands, reaching elevations of up to 480 feet. It's characterized by high clay banks and steep, forested shores. A sand spit is found on the island's southwest corner. An active eagle's nest is situated on the island's south shore, and bears find refuge on this island. The remains of five logging camps have been found here.

Over ten miles of trail traverse the island. A dock on the island's western shore provides access to four group campsites, privies, and a well. An additional eight designated campsites are dispersed along the shoreline. Beaches dot the island.

BASSWOOD ISLAND
1,917 acres

Oval-shaped Basswood Island is easily accessible due to its proximity to Bayfield's marinas. The island is heavily wooded, and has a rocky shoreline with interesting formations on the eastern shore. A natural rock landing can be found on the island's southern corner.

Basswood offers four designated campsites located near the island's historic brownstone quarries on its southeastern end. A group campsite and two more campsites are located near a dock on the island's western shore, served by a well and privy. A five-mile hiking loop connects the campsites to a pair of homestead sites and an old farm. Thanks to its relatively easy access, winter camping remains an option here for hearty explorers.

MANITOU ISLAND
1,363 acres

Manitou is one of the lowest islands in the Apostles. Remains of a historic fishing camp are found near the island's gravel beach, and a dock is situated on Manitou's southwestern end. One of the old cabins serves as the seasonal home to a ranger who interprets the island's history.

A 1/2-mile trail leads from the fish camp to an archaeological site on the southeast side of the island. Campsites are currently found along the western shore of the island, and plans call for these sites to be linked with the fish camp, dock, and archaeological site.

STOCKTON ISLAND
10,054 acres

Many visitors consider Stockton to be the most beautiful of the Apostle Islands. At 7.5 miles long and 2.5 miles wide, it's the largest of the islands within the national lakeshore, and the second-largest within the entire Apostle chain. Several sand beaches dot the island's forested shoreline, and a large lagoon provides habitat for beavers. Bears also inhabit the island. On the southeastern end, a low, sandy tombolo connects rocky Presque Isle Point with the rest of the island.

Stockton Island is the most-visited of the national lakeshore islands. Concrete piers at Presque Isle Bay on the island's south side are used by visitors arriving via tour boats or private vessels. Many arrive to hike the island's 14.5 miles of trail, which include a 1/2-mile, self-guided nature trail along Julian Bay, where the historic wreck of the *Noquebay* rests. This shipwreck is a favorite destination for scuba divers, but all must register with the park prior to making a dive.

A 19-site campground overlooking Presque Isle Point serves overnight visitors to the island. A well and privies are provided. A ranger station and interpretive displays assist visitors in their enjoyment of the island. There are four group campsites, a well, and a privy west of Presque Isle Bay.

Backpackers will find three designated campsites on the northeast corner of the island at Trout Point, site of a 1917 logging camp. These sites are accessible by hiking trail from Presque Isle Bay.

LONG ISLAND
300 acres

Long Island is a prime example of an unspoiled barrier spit, quite rare on Lake Superior. It was included within Apostle Island National Lakeshore in 1986, and is the only island within the lakeshore that receives electrical power from the mainland.

To protect the sensitive species that utilize its resources, notably the endangered piping plover, there are no visitor facilities offered on Long Island.

YORK ISLAND
320 acres

York Island was once two islands, but the two are now connected by a low stretch of sand. There are no docking facilities, but the one-mile-long island is a popular destination for sea kayakers who land on its northwestern end. An active bald eagle site is found on the island.

There are five campsites located along the sandy north beach, but there is no well or privy. No camping is allowed on the island's fragile sand spit.

HERMIT ISLAND
778 acres

Two-mile-long Hermit Island is steep and rocky. The primary landing spot is along the sand beach of the island's north shore.

An abandoned brownstone quarry, located on the island's southeast side, can be viewed from Lake Superior. Massive cribs are the only remains of an old dock that once served the quarry, and they can be seen just below the water's surface from the seat of a kayak.

BEAR ISLAND
1,824 acres

There are no docking facilities on the two-mile-long, 1.75-mile-wide Bear Island, but those who make the effort to visit will find a sand spit, rocky shores and clay bluffs.

The highest point on Bear Island is 250 feet above Lake Superior, making it the second-highest island in the Apostles chain. The island also contains a virgin stand of hemlocks and a bog. The remains of a logging camp from the 1930s are located on the northeast side of the island.

OTTER ISLAND
659 acres

The north and northwest shorelines of Otter Island are lined with rock cliffs, while the rest of its shoreline is mostly low-lying. There is a natural rock landing on the north side of this two-mile-long island, plus a small sand spit on the southeast end.

A U-shaped dock on the southeast corner of the island provides access to three designated campsites, a well, a privy, and a two-mile hiking trail. A historic 19th-century fishing or logging camp and an archaeological site are located near the trailhead.

IRONWOOD ISLAND
659 acres

A sand beach landing and a single designated campsite on the south tip of Ironwood Island provide a welcome treat for sea kayakers. Past logging activities have damaged the island's sand spit, and several old logging roads lace the island.

There are no designated or maintained trails, but backcountry camping is permitted.

CAT ISLAND
1,348 acres

The south end of Cat Island has sand beaches, while the north end consists of rocky shoreline. The south sand spit provides an excellent sand beach landing spot, along with two designated campsites and a well.

Old logging roads and an old cabin are found on the island, but there are no maintained hiking trails.

SOUTH TWIN ISLAND
360 acres

One-mile-long South Twin Island is predominantly covered with sand and has no rock formations, but due to its protected waters and Park Service facilities, the island is heavily used.

On the west side of the sand spit, boardwalks connect a dock with a fire ring and a district ranger residence. A well and privy serve the five campsites located around the parameter of the island.

The anchorage between South Twin and Rock islands is popular with sailboaters, because it offers a safe, protected place to moor.

ROCKY ISLAND
1,099 acres

Rocky Island offers a great deal of variety, with a rocky shoreline on the south, sand beaches on the east and northwest, and a sand spit on the southeastern shore.

The protected waters between Rocky and South Twin islands draw the second-highest boater use in the area, exceeded only by the waters around Stockton Island.

A two-mile trail from the docks situated on the east side of the island leads to a sand spit and seven campsites along the shore. A second trail leads from the dock to the west side of the island, passing the Niews fish camp, which is interpreted via wayside exhibits.

DEVILS ISLAND
318 acres

Devils Island is the northernmost of the Apostle Islands, and it receives the full brunt of Lake Superior's wrath. The constant pounding of waves has created spectacular caves in the rocky sandstone bluffs along the northeast shoreline. These caves are a highlight of excursion boat tours, and a challenge to visit by sea kayak. An active bald eagle's nest is located on the southeastern side of the island.

The historic light station on the north end is served by a natural rock landing site. A 1.2-mile historic road links the light station to a dock and small boathouse on the south end of the island. There is one designated campsite at the south landing. Backcountry camping is not permitted on Devil's Island.

OUTER ISLAND
7,999 acres

At 6.5 miles long by 2.5 miles wide, Outer Island is the third largest of the Apostle Islands, and the second largest within the archipelago. Low rock cliffs face the east shoreline and clay bluffs line the western shore. There are several natural rock landings along the coast, and the south end of the island has a large sand spit that encloses a mile-long lagoon. The island also features a large stand of virgin hemlock, a beaver population, and an active bald eagle's nest.

A seven-mile trail connects the light station with a sand spit, and here you'll find a sand beach landing and one campsite.

MICHIGAN ISLAND
1,581 acres

A large sand spit on the southwestern end of Michigan Island encloses a lagoon, but most of the rest of this 3.5-mile-long, 1.25-mile-wide island is characterized by high clay bluffs.

A dock completed in 1987 services visitors exploring the island's historic light station. Campsites are located near the island's sand spit, about one mile from the light station.

NORTH TWIN ISLAND
175 acres

GULL ISLAND
3 acres

EAGLE ISLAND
28 acres

There is no public access to remote North Twin, Gull, and Eagle islands. These are important nesting sites for sensitive shorebirds, including bald eagles, double-crested cormorants, and great blue herons. Please respect their privacy, especially during critical nesting periods.

MADELINE ISLAND
Chamber of Commerce
P.O. Box 274B
La Pointe, WI 54850
715/747-2801

Creature comforts, summer homes, and stunning sunsets bring thousands of visitors to Madeline Island from Bayfield each summer.

The Madeline Island Ferry Line offers several daily departures for the 15-minute ride from Bayfield on the mainland to La Pointe on the island. At La Pointe, you'll find a year-round population accommodating visitors with restaurants, lodging, and nightclubs. Walking is a great way to enjoy historic La Pointe, as all of the town's attractions are within walking distance from the ferry dock, including a picnic area and swimming beach.

The Ojibwa gave Madeline Island a name meaning "home of the golden-breasted woodpecker." To Ojibwa the island holds special significance, because their legends recall that life itself began here.

Madeline Island is well-known to sailors, and chartering a boat or hiring a captain is a great way to enjoy the Apostle Islands. Before setting sail, however, be sure to pay a visit to the Madeline Island Museum. Operated by the Wisconsin State Historical Society, the museum offers a fascinating look at frontier life in Old La Pointe.

If you have a car or bike, you'll enjoy a trip to Big Bay State Park (listed separately), located seven miles from La Pointe. The town also operates a campground on the island called Big Bay Island Park, which is easily confused with the state park. This 44-unit campground is located on the north side of Big Bay, adjacent to the state park. Campsites here are available on a first-come, first-served basis.

GETTING THERE

It's a 15-minute, 2.6-mile crossing by ferry from Bayfield to historic La Pointe. Year-round daily departures are available aboard safe, modern car ferries.

Many visitors make the crossing only to have dinner, visit the island's museum, or sample the salty flavor of life on Madeline Island. Those wishing to avoid the extra cost of bringing a car aboard the ferry should consider bringing a mountain bike instead. The cost is only about $3 roundtrip, and the wide tires of an all-terrain bike are ideal for navigating the entire length of the island. If you must bring a car, budget $12 plus $6 for each passenger.

From January through March, the Madeline Island Ferries are normally ice-bound. Depending on ice conditions, residents must cross the ice on foot, by snowmobile, or by car on an ice bridge. At the beginning and end of winter, travelers go to and from Madeline Island on a windsled. This boat is driven by an air propeller that scoots across the ice. It can also climb out of pockets of open water if necessary.

BIG BAY STATE PARK
Box 589
Bayfield, WI 54814
715/779-3346

From thundering spray to placid lagoon, the many moods of Lake Superior can be enjoyed at Big Bay State Park.

Getting to the park, which is located on the eastern shore of Madeline Island, can be an adventure in itself. Daily ferries frequently depart the mainland for the 2.6-mile crossing from Bayfield to La Pointe, but once you're at La Pointe, it's a seven-mile hike or ride to Big Bay State Park. When you finally arrive, 55 campsites, a glorious, 1.5-mile swimming beach, and 2,358 acres of parkland greet you. Before boarding the ferry, secure reservations or call the park to be sure there are campsites available.

Day visitors will enjoy touring Madeline Island and Big Bay State Park by mountain bike. Quiet travelers may encounter shy white-tailed deer peering from the safety of the rural island landscape. Remember that not all of Madeline Island's 45 miles of road are paved. Wide-tired bikes are quite helpful when you're negotiating the gravel stretches.

The park's long sand beach on Big Bay, located just a short hike from the campground, serves as its greatest natural attraction. Just behind the beach, a well-protected lagoon provides opportunities to drop a canoe in and try your luck at fishing for resident northern pike.

Meanwhile, the most dramatic scenery on the island can be found within the park at the Big Bay Point Picnic Area. When the lake is calm, you can freely enjoy the area's shoreside cliffs. But when Lake

Superior is rough, waves rush the shoreline with a thunderous crash, anointing those who venture too close with a soaking spray.

If you're unable to secure a campsite at Big Bay State Park, try landing a tent pad at the adjacent Big Bay Town Park.

AMNICON FALLS STATE PARK
Highway 35, Rt. 2
Box 435
Superior, WI 54880
715/399-8073

The Amnicon River divides into two streams as it dances over a series of waterfalls in the center of Amnicon State Park.

The warm water of the Amnicon provides an important spawning ground for Lake Superior fish. During spring, walleye, smelt, and rainbow trout (steelheads) migrate up the Amnicon to spawn. Coho salmon (or silver salmon) spawn here in the autumn, along with the Chinook salmon that were recently stocked in the river. Lucky anglers also land an occasional northern pike or muskie, so pack along your fishing gear if you're feeling lucky.

The park and surrounding area lie on ancient lava flows that gushed from cracks in the earth in the Lake Superior region over one billion years ago. Over the eons, a huge block of lava settled downward, or faulted, in this area after a great earthquake. The geological feature is known as the Douglas Fault, and it's best observed in Amnicon Falls State Park. Today, the Amnicon River is still eroding the sandstone and exposing the lava.

Undoubtedly the most famous manmade feature of Amnicon Falls State Park is the covered bridge overlooking the falls. Hikers pause here on their way to the island across the Amnicon River, and the bridge is a favorite subject for photographers.

Swimmers can often be found taking a dip in the pools below the falls, but no lifeguards are on duty, so children must be supervised.

Amnicon Falls State Park is a seasonal park, typically open from early May through the first weekend of October. Its 36 rustic campsites include two walk-in sites for those wishing a bit more seclusion.

PHOTO CREDITS

Other Nature and Travel Books You'll Enjoy from

NorthWord Press, Inc.

America's Nature Publisher

Guide to Wisconsin Outdoors

Guide to Minnesota Outdoors

Wild Wisconsin

Wild Michigan

Spirit of the North

True North: Journal of a North Country Year

Northwoods Wildlife: A Watcher's Guide to Habitat

Traveler's Guide to Native America: The Great Lakes Region

NorthWord also offers calendars, posters, audiotapes, and gifts related to nature and wildlife. For a free catalog, call 1-800-336-5666.